Introduction to pupils: how to use this book

This book has been carefully divided up so that each topic fits on one double page.

- [ ] The **text** gives you the information and background which you need. Words in **bold** type are used to highlight important names and ideas.

- [ ] The **pictures** are an important part of each topic, and many of them tell a story of their own.

- [ ] You can find a topic by looking at the **Contents** pages at the start. The topics are grouped into sections. Basic chemical ideas and principles come first. Details and facts come later, and the mathematical aspects are near the end.

- [ ] To find out something more specific, you should look up the key word using the **Index** at the back. This is arranged alphabetically.

- [ ] Near the end, you will find the **Datapages**. These contain a large number of facts and figures. Don't worry! You are not expected to learn them by heart. They will help you to understand how chemistry affects what goes on in the world.

- [ ] The **questions** in this book are of several kinds. The ones on the text pages are there to prompt you as you go along, and to give practice in handling information for yourself. The ones at the end of the chapters test the different skills required by the GCSE examinations. To give you an idea of how much is expected, they have been given star-ratings. 3-star questions are the hardest, or require the most detailed answers.

- [ ] The following **abbreviations** are used in this book:

Abbreviations	Meaning
aq	short for the word 'aqueous', meaning 'a solution in water', usually as (aq)
A	mass number, the number of protons plus the number of neutrons in the nucleus of an atom
A_r	relative atomic mass
C	as in °C, degrees on the Centrigrade or Celsius scale of temperature
cm^3	cubic centimetre, a unit of volume equal to 1 millilitre (1/1000 litre)
g	gram, the unit of mass or short for the word 'gas', usually as (g)
J	Joule, a unit of heat energy
k	'kilo−', meaning 1000x, as in 1 km = 1000 metres 1 kg = 1000 grams; 1 kJ = 1000 Joules
K	Kelvin, the unit of temperature on a scale which takes +273° as the freezing point of water
l	short for the word 'liquid', usually as (l)
L	litre, a unit of volume equal to 1000 cm^3
m	metre, m^3 = cubic metre
M_r	relative molecular mass
M	'mega−', meaning 1000 000x, as in 1 Mt = 1 million tonnes
s	short for the word 'solid', usually as (s) or for 'second(s)', the unit of time
T	short for the word 'temperature'
t	short for the word 'time', or the unit of mass 'tonne' (the metric tonne, which is 1000 kg)
Z	atomic number, the number of protons in the nucleus of an atom

Contents

CHEMISTRY FOR · GCSE

COLIN JOHNSON

Heinemann Educational Books

Heinemann Educational Books Ltd
22 Bedford Square, London, WC1B 3HH
LONDON EDINBURGH MELBOURNE AUCKLAND SINGAPORE
KUALA LUMPUR NEW DELHI IBADAN NAIROBI JOHANNESBURG
PORTSMOUTH (NH) KINGSTON

ISBN 0 435 64440 8

Front cover photo by Mike McNamee, Science Photo Library.
It is a polarised light micrograph of sulphur crystals.

Designed and typeset by FD Graphics.
Printed and bound in Spain by Mateu Cromo Artes Gráficas, S.A.

Preface

The purpose of this book is to assist students who are preparing for the written papers of **GCSE examinations** in science. It covers the published syllabuses for **chemistry**, and in so doing also provides for those candidates whose study of chemistry is part of an integrated or modular course.

The subject matter has been divided into **topics**, each occupying a double-page, and following a standard format. This should allow students to find their way easily through the text, and to derive maximum benefit from the numerous pictures and diagrams, which have been chosen, not for their pictorial value alone, but also as a direct complement to the text.

The **questions** in this book are of several kinds. Those in the text provide tests of understanding, and also a variety of tasks which should help students to make sense of new ideas and information for themselves. At the end of each chapter there are questions graded in difficulty, using a 'star' system, and grouped according to GCSE criteria.

Many students find the **quantitative aspects** of chemistry difficult, and a special **appendix** of worked examples has been included for use either by the teacher or for private study. The main text is thus left clear of this material.

Among the novel aspects of the GCSE is the requirement that pupils should become more adept at **handling information**. The **Datapages** at the end of this book provide raw material which teachers may use as the basis of their own questions, and as a detailed source of reference for use throughout a chemistry course.

The **Index** has been designed to give maximum help to all users, both students and teachers. Three aspects of the GCSE approach to chemistry have been given special prominence:

☐ Applications, social and environmental aspects
☐ Historical material
☐ Industrial processes

These have been separately indexed, for the benefit of teachers seeking further material with these particular emphases.

Lastly, a few words of thanks: even when there is only one name on the cover, a new book reflects the efforts of a large number of people. I have been deeply fortunate in the help and encouragement which I have received throughout the writing of this book. The science publishing team at Heinemann has given me every possible support. I would also like to thank Rex Hendricksen, Lesley Good and David Swinden who read large parts of the manuscript in draft, and to assure them that I take full responsibility for what now appears in the final version! Jennifer Johnson sought out most of the photographs, and single pictures or pieces of information came my way through numerous individual kindnesses, for which I am most grateful. Steve Donaldson and Gill Owen gave me invaluable help with photography. Above all, special thanks are due to Helen and Sarah, my wife and daughter, without those forbearance this work would not been possible.

Colin H. Johnson
July, 1987

Acknowledgements

The publishers wish to thank the following for permission to reproduce photographs:

1.1 Fig. 1 ICI, fig. 2 Will McIntyre/Science Photo Library, fig. 3 Araldite, fig. 4 Maggie Murray/Format, fig. 5 Frants Hartman/Frank Lane Agency, fig. 6 Safeway Food Stores. 1.2 Fig. 1 Adam Hart Davies, fig. 2 Ann Ronan, fig. 3 Royal Institution, fig. 5 Sporting Pictures (UK) Ltd, fig. 6 Colin Johnson. 1.3 Fig. 2 Andrew McClohagham/Science Photo Library, fig. 3 Colin Johnson, fig. 5 Christiana F Carvalho/Frank Lane Agency, fig. 6 J Allan Cash. 1.4 Figs. 1, 2 Ann Ronan, fig. 3 Dept of Chemistry/University of York, fig. 4 Vivien Fifield 1.5 Fig. 3 Erwin Mueller/Science Photo Library, fig. 4 Dr Tony Brain & David Parker/Science Photo Library 1.6 Fig. 1 J Allan Cash, fig. 5 Vivien Fifield, fig. 6 Unilever 1.7 Figs. 1, 2, 4 Colin Johnson, fig. 3 RIDA, fig. 4 J Allan Cash, David Leah/Science Photo Library. 1.8 Fig. 1 De Beers, figs. 2, 5, 6 Colin Johnson, fig. 3 Osram 1.9 Figs. 1, 2, 3 Colin Johnson, fig. 4 ICI. 1.10 Fig. 1 Colin Johnson. 1.12 Figs. 1, 4 Colin Johnson, fig. 3 Arthur Christiansen/Frank Lane Picture Agency, fig. 5 Alan Burgess Associates, fig. 6 Martin Dohrn/Science Photo Library 1.14 Fig. 2 UKAEA, fig. 3 J Allan Cash, fig. 4 Vivien Fifield. 1.15 Figs 2, 4, 5 UKAEA. 2.1 Figs. 2, 4 Colin Johnson, fig. 3 Canada Dry. 2.2 Figs. 1, 2, 3, 5 Colin Johnson, fig. 6 RIDA. 2.3 Fig. 1 RIDA, fig. 2 Colin Johnson, fig. 3 National Dairy Council, fig. 4 Alcan, fig. 5 Wool Secretariat. 2.4 Fig. 1 Jerome Yeates/Science Photo Library, fig. 2 J Allan Cash, fig. 3 Jones Cranes, fig. 4 A Shell Photograph, fig. 5 London Fire Brigade. 2.5 Fig. 1 Sporting Pictures (UK) Limited, fig. 2 J Allan Cash, fig. 3 Ronald Sheridan. 2.6 Fig. 1 Science Photo Library, fig. 2 Colin Johnson, fig. 3 National Coal Board, fig. 4 Rex Features 2.7 Figs. 1, 2 Colin Johnson. 2.8 Figs. 3, 4 Colin Johnson. 2.9 Fig. 1 Maggie Murray/Format, fig. 2 Colin Johnson. 2.10 Fig. 1 Royal Institution, fig. 4 Holt Studios. 3.1 Fig. 3 Daily Telegraph Colour Library, fig. 6 Farmers Weekly. 3.2 Fig. 1, Ann Ronan, fig. 2 Colin Johnson, fig. 3 J Allan Cash, fig. 4 ICI, fig. 5 British Steel, fig. 6 Daily Telegraph. 3.3 Fig. 1 Air Products, fig. 2 Osram, fig. 5 Trinity House, fig. 6 Airship Industries. 3.4 Fig. 2 Andrew McClenagham/Science Photo Library, fig. 3 Jeremy Burgess/Science Library, fig. 5 Picturepoint. 3.5 Figs. 1, 2 Colin Johnson, fig. 3 David Redfern. 3.6 Fig. 1 Colin Johnson, fig. 2 ICI, fig. 3 Bayer UK Limited, figs. 4, 5 Colin Johnson, fig. 6 British Museum/Natural History. 3.7 Figs. 2, 3 Topham, figs. 4, 5 Ann Ronan. 3.8 Figs. 1, 2, 4 Colin Johnson, fig. 3 NASA. 3.9 Figs. 1, 2 Colin Johnson, fig. 3 De Beers, fig. 5 National Coal Board. 3.10 Fig. 1 ICI, fig. 2 Science Museum, fig. 3 Tropical Development & Research Institute, figs. 5, 6 J Allan Cash. 3.11 Figs. 2, 3, 6 ROSPA, fig. 4 London Fire Brigade. 3.12 Fig. 2 British Sulphur Corporation Limited. 3.13 Figs. 3, 5 Colin Johnson. 3.15 Fig. 2 Associated Octel Co Ltd, London, fig. 4 The Associated Press, fig. 3 J Allan Cash. 4.1 Fig. 3 Colin Johnson. 4.2 Fig. 1 Ann Ronan, fig. 3 IBM, fig. 4 British Museum/Natural History. 4.3 Fig. 1 Michael Holford, fig. 2 Ronald Sheridan Photo Library. 4.4 Fig. 1 Canning Advisory Council, fig. 3 Thermit Welding, fig. 4 Austin Rover. 4.5 Fig. 1 Michael Holford, fig. 2 Press Association, fig. 3 Picturepoint, fig. 4 Sporting Pictures UK Ltd, fig. 5 ICI, fig. 6 Metropolitan Police. 4.6 Fig. 4 Camera Press, fig. 5 FUJI, fig. 6 NASA. 4.7 Figs. 1, 3 Colin Johnson, fig. 2 Central Electricity Generating Board. 4.8 Fig. 3 ICI. 4.9 Figs. 2, 4 Canning Metals Limited, fig. 3 Colin Johnson. 4.10 Fig. 2 John and Penny Hubley. 4.11 Fig. 1 Metal Box, fig. 2 Automobile Association, fig. 3 Geoff Evans/Strength Athlete Magazine, fig. 4 Colin Johnson. 5.1 Fig. 3 J Allan Cash, fig. 4 Colin Johnson. 5.2 Fig. 1 Colin Johnson, fig. 2 Geoscience Features, fig. 3 ICI, fig. 4 City of Cardiff, fig. 6 J Allan Cash. 5.3 Fig. 2 Numbus Records CD Pressing Plant England, fig. 3 Central Electricity Generating Board, fig. 5 Anglesey Aluminium Metal Limited. 5.4 Fig. 1 Colin Johnson, figs. 2, 4 British Steel. 5.5 Figs. 1, 3 J Allan Cash, fig. 2 John & Penny Hubley, fig. 4 Z. Guard Zinc Anodes. 5.6 Fig. 1 Colin Johnson, fig. 2 Ford, fig. 3 J Allan Cash, figs. 4, 5 British Steel. 5.7 Fig. 2 Colin Johnson, fig. 3 Armitage Shanks. 5.8 Figs. 1, 2 Michael Holford, fig. 3 John & Penny Hubley. 5.9 Fig. 1 J Allan Cash, fig. 2 Royal Mint, fig. 3 Miles Laboratories Ltd, fig. 4 Colin Johnson, fig. 5 Holt Studios. 5.10 Fig. 1 Armitage Shanks, fig. 2 Science Photo Library, fig. 3 Science Photo Library, fig. 4 ICI, fig. 5 Royal Mint. 6.1 Fig. 1 Science Photo Library, fig. 2 British Petroleum, fig. 3 Colin Johnson, fig. 4 National Coal Board, fig. 5 Richard Folwell/Science Photo Library. 6.2 Figs. 1, 4 British Museum/Natural History, fig. 2 Royal Society of Chemistry, fig. 3 Colin Johnson. 6.3 Figs. 1, 2, 4, 5, 6 National Coal Board, fig. 3 British Steel. 6.4 Fig. 2 Ann Ronan, fig. 4 photo by British Petroleum, fig. 5 Richard Folwell/Science Photo Library. 6.5 Figs. 1, 2 a Shell photograph, figs. 4, 5, 6 photos by British Petroleum. 6.6 Fig. 1 a British Petroleum picture. 6.8 Figs. 1, 4 British Gas, fig. 2 Tropix, fig. 3 J Allan Cash, figs. 5, 6 Colin Johnson. 6.9 Fig. 4 Fyffees Group Ltd, fig. 5 BXL Plastics, fig. 6 Colin Johnson. 6.10 Figs. 1, 2 British Museum/Natural History, fig. 3 J Allan Cash, fig. 4 De Beers, fig. 5 Topham. 6.11 Fig. 2 Lead Development Association, fig. 3 Glass Manufacturers Federation, figs. 4, 5 British Geological Survey, fig. 6 Geoscience Features. 6.12 Figs. 1, 4 Welsh Water Authority, fig. 5 Jean Lane/Frank Lane Picture Agency. 6.13 Figs. 1, 2 Welsh Water Authority, fig. 4 The Times Newspapers, figs. 5, 6 Friends of the Earth. 6.14 Figs. 1, 2, 3 Permutit, fig. 4 J Allan Cash. 6.15 Fig. 1 Geoscience Features, fig. 2 Colin Johnson, fig. 3 Permutit. 7.1 Fig. 1 ICI, fig. 2 John Schmid/Tropix, fig. 3 Mark Bouton/ICCE, fig. 4 Consolidated Gold Fields PLC. 7.2 Fig. 2 Holt Studios, fig. 4 Museum of Rural Life, fig. 5 Frants Hartman/Frank Lane Agency. 7.3 Figs. 1, 2 Colin Johnson, fig. 4 ICI. 7.4 Fig. 2 Johnson-Mathey, figs. 3, 4 ICI, fig. 5 Vivian Fifield. 7.5 Fig. 1 Mansell, figs. 2, 6 J Allan Cash, fig. 4 Farmers' Weekley, fig. 5 Geoscience Features. 7.7 Fig. 1 Science Photo Library, fig. 2 British Gypsum, fig. 3 Ronald Sheridan Photo Library, fig. 4 Ann Ronan, fig. 5 Colin Johnson. 7.8 Fig. 1 Thames Water, fig. 2 Topham, fig. 3 Colin Johnson, fig. 4 ICI. 7.9 Fig. 1 Science Photo Library, fig. 2 J Allan Cash, fig. 3 Colin Johnson, figs. 4, 5 ICI. 7.10 Figs. 1, 2 ICI. 7.11 Fig. 1 J Allan Cash, figs. 2, 5 Colin Johnson, fig. 3 Alpine Refrigerated Distribution (part of NFC Distribution Group), fig. 4 Barnaby's Picture Library. 7.12 Fig. 2 John & Penny Hubley, fig. 3 ICI, fig. 4 Safeways Foodstore, fig. 5 Van den Berghs & Jurgens. 7.13 Fig. 1 Prato/Bruce Coleman, fig. 2 ICI, fig. 3 British Petroleum, fig. 4 Science Museum, fig. 5 Telefocus, fig. 6 The Warmer Campaign. 7.14 Fig. 1 a Shell photograph, figs. 2, 3 ICI, fig. 4 Formech, fig. 5 British Petroleum.

All about matter

The world of chemistry

Fig. 1 Is this the world of chemistry?

*Fig. 2 Is **this** the world of chemistry?*

Fig. 3 How about this?

All the photos on this page suggest something about the world of chemistry. But what does the "world of chemistry" mean to you? To many people it means a chemist's shop, a chemistry laboratory, or perhaps a large chemical works. All of these are part of the world of chemistry, but it's a world which stretches much further than that — it comes into the daily lives of us all.

Some people imagine that chemistry is only the business of scientists — men and women in white coats with mysterious jobs to do in strange laboratories. Others tend to think of it as something rather dangerous and unpleasant. They do not realise that chemistry also plays a vital part in the supply of food, water and fuel to our homes, in looking after our health and comfort, and in the production of materials as different as paper, fabrics, plastics and steel.

Most people with a knowledge of chemistry find it helpful in one way or another. For instance, knowing some chemistry helps with many everyday tasks: feeding a family, using cleaning materials and disinfectants, looking after a garden, treating simple accidents and illnesses, and living safely with all the household products which are now available. It also helps in reaching an opinion about some of the important issues which affect the future of us all.

What is chemistry about?

Chemistry sets out to answer certain kinds of questions. For example:

- [ ] What are substances made of?
- [ ] Why do they behave as they do?
- [ ] Can we make new substances which will be useful to us?
- [ ] Can we use our understanding of one substance to predict how another one will behave?
- [ ] How can we extract and use materials from the earth?

Of course, there are hundreds of possible questions, but the main point about them is this:

- [ ] Chemistry is the study of the materials which make up our world, both living and non-living.

Asking questions in chemistry

Any study of science involves asking lots of questions. These may be questions about facts, or about ideas and theories, or basic principles. Very often they are questions about how to do things, and how to communicate the answers. The questions in this book are there to help with all these tasks. Some of the questions can be answered by reading the text on the same page. Others may send you looking elsewhere in the book, or even to a library.

The questions are there to help you to learn and understand some chemistry. They are *also* to give you practice in finding things out, and in presenting your answers to other people. Where there are facts and figures to be sorted out, there may be just one 'right answer', but it is important to realise that some questions are different. Do not be put off if the question leaves you some choice in the way you answer. The way of tackling the question may be as important as the answer itself!

Fig. 4 Well?

Fig. 5 Still thinking?

Fig. 6 There's as much chemistry here, as in any of the other pictures!

Looking at the pictures

The pictures in this book are there to help you understand the text, but they also tell a story of their own. Chemistry does not happen in some isolated spot, untouched by the world in which we live, or by the passage of time. It plays its part in the economic health of our society, and it helps to shape the environment in which we live — for good and ill. It is part of the daily lives of people all over the world. The pictures in this book will help you to see how this has come about.

Q1 If your teacher agrees, illustrate the cover or the front page of your chemistry notebook by using cuttings from magazines which show what chemistry means to you. The questions on this page will give you some ideas, or you may prefer to choose a theme of your own.

What is 'matter'?

The word 'matter' is used to cover all the substances and materials from which the universe is made. Many millions of different substances are known. All of them are either solids, liquids or gases.

Solids, liquids and gases

If you look carefully at Fig. 1 (or even better, at an actual candle!) you will see that the candle itself is made from **solid** wax. There is some **liquid** wax at the base of the wick, and perhaps running down the side. Wax in the form of **gas** is just a little more difficult to see. If you look closely you will notice that the outer part of the flame actually surrounds a greyish patch. This greyish part of the flame is unburned gas, just like the 'blue cone' at the centre of a Bunsen flame.

Fig. 1 Wax – as solid, liquid and gas.

	a		**b**	
candle wax	⇌	**melted wax**	⇌	**centre of flame**
(solid)	**d**	(liquid)	**c**	(gas)

As the temperature rises, the separate changes are:

a the solid wax **melts** to become a liquid

b the liquid wax **evaporates** to become a gas (or vapour)

and – in reverse – as the temperature falls:

c the gas **condenses** to become a liquid (which you may have noticed when you snuff out a candle between finger and thumb), and

d the liquid **solidifies** (i.e. **'freezes'**) to become a solid.

You will be able to think of other examples. The best known one is

	melts		evaporates	
ice	⇌	**water**	⇌	**steam**
(solid)	freezes	(liquid)	condenses	(gas)

Water, wax and very many other substances can exist in the **three states:** solid, liquid and gas. It is usual to represent these by (s), (l) and (g) for short.

Fig. 2 Michael Faraday (1791–1867), whose work led to a much better understanding of solids, liquids and gases.

What happens when substances change their state?

Water can exist as a solid, a liquid, or a gas, depending on the conditions. Almost every other material can exist in these three states. What is it about substances that makes this possible?

All the evidence points towards the idea that every substance is made up of tiny particles. All that happens when substances change from solid to liquid to gas is that the particles arrange themselves differently, as shown in Fig. 4.

In a solid, the particles are tightly packed together and arranged neatly in rows and columns.

In a liquid, the particles are still touching, but they are not neatly packed together, and they can move around.

In a gas, the particles are far apart, and they move *very* rapidly in all directions. They continually collide with one another and with the walls of the container, creating the effect called **pressure**.

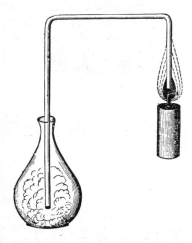

Fig. 3 A drawing of one of Michael Faraday's experiments on gases (see Q1).

Q1 The illustration in Fig. 3 came from a famous book called *The Chemical History of a Candle* by Michael Faraday, published in 1861.
Explain what you think is going on here.

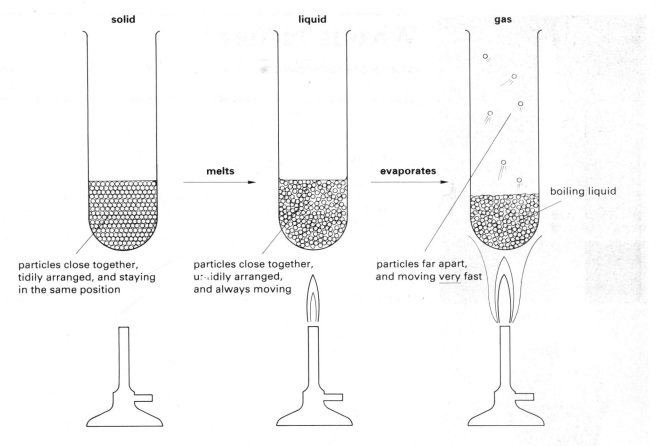

solid   liquid   gas

melts   evaporates

boiling liquid

particles close together, tidily arranged, and staying in the same position

particles close together, untidily arranged, and always moving

particles far apart, and moving <u>very</u> fast

Fig. 4 Particles in a solid, a liquid and a gas: notice how heat energy needs to be supplied to make the material change from solid to liquid to gas.

Sublimation

A few substances, when heated and allowed to cool, 'miss out' the liquid state altogether. Iodine, for instance, behaves like this:

               heat   allow to cool
solid iodine $\rightarrow$ iodine **gas** $\rightarrow$ **solid** iodine

The iodine **sublimes**, and the crystals you can see in Fig. 5 are called the sublimate. The warmth of the room is often enough to cause iodine crystals to sublime in the bottle.

☐ The process taking place when a heated solid turns directly to a gas, without melting, is called **sublimation**.

Fig. 5 Iodine crystals subliming.

> **Q2** Figure 6 shows a rugby match in progress. Some spectators are seated in rows, and keep to fixed positions all through the match. Others are standing on the terraces, and mingle with one another, perhaps even 'flowing' from place to place. The main space is occupied by a small number of players, running around colliding with one another.
> What has all this to do with solids, liquids and gases?

Fig. 6 A rugby match in progress. What has this to do with particles? (See Q2.)

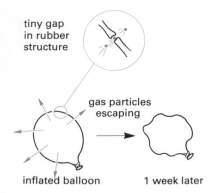

gas particles
escaping

inflated balloon   1 week later

*Fig. 1 Gas particles diffuse through the
surface of a balloon.*

1.3

More about gases, liquids and solids

Gases are quite different from liquids and solids because the particles in a gas are moving about rapidly all the time. The particles in the air around you are moving – on average – at about the cruising speed of Concorde.

> **Q1** You cannot feel the impact of gas particles in the air when they collide with you, although they are moving with great speed.
> Suggest some possible reasons for this.

Diffusion

A sealed balloon gradually 'goes down' because the rapidly moving gas particles escape through tiny holes in the rubber. This is an example of **diffusion** (Fig. 1). The lighter the gas particles, the more rapidly they move, and the more quickly they diffuse away.

> **Q2** Diffusion can also take place in liquids, but it is slower. Use the ideas about particles to suggest why this is.

*Fig. 2 Diffusion: the gas particles in bromine
and air mix completely when the glass plate
separating the containers is removed.*

You can sometimes see the movement of particles as they move among one another – if they are big enough. This is called **'Brownian movement'**, and is named after the Scottish scientist Robert Brown. It occurs when the visible particles are jostled by huge numbers of fast-moving smaller particles. Imagine leaving a trolley in a crowded supermarket. If you return to it later, the trolley will be in a different spot, simply because it has been pushed around by all the passers-by. The particles in gases and liquids jostle one another in just the same way, and this is how diffusion occurs.

Gas pressure: what happens when you squash a gas?

> **Q3** Gases can be compressed, but liquids and solids cannot. Explain this, bearing in mind the diagrams in 1.2, Fig. 4.

The particles of a gas are colliding all the time with the walls of their container. All these tiny impacts produce a force on the inside surface of the container. The force on a given area of this surface is the gas **pressure**. If you change the size of the container, without changing the number of gas particles, then the pressure is altered. The pressure becomes greater when the same number of particles are crowded into a smaller space.

> **Q4** When a gas is heated, the particles move more rapidly. Explain what will happen to the volume of the heated gas, if the pressure is not allowed to change.

*Fig. 3 Sugar will dissolve slowly even if you
don't stir – because of diffusion.*

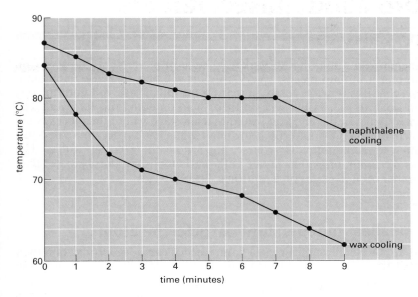

Fig. 4 *This graph shows how the temperatures of liquid naphthalene and liquid wax change when they are allowed to cool until they become solids.*

Looking at changes of state

The graph in Fig. 4 was drawn by plotting the temperatures of two substances every minute, as they cooled. These were the figures:

Time (mins)	0	1	2	3	4	5	6	7	8	9
Temperature (°C)										
naphthalene	87	85	83	82	81	80	80	80	78	76
wax	84	78	73	71	70	69	68	66	64	62

Fig. 5 *Melting ice and water: a change of state.*

You can see from both curves that changes of state have taken place. Both naphthalene and wax are liquids when the temperature is first measured. As the liquids cool, the temperatures drop steadily at first. As the temperatures get lower the liquids cool down more slowly. Then you notice that the curves change: the naphthalene stops cooling altogether for a while, and the wax cools more slowly than you would expect. During these periods of time a **change of state** is taking place. The **liquids** are turning to **solids**.

> **Q5** Read off from the graph
> (a) the melting point (= freezing point) of naphthalene, and
> (b) the melting range of the wax used in this experiment.

Naphthalene is a single substance, and has a 'sharp' melting point. Wax, like many other mixtures, melts and freezes gradually.

> **Q6** Some water is cooled for 20 minutes. During this time its temperature goes down from +10°C to −10°C. Draw axes, and sketch the curve you would see when these results are plotted.

Fig. 6 *Boiling water and steam: a change of state.*

Atoms and molecules

Let's begin with a milk bottle top! It is made of aluminium. Suppose you start to tear it up into pieces. Every little bit will be a piece of aluminium. Imagine that it is possible to go on tearing the milk bottle top until the bits are too small to see. Could you (in theory) go on doing this for ever? The answer is 'No!'. In the end you would reach a stage where the pieces could get no smaller. You would reach this limit when each piece contained just one **atom** of aluminium. Of course, the whole thing is impossible. The number of aluminium atoms in one milk bottle top is ten times greater than the number of sand grains on all the beaches of Britain!

Fig. 1 John Dalton (1766–1844), who suggested the symbols for elements and compounds shown in Fig. 2.

Fig. 2 Dalton's symbols for some elements and compounds show his ideas about atoms and how they joined up.

The smallest independent particle: the atom

Atoms are the smallest particles in nature which can normally exist on their own. All the substances and materials we know about are made up from atoms, very often groups of atoms linked together in some way. The copper in an electric wire consists entirely of copper atoms, the mercury in a thermometer consists of mercury atoms, and the helium which is used to fill balloons at a fairground consists of helium atoms. Atoms are the 'building blocks' of nature.

Q1 Ninety-two different kinds of atom are found naturally on the earth. Just a few of these types make up 98.5% of the earth's crust. Use *Datapage I1* to find out which they are, and show them in a suitable chart or table.

Atoms linked together: molecules

Although some elements, such as helium, have atoms which can exist on their own, it is far more common for atoms to link up with one another. When two or more atoms become linked together they form a new kind of 'building block', called a **molecule**. If you tear up a polythene bag instead of a milk bottle top, the smallest bit of plastic you can reach is a polythene molecule. This particular molecule is built up from many atoms of carbon and hydrogen linked together. It is a fairly complicated one, but many molecules are much simpler. Molecules of water, for instance, contain just two atoms of hydrogen and one atom of oxygen linked together.

John Dalton and the atom

Dalton became a teacher in his own village school at the age of 12. As a young man he moved to Manchester, where he studied and worked as a lecturer for the rest of his life. His ideas about atoms came from studying the proportions by weight in which elements combine to form compounds.

Q2 John Dalton's symbols for atoms and molecules are shown in Fig. 2.
(a) Copy the drawing for one carbon dioxide molecule (he called it 'carbonic acid'), and label it to show what each part represents.
(b) Invent your own symbol for a hydrogen atom, and make a drawing which shows a water molecule.
Dalton got it wrong (see Fig. 2). What was his mistake?

Q3 The pictures on these pages show some famous people whose work has helped us to understand atoms and molecules. As a library project, find out what you can about the life of any one of them.

Fig. 4 Ernest Rutherford (1871–1937), whose picture of the atom we now use, seen here on the right.

Fig. 3 Prof. Dorothy Hodgkin (b. 1910) and her research group worked out the structure of this molecule, which contains hundreds of atoms. It is insulin, the substance which controls the glucose level in our blood. Injections of it are used to treat diabetes.

The structure of atoms

Most people think of atoms as the smallest particles which exist. In a way that is true. The smallest bit of a wall which can exist is one brick. You could smash up a brick into fragments, but then you wouldn't have anything to rebuild the wall with. In the same way, the smallest bit of a gold ring is a gold atom. The atom *can* be broken up, but it's no longer gold when you have done that, and you would not be able to use the fragments for re-making the ring. So it is true, in a sense, that atoms are the smallest particles which can exist. If the atoms are broken up you no longer have a recognisable substance.

We know quite a lot more about atoms:

☐ we know how big most of them are
☐ we can tell what they weigh
☐ we know that most of their mass is at the centre
☐ we believe that even atoms themselves are mostly empty space
☐ we know something about the even smaller particles from which atoms are made
☐ we know something about the forces which hold an atom together.

If atoms are so tiny, how can we possibly know about fragments of atoms, which are even smaller? The answer is that we have to rely on 'indirect evidence'. That's not so difficult: you do it all the time. If you see a big lorry going uphill you don't have to look inside to see if it is loaded. You don't even have to look at it directly at all. If you can hear the bodywork clattering and bumping, you know that it is probably empty. The sound of the engine will give you some indirect evidence as well. Indirect evidence about atoms is rather more difficult to come by, but we have quite enough to be able to build up a reasonable picture of what atoms are like.

Fig. 5 Indirect evidence: we can tell without looking at it that this lorry is heavily laden.

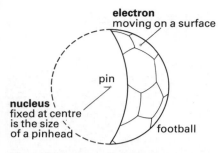

Fig. 1 *If the nucleus of a hydrogen atom was to become the size of a pinhead, the orbit of its electron would be about the size of a football.*

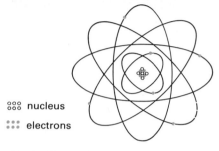

○○○ nucleus
∷∷∷ electrons

Fig. 2 *All atoms have this type of structure, with protons and neutrons in the centre, with electrons 'whizzing' round the outside.*

Fig. 3 *This is as near as we can get to photographing atoms. This is the metal iridium, and the light spots show the position of its atoms.*

Looking closely at atoms

No-one has ever seen an atom, but there is enough indirect evidence to give quite a good picture of what an atom is like.

Empty space

First of all, an atom is mostly empty space! There is a bit at the centre, called the **nucleus**. Then there is a lot of space, and whizzing around in this space are a number of **electrons**. In the simplest atom, hydrogen, there is just one electron. Figure 2 gives you some idea of the amount of space in a hydrogen atom. Imagine this one electron moving about on the surface of something the size of a football. On this hugely enlarged scale, the nucleus at the centre would be about as big as a pinhead. The rest is space.

The nucleus

As shown in Fig. 2, the nucleus is:

☐ 'fixed' at the centre of the atom
☐ the heavy part of the atom
☐ positively charged.

It contains two kinds of particle: **protons** and **neutrons**. Protons are the particles which have a positive charge. Neutrons have no charge. These two particles in the nucleus have almost exactly the same mass, but the neutron is slightly heavier.

The electrons

The electrons are:

☐ 'moving' in the outer part of the atom
☐ much lighter than the particles in the nucleus
☐ negatively charged.

The mass of an electron is small: about 1836 electrons would have the same mass as 1 proton.

Q1	Copy and complete the following table.			
	Name of particle	Where found in atom	Relative mass	Charge
	proton	– – – – –	– – – – –	+1
	neutron	in nucleus	– – – – –	– – –
	electron	– – – – –	1/1836	– – –

Making atoms visible

Figure 3 is a photograph of a tiny piece of the metal iridium, magnified by more than a million times. To take this picture the point of an iridium needle was bombarded with helium. The atoms of helium lost electrons as they collided with the iridium atoms, and then they bounced off in straight lines towards a photographic film. Each bright spot on the photograph shows the position of an iridium atom where one of these collisions took place.

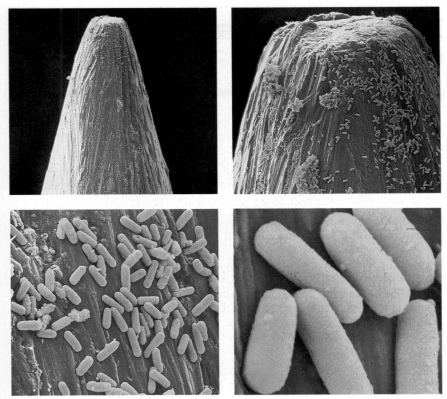

Fig. 4 *These pictures show the same pin head. Even at the highest magnification (× 10 000) it is not possible to see any atoms.*

How many of these particles are in an atom?

The list on *Datapage B* gives the elements arranged in order of mass. Hydrogen is the first element, because it has the smallest mass. Its nucleus contains just one proton, so it is element number 1.

The first three elements in order of mass

Element	Symbol	No. of protons	No. of neutrons	No. of electrons
hydrogen	H	1	0	1
helium	He	2	2	2
lithium	Li	3	4	3

Notice that the number of electrons in an atom is always equal to the number of protons. This means the positive charges in the nucleus are exactly balanced by an equal number of negative charges on the electrons. The atom itself has no overall electric charge.

☐ The number of protons in an atom is known as its **atomic number**. It is usually represented by the capital letter Z.

☐ The total number of protons *and* neutrons in an atom is known as its **mass number**. It is usually represented by the capital letter A.

☐ The full symbol for an atom X is written $^A_Z X$. For example, the atoms of the first three elements shown in the Table above are written: $^1_1 H$, $^4_2 He$, and $^7_3 Li$.

Q2 Find out from *Datapage A,B* the values of Z and A for the elements carbon, silicon, tin and lead. Write their symbols in full.

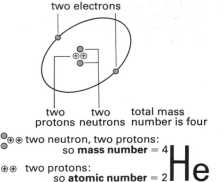

Fig. 5 *A helium atom $^4_2 He$ (not to scale).*

More about the structure of the atom

The electrons are the most important part of an atom from a chemical point of view. One or more of the electrons are always involved in some way when a chemical reaction takes place.

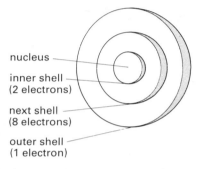

Fig. 1 'Sodium lamps' glow yellow as electrons move in and out of their normal places in the sodium atom.

nucleus

inner shell (2 electrons)

next shell (8 electrons)

outer shell (1 electron)

Fig. 2 A sodium atom, showing its 11 electrons.

How are the electrons arranged in an atom?

One common picture of an atom is like a miniature 'solar system', with the nucleus at the centre and the electrons moving like planets in orbits around it. This is by no means the whole story, but there is some evidence to support the idea. This evidence comes from measurements of the amount of energy needed to 'pull away' the electrons from an atom.

A sodium atom has 11 electrons. Starting from the outside, the amounts of energy needed to remove those electrons, one at a time, are:

Electron	1st	2nd	3rd	4th	5th	6th	7th	8th	9th	10th	11th
Energy to remove it	0.5	5	7	10	13	17	20	25	29	141	159

Q1 Plot a graph of these figures, using equally spaced points along the horizontal axis for the 11 electrons.

Electrons in 'shells'

You can see that much less energy is needed to remove the 1st electron than to remove the others. It is also obvious that very much more energy is needed to remove the last two electrons – numbers 10 and 11. These observations have led to the idea which is shown in Fig. 2: that the electrons in an atom are arranged in 'shells', like the layers of an onion. The electrons in the outer shell can be removed most easily, and take part in chemical reactions. The inner electrons are *very* hard to remove.

In the sodium atom the electrons are thought of as being arranged in three shells:

Outer shell 1 electron (1st electron)
Next shell 8 electrons (2nd–9th electrons)
Inner shell 2 electrons (10th and 11th electrons)

The 'electron arrangement' of a sodium atom is therefore usually written $_{11}Na,2,8,1$.

When the outer shell of electrons in an atom is 'full', chemical reactions are difficult, since the energy required to remove an electron is considerable. For example, the noble gas atoms He and Ne have electron arrangements $_2He,2$ and $_{10}Ne,2,8$. The electrons in the first eighteen elements are arranged into 'shells' like this:

Fig. 3 Niels Bohr (1885–1962), who suggested the idea of electron 'shells'.

H 1							He 2
Li 2,1	Be 2,2	B 2,3	C 2,4	N 2,5	O 2,6	F 2,7	Ne 2,8
Na 2,8,1	Mg 2,8,2	Al 2,8,3	Si 2,8,4	P 2,8,5	S 2,8,6	Cl 2,8,7	Xe 2,8,

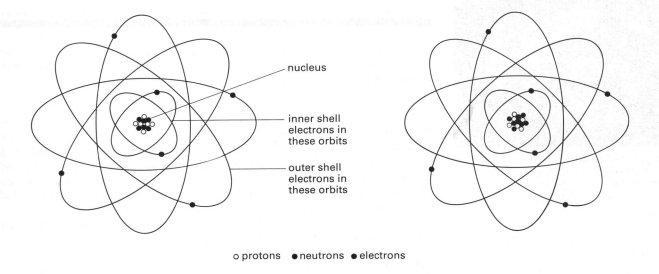

nucleus

inner shell electrons in these orbits

outer shell electrons in these orbits

o protons ●neutrons ●electrons

Fig. 4 *Two isotopes of carbon: carbon-12 and carbon-14.*

Isotopes

Two kinds of particle are found in the nucleus of an atom: protons and neutrons. The number of protons determines which kind of atom it is. All atoms with 1 proton are hydrogen, all atoms with 6 protons are carbon, all atoms with 17 protons are chlorine, and so on.

The number of neutrons in atoms of the same element is not always the same, however. For example, there are three different kinds of hydrogen atom. All three have just 1 proton in the nucleus, but one has 1 neutron, another has 2 neutrons, and yet another has 3.

☐ Atoms which have the *same atomic number (Z)* but *different mass numbers (A)* are known as **isotopes**.

Q2 Write down the values of the mass number and the atomic number for these three different types of hydrogen atom. Then write out their symbols in full.

Q3 Here is some information about the isotopes of chlorine:

Name of isotope	No. of protons (atomic number, Z)	No. of neutrons and protons (mass number, A)
chlorine-35	17	35
chlorine-37	17	37

(a) Work out the number of neutrons present in each of the isotopes of chlorine.

(b) Write down the full symbol for one atom of each isotope.

Fig. 5 *A modern mass spectrometer, used for analysing isotopes of all kinds.*

Many substances: elements and compounds

Fig. 1 *These are all single substances.*

The objects around you are made of many different substances. Some are very simple, and others are extremely complicated, but just by looking at them you have no way of telling that.

What is the universe made of?

If you look around, it is hard to believe that there is any answer to this question. Everything seems so different. What can water, wool and wood have in common? Or trains, turnips and tadpoles? The first part of the answer is that they are all built from a range of different **substances**. Water is one kind of substance. Wood is a mixture of several substances. Tadpoles contain thousands!

Everything which exists – living, non-living or dead – is made from one single or many different substances.

One substance or many?

Item	'Substances' it contains	Single substance or many?
drinks can	aluminium	single substance
sugar lump	sucrose	single substance
pure water	water	single substance
coin	an alloy, e.g. copper and nickel	mixture of single substances
cup of tea	water, milk, sugar	mixture of substances
glass of milk	water, fats, salts, protein	mixture of substances
sheet of paper	wood or cloth fibres, filler, gum	mixture of substances
pencil	wood, graphite, clay	mixture of substances

Fig. 2 *These are all mixtures.*

What are substances made of?

You can see from the table above that aluminium is a *single* substance. In other words, it is the same all the way through. Copper and nickel are both single substances, too. You can mix them up to make something (like the metal in the coin) which *looks* like a single substance, but is in fact a mixture. Many everyday things are very complicated mixtures. Even to make a cup of tea you must mix some single substances with another substance (milk) which is already a mixture.

☐ Single substances contain just one kind of atom, one kind of molecule, or the same structural unit – all the way through.

☐ Mixed substances contain more than one kind of atom or molecule.

Mixed substances can sometimes be separated quite easily, as explained in more detail in 2.6 and 2.7.

Two kinds of single substance: elements and compounds

All the millions of known substances are built up from just 92 simple substances, called the **elements**. These elements are different from all other substances in one way: each one is made up from just one kind of atom.

☐ A copper wire consists of copper atoms all the way through. The mercury in a thermometer contains nothing but mercury atoms. The gas neon contains neon atoms only. Mercury and neon are elements.

Fig. 3 *This granite is a mixture.*

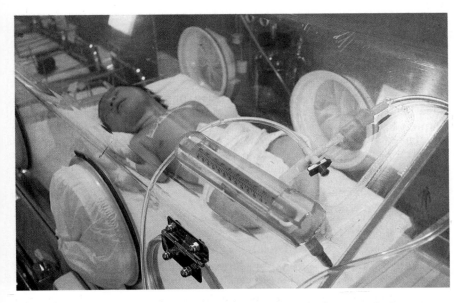

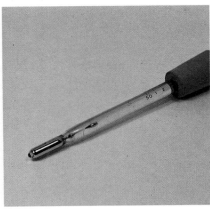

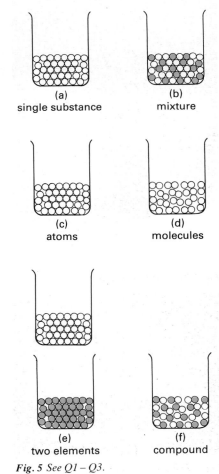

Fig. 4 *Can you name the 'elements at work' in these pictures?*

(a)
single substance

(b)
mixture

When the atoms of two or more different elements are linked together in some way, the substance they form is known as a **compound**. A compound is a single substance, because it contains the same kind of particles all the way through. It's just that each individual particle contains more than one element.

☐ If an atom of the element carbon is linked to two atoms of the element oxygen, the new particle they form is a molecule of carbon dioxide. Carbon dioxide is a single substance, but its particles each contain two elements. Carbon dioxide is a compound.

(c)
atoms

(d)
molecules

Q1 Look at diagrams (a) and (b) in Fig. 5, which represent single substances and mixed substances. How can you tell that diagram (b) does not represent a single substance?

Q2 Look at diagrams (c) and (d) in Fig. 5. Each single 'blob' represents one atom. What does diagram (d) tell you about the differences between an atom and a molecule?

Q3 Look at diagrams (e) and (f) in Fig. 5, which represent elements and compounds. What do these diagrams tell you about the differences between an element and a compound?

Q4 Draw diagrams to show the difference between a mixture of iron and sulphur (two *elements*) and iron sulphide (a *compound* of iron and sulphur).

(e)
two elements

(f)
compound

Fig. 5 *See Q1 – Q3.*

23

Chemical symbols and formulae

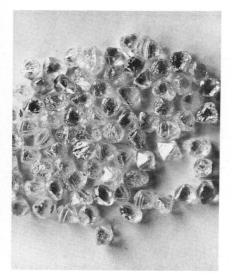

Fig. 1 Diamonds are a form of the element carbon, symbol C – the first letter of its name.

Fig. 2 These old cooking pots are made of iron, symbol Fe from its Latin name ferrum.

Fig. 3 The filament in this light bulb is made of tungsten, symbol W from its old German name wolfram.

Most elements have fairly long and awkward names. In past centuries there have been several suggestions for getting round this problem. The best known idea was John Dalton's (see 1.4, Fig. 2). Today we represent each element by one or two letters, known as its **chemical symbol**. A full list of chemical symbols is given on *Datapage B*, and there are a few examples below. These symbols are internationally agreed, and used in all countries of the world.

Some chemical symbols

Element	Symbol	Notes
carbon	C	first letter of name
calcium	Ca	first two letters of name, to avoid confusion with carbon
cobalt	Co	first two letters of name
copper	Cu	first two letters of Latin name (cuprum), to avoid confusion with cobalt

All the symbols follow certain rules:

☐ All symbols consist of one or two letters, never more than two.
☐ The first (or only) letter is always a *capital* letter.
☐ The second letter, if there is one, is always a *small* letter.
☐ Strictly speaking, the chemical symbol represents *one atom* of the element. It should not really be used as an abbreviation for the name.

Where possible, symbols have been made up with letters from the English name. In a few cases the Latin name has been used instead.

Some chemical symbols from Latin names

Element	Symbol	Latin name from which symbol is taken
silver	Ag	*argentum*
gold	Au	*aurum*
copper	Cu	*cuprum*
iron	Fe	*ferrum*
mercury	Hg	*hydrargyrum*
sodium	Na	*natrium*
lead	Pb	*plumbum*
tin	Sn	*stannum*

[There is more about the names of elements on Datapage T, U.]

Writing the chemical formula of an element

The formula of a substance is made up from the symbols of the atoms it contains. The formula gives more information than this, however. It shows the **numbers** of atoms which are present in the smallest particle of the substance.

The chemical *symbol* for an element is not necessarily its chemical *formula*. In the case of metals, carbon and some gases the symbols and formulae are the same, because the smallest particle of the substance itself is just one single atom.

Non-metals usually consist of molecules in which two or more atoms are linked together. The chemical formula must show this as you can see in the table opposite and in Figs. 5 and 6.

دراسة تأثير ظروف المعالجة على نشاطية
واختيارية حفاز Pt/Al_2O_3

上述反应中 ZnO(a) 和 ZnO(p) 分别表示活性和钝性的氧化锌，
$(O)_{ad}$ 表示吸附在电极表面层的锌原子上的氧原子

根据以上的反应机理，可以推导出锌在KOH溶液中阳极溶解

КТ обозначает действительный катализатор, который образуется на основе $HgCl_2$ и реагентов. Стадия (П) является лимитирующей ста-

溶液にNaOHを加えて室温でN_2ガスを吹きこみかくはんを続けて濃緑色溶液を得た。反

Fig. 4 *Chemical symbols are the same the world over. Can you find the formulae for 3 elements and 5 compounds?*

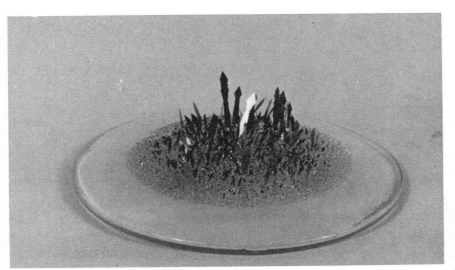

Fig. 5 *Iodine has the symbol I. Two atoms link together to make the smallest particle of iodine, so it has the formula I_2.*

Some elements with a formula which is not the same as the symbol

Element	Symbol	Formula	No. of atoms linked in one molecule
hydrogen	H	H_2	2
iodine	I	I_2	2 (Fig. 5)
oxygen	O	O_2	2
phosphorus	P	P_4	4 (Fig. 6)
sulphur	S	S_8	8

Q1 Explain why the chemical formula for sulphur is written as S_8, and not just S.

Q2 Chlorine gas consists of molecules, each containing two atoms. Write the symbol and the formula for chlorine.

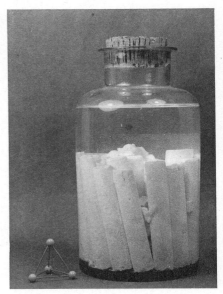

Fig. 6 *Phosphorus has the symbol P. Four atoms link together to make the smallest independent particle of phosphorus, formula P_4.*

What is a chemical reaction?

When two substances are mixed, their particles may or may not affect one another. If they simply mix, there is no permanent change, and they can usually be 'un-mixed' quite easily. However, when a chemical reaction takes place, there are changes to the particles of the substances which are present. Sometimes a chemical reaction is no more than the transfer of a single electron from one atom to another. Other chemical reactions are extremely complex processes.

Thinking about chemical reactions

Suppose you had a beaker containing a dozen balls – six white and six blue. These represent the particles of two substances mixed together (Fig. 1). When you shake the beaker the balls are re-arranged. You have the same mixture, but it is differently arranged (Fig. 2).

Now imagine that the white balls each have a small patch of cloth attached to them, and that the blue balls each have a 'sticky' patch of 'Velcro' on them.

> **Q1** What happens if you shake the beaker now? Without reading ahead, write down all the possibilities, explaining how each may arise.

After a few minutes shaking you might expect to find:

(1) some white balls on their own
(2) some blue balls on their own
(3) some 'pairs' of blue and white balls
(4) some 'pairs' of blue balls (since one piece of Velcro will stick to another)
(5) just possibly a 'trio' of two blue balls stuck to one white one, or two white ones stuck to a single blue.

How is a chemical reaction represented in print?

The white balls represent one kind of atom, symbol Wh. The blue balls represent another kind of atom, symbol Bl. In cases (3), (4), and (5) a 'new substance' has been formed, and this is what happens when a **chemical reaction** takes place. Reaction (3) is illustrated in Fig. 5. During the reaction, atoms have become linked together. These links are called **chemical bonds**.

These particular 'reactions' could be represented as a 'chemical equations'. A chemical equation is a way of summing up what happens in a chemical reaction, either in words or by using symbols and formulae. This is explained on p. 217 in the Appendix. The equations for these reactions can be written:

(3) $Wh + Bl \rightarrow WhBl$ (a new substance has been formed)

(4) $Bl + Bl \rightarrow Bl_2$ (a new substance has been formed)

(5) $Wh + 2Bl \rightarrow WhBl_2$ (a new substance has been formed)

> **Q2** Write the 'chemical equation' for what happens when one blue ball links with two white ones to form a new substance.

Fig. 1 These balls represent particles of two different substances.

Fig. 2 When the substances are shaken, the particles might re-arrange to make a mixture like this.

Fig. 3 New substances are formed when white and blue particles link together. These represent some possible ones.

Fig. 4 *Some chemical reactions are extremely vigorous. Chemical bonds are being broken and re-formed very rapidly in this extreme heat.*

Different types of chemical reaction

Some books give long lists of different kinds of chemical reaction. But all you need to know is this: when the bonds between atoms are re-arranged, a chemical reaction has taken place. New substances are always formed in a chemical reaction. In example (3) above there was a simple change in which white 'atoms' linked up with blue 'atoms' to form 'white-blue molecules':

$$\text{'white atoms' + 'blue atoms'} \rightarrow \text{'white-blue molecules'}$$
$$\text{Wh + Bl} \rightarrow \text{WhBl}$$

The substances which react together are known as the **reactants**. The new substances formed are known as the **products**. So a chemical reaction may be summed up as:

$$\text{reactants} \rightarrow \text{products}$$

Making and breaking chemical bonds

Every time a chemical reaction takes place, two things must happen:

☐ bonds holding particles in the reacting substances together must be broken;
☐ new bonds, linking together the particles in the new substance, must be formed.

Another way of saying this is that 'bonds in the *reactants* must break before bonds in the *products* can form'. Chemical bonds are formed and broken when the outer electrons of one atom come under the influence of another. There is more about this in 1.10.

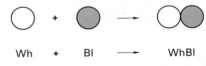

Wh + Bl ⟶ WhBl

Fig. 5 *A 'white atom' combines with a 'blue atom' to form a 'white–blue molecule'.*

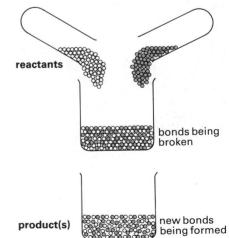

reactants

bonds being broken

product(s)

new bonds being formed

Fig. 6 *Bonds in the reactants must be broken before new bonds can be formed to make the product(s).*

27

Bonds between atoms – I

The 92 naturally occurring elements can form millions of different compounds. They can do this because their atoms are able to link with one another. It is difficult at first to see why atoms should link together, when you remember how they are constructed (see 1.5). They have a small positively charged part in the middle (the **nucleus**), and a number of negatively charged particles around this (the **electrons**).

When two atoms come close together their outer electrons almost meet. Since particles with the same electric charge repel each other, you would expect the atoms to move away from one another again. Very often this is all that happens. Under some circumstances, however, atoms do link together and chemical bonds are formed.

No bonds: atoms of helium

Each helium atom contains 2 protons, 2 neutrons and 2 electrons, as shown in Fig. 2. The nucleus is stable, and the electron shell is 'full'. There is no way in which the helium atom can become more stable by linking with another atom. So when two atoms collide, they bounce apart, and continue along new paths until they collide again. Helium is a 'noble gas' – there is more about these in 3.3. All noble gas atoms have full electron shells, including the outermost one. They do not link with one another to form molecules.

Evidence: Helium has the lowest boiling point of any substance. The forces between its particles must therefore be very weak indeed. No-one has ever been able to detect a helium particle which appears to contain more than one nucleus.

Covalent bond: molecules containing two atoms of hydrogen

Each atom of hydrogen contains 1 proton and 1 electron, as shown in Fig. 3. The nucleus is stable, but there is a 'vacancy' in the electron shell. When one hydrogen atom approaches another, its electron is attracted to the nucleus of the other atom. Similarly, its own nucleus attracts the electron of the other hydrogen atom. As both electrons come under the influence of both nuclei, it becomes impossible to distinguish which electron belongs to which nucleus. The two atoms end up by sharing the two electrons equally between them. This situation is known as a **covalent bond**.

□ Covalent bonds are formed by a process of **electron sharing**.

□ One shared **pair** of electrons makes up a **single** covalent bond.

□ When **two** shared pairs of electrons form the link between two atoms, this is known as a **double covalent bond**.

Evidence: It is possible to make measurements of the 'electron density' in a hydrogen molecule . A 'map', with 'contour lines' of equal electron density, can be plotted (see Fig. 4). This shows a symmetrical pattern in which the electrons are equally shared.

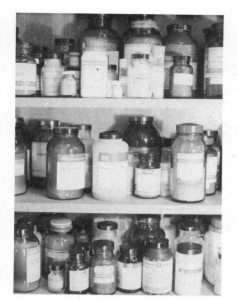

Fig. 1 Most of the ninety-two elements can join together to make up millions of different compounds. These chemistry lab shelves show only a few of them.

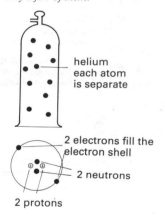

helium each atom is separate

2 electrons fill the electron shell

2 neutrons

2 protons

Fig. 2 Helium is one of the few elements which cannot become more stable by linking with other atoms. So helium gas contains helium atoms.

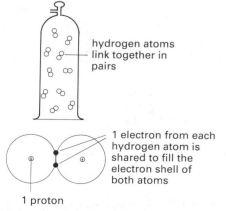

hydrogen atoms link together in pairs

1 electron from each hydrogen atom is shared to fill the electron shell of both atoms

1 proton

Fig. 3 Hydrogen atoms combine with each other (and other elements) to become stable. Hydrogen atoms link up in pairs so hydrogen gas contains hydrogen molecules.

Q1 What is the formula of the hydrogen molecule?

Q2 Write down the formulae of some other elements which form molecules in the same way.

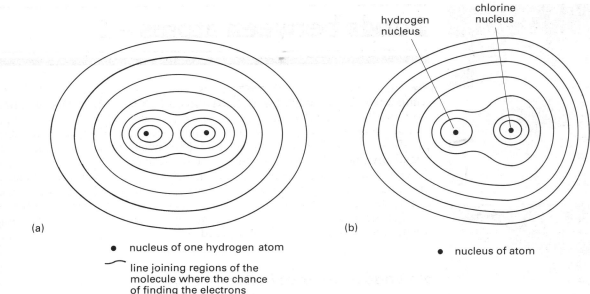

(a)

(b)

hydrogen
nucleus

chlorine
nucleus

● nucleus of one hydrogen atom

⌒ line joining regions of the
molecule where the chance
of finding the electrons
is the same

● nucleus of atom

Fig. 4 (a) This 'map' shows where the electrons are most likely to be found in a hydrogen molecule. *(b)* This 'map' shows where the electrons are most likely to be found in a hydrogen chloride molecule. Notice that the electrons are more likely to be near the chlorite atom.

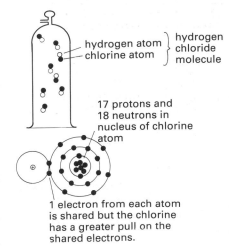

chlorine atoms
link together
in pairs

17 protons and
18 neutrons in
nucleus of chlorine
atom

1 electron from each atom
is shared, to form a covalent bond

Fig. 5 Chlorine gas contains chlorine molecules: two chlorine atoms share two electrons equally.

Covalent bond: molecules containing two atoms of chlorine

Each atom of chlorine contains 17 protons and 17 electrons. There is one 'vacancy' in the outer electron shell. When one chlorine atom approaches another its electrons are attracted to the nucleus of the other atom. The two atoms form a covalent bond by sharing two electrons equally, as shown in Fig. 5.

Polar covalent bond: molecules containing a hydrogen atom and a chlorine atom

When a hydrogen atom approaches a chlorine atom, covalent bonding can again occur. The only difference this time is that the chlorine atom has a greater pull on the shared electrons than the hydrogen atom does. Therefore the covalent bond is not equally shared. Hydrogen loses more than a half share in its electron. This bond is known as a **polar covalent bond.**

Evidence: First, the electron density map (Fig. 4(b)) shows that the shared electrons forming the covalent bond are unequally shared. They are likely to be found nearer to the chlorine atom than to the hydrogen atom. Secondly, hydrogen chloride reacts with water to form a solution which conducts electricity (as shown in 7.8). This kind of reaction can only happen between molecules with unequally shared electrons.

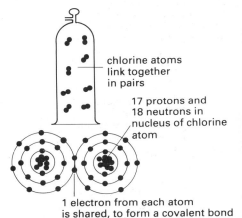

hydrogen atom
chlorine atom

} hydrogen
chloride
molecule

17 protons and
18 neutrons in
nucleus of chlorine
atom

1 electron from each atom
is shared but the chlorine
has a greater pull on the
shared electrons.

Fig. 6 Hydrogen chloride gas contains hydrogen chloride molecules. The hydrogen and chlorine atoms share a pair of electrons unequally – the electrons are more attracted to the chlorine.

> **Q3** Draw diagrams to show how the covalent bonds are formed in the following molecules: fluorine, ammonia, hydrogen fluoride (HF), ammonia, water, and methane.
>
> **Q4** Each of the bonds in carbon dioxide, CO_2, contains *two* shared pairs of electrons. Draw a diagram to show this information.

Bonds between atoms – II

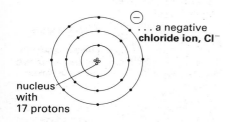

sodium atom, Na
with 1 electron in
its outer shell . . .

nucleus
with
11 protons

. . . transfers
this electron
to . . .

nucleus
with
17 protons

. . . a chlorine atom,
Cl, with 7 electrons
in its outer shell . . .

. . . forming . . .

. . . a positive
sodium ion, Na⁺,
and . . . .

nucleus
with
11 protons

. . . a negative
chloride ion, Cl⁻

nucleus
with
17 protons

Fig. 1 An ionic bond forming between a sodium atom and a chlorine atom. Na⁺ and Cl⁻ ions are formed as the electron is transferred.

Ionic bonds: linking a sodium atom and a chlorine atom

A sodium atom has 11 protons and 11 electrons, arranged in three shells: 2,8,1. A chlorine atom has 17 protons and 17 electrons, arranged in three shells: 2,8,7. When the two atoms collide, all the electrons again come under the influence of both nuclei. The chlorine atom has the greater pull on the electrons. The one electron in the outer shell of the sodium atom is pulled right into the single vacancy in the outer shell of the chlorine atom. This is shown in Fig. 1.

This leaves the sodium atom 'one electron short'. It now has 11 positive charges in the nucleus, and 10 negative charges on the surrounding electrons. It has acquired an overall charge of +1. It has become a **positive ion**. The chlorine atom, on the other hand, has gained an extra electron. It still has 17 positive charges in the nucleus, but there are now 18 negative charges surrounding it. Its overall charge is now –1; it has become a **negative ion**.

Because these ions are oppositely charged they attract one another strongly. The link which forms between them is known as an **ionic** (or **electrovalent**) **bond**. The bond is formed by a process which is often referred to as **electron transfer**.

The electron arrangement in the sodium ion, Na⁺, is 2,8,0 (the same as in the noble gas neon). In the chloride ion, Cl⁻, it is 2,8,8 (the same as in the noble gas argon). The following notation is sometimes used:

$$_{11}Na^+, 2,8,0 \qquad _{17}Cl^-, 2,8,7$$
$$_{10}Ne, 2,8 \qquad _{18}Ar, 2,8,8$$

Ions like these, and noble gas atoms, are believed to be stable for the same reason: they both have completed (or 'full') outer shells of electrons.

Evidence:

☐ X-ray photographs of the sodium chloride crystal give information about the way the ions are packed together. The arrangement is known to be as shown in Fig. 2. It is even possible to measure the distances between the ions.

☐ Molten sodium chloride conducts electricity. This can only happen because solid sodium chloride is made up from charged particles which are set free when it is melted.

☐ The melting point of sodium chloride is quite high (801°C), compared with the melting point of sodium (98°C) and chlorine (−101°C). It is known from comparisons with other substances that if sodium chloride were a covalently bonded substance, its melting point would be much lower.

Q1 Potassium fluoride, KF, is an ionic substance. Explain fully what happens when a potassium atom and a fluorine atom combine to form a pair of ions.

Q2 Show how ionic bonding takes place in the following compounds: sodium fluoride, NaF; calcium fluoride, CaF_2; lithium oxide, Li_2O.

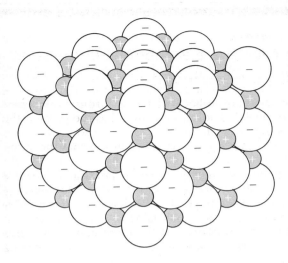

Fig. 2 The ions in a sodium chloride crystal pack together like this.

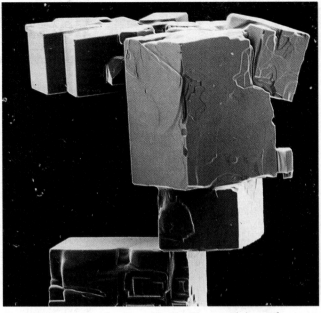

Fig. 3 Cubic crystals of sodium chloride. The crystal shape of a substance depends on how its particles pack together.

Metallic bonds: linking metal atoms

There is no obvious reason why two atoms of the same metal should link with one another. There is no difference between their nuclei, or their numbers of electrons. What seems to happen is this. When the atoms meet, *all* the electrons come under the influence of *all* nearby nuclei. If there are electrons which are not very strongly held by 'their own' nucleus they can be drawn towards the nuclei of other atoms.

Metals have only small numbers of electrons in their outer shells, and these electrons are quite easily released. It is believed that in a piece of metal the outer shell electrons of each atom become shared out equally among all the nuclei. In this way the atoms become linked together by **metallic bonding**. The spreading out of electrons in a metallic bond is sometimes known as **delocalisation**. It is important to note that only the outer electrons are 'delocalised'. The nuclei of the atoms stay in a regularly packed arrangement.

The overall result is no different from a single atom, since – on average – each individual atom has the same number of outer shell electrons as it would have on its own. However, the 'population' of outer shell electrons is free to move throughout the metal, and indeed does move if a charge is applied at some point.

Evidence: An electric current is a flow of charge. Metals will carry an electric current. This can only happen because the electrons are free to flow through the metal.

Representing chemical bonds

Covalently bonded substances may be represented in several ways. Here are some examples you will find in this book, and elsewhere.

Substance	Formula of molecule	Structural formula
hydrogen	H_2	H-H
hydrogen chloride	HCl	H-H
water	H_2O	O
methane	CH_4	H H

overhead line made from copper

copper atoms

electrons which are free to move from one atom to the next

train 'pantograph' which picks up current from the overhead line to power the engine

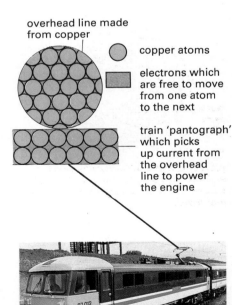

Fig. 4 Current can flow from the overhead lines to this engine because some of the electrons in the metal are free to move.

Relating properties to structure

Some people would say that being able to relate the way a substance behaves to the way it is constructed is the true purpose of chemistry. Certainly it is a very important 'chemical activity'. What sort of clues do substances give us about their underlying structure?

☐ The outward appearance of a substance *may* be quite helpful, although it can also be misleading. The colour, the crystalline shape, and even the hardness can be informative.

☐ The effect of heat is often a very useful guide. Substances which melt easily have comparatively weak forces between their particles. Substances which melt gradually over a temperature range, rather than at a sharp melting point, are mixtures. They may be mixtures of molecules of similar kinds (e.g. large molecules of the same type, but different lengths) or mixtures of molecules of different kinds.

☐ The effect of water can be a helpful guide. Substances which dissolve in water may contain ions or polar covalent bonds. Substances which react with water usually contain covalently bonded molecules.

Fig. 2 The layer structure of this graphite is a clue to the way it behaves.

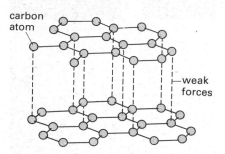

Fig. 1 This wax melts easily, showing that the forces between its molecules are weak.

Simple molecular substances

Many common substances consist of small molecules which are held together by covalent bonds. These are called **simple molecular** substances. The bonds which hold the molecules together are strong, but the attraction between one molecule and the next is weak. Simple molecular substances therefore melt and boil at low temperatures. Many are gases or liquids under normal conditions. When solid, they are often soft or waxy. Because they contain no ions they do not conduct electricity when molten or dissolved.

Examples: wax, sugar, methane, steam, ammonia, napthalene.

Giant molecule (or macromolecular) substances

Some substances are continuous structures of atoms which are covalently linked together. Each piece is one enormous molecule. These are called **giant molecule** or **macromolecular** substances. Graphite and diamond both consist of endless lattices, built from carbon atoms which are linked by covalent bonds. Sand, which is a form of silicon oxide, has a similar structure. Owing to the strong bonds which lock the structure together, giant molecule substances have some of the highest melting points of all. Many are also very hard. They do not dissolve in water, nor (except for graphite) do they conduct electricity.

Examples: quartz, zinc blende, carborundum.

Fig. 3 How do the properties of this graphite relate to its 'layer structure' (Fig. 2)?

Ionic substances

Substances which contain ions are often called **ionic**. All ionic substances will conduct electricity when molten, or when dissolved. Many, but not all, ionic substances will dissolve in water. Ionic substances are solids at room temperature. Their melting points are mostly high (above 500°C) because the ions form a giant lattice. In many cases, a good deal of energy is needed to overcome the forces between the ions in this lattice.

Examples: sodium chloride, magnesium oxide, sodium hydroxide.

Fig. 4 Sand is a giant molecular substance.

Fig. 5 The facade of the Birmingham Hippodrome is made from a composite material called glass-reinforced polyester (GRP). It has the lightness of the plastic with the added strength of the glass fibres.

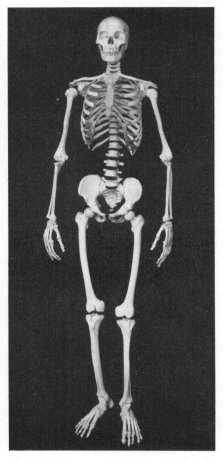

Fig. 6 Our bones are also a composite material: the mineral part is reinforced with strands of protein.

Composite materials

Most everyday substances are mixtures, or **composite** materials. The properties of composite materials are often combinations of the features of the separate substances they contain – together with some new features of their own. GRP (glass-reinforced-polyester) is a well-known composite material which consists of a plastic containing strands of glass fibre (Fig. 5). The product has the lightness of the plastic, but is much strengthened by the glass fibres. Wood is a natural composite material which consists of fibres embedded in a flexible substance.

Q1 Draw a table with the following headings:

'Structures' (across the page): molecular, ionic, macromolecular, composite.

'Properties' (down the page): melting point, solubility, hardness, electrical conductivity.

Rule a grid, and fill in each space using words like 'high', 'low', 'good', 'poor', etc.

Q2 Use the index and *Datapages* to find information about the following substances, and decide which kind of structure they have: sodium chloride, ammonia, copper, hydrogen chloride, octane, sulphur, quartz.

Writing formulae for compounds

Fig. 1 Copper oxide, a compound with the formula CuO: one copper atom and one oxygen atom in every molecule.

The chemical formula for a compound shows the *number* of atoms of *each type* which are present in the smallest particle of that compound. For instance:

☐ Copper oxide contains the elements copper (Cu) and oxygen (O). The smallest particle contains one atom of each, so its formula is CuO (Fig. 1).

☐ Carbon dioxide contains the elements carbon (C) and oxygen (O). One molecule of carbon dioxide has two oxygen atoms linked to one carbon atom, so its formula is written CO_2. The small '2' below the line means that there are two atoms of oxygen present (Fig. 2).

☐ Hydrogen peroxide contains two atoms of hydrogen (H) and two atoms of oxygen in each molecule, so its formula is H_2O_2 (Fig. 3).

Q1 Write the formula of each of the following substances.

Substance	Numbers of atoms present in one molecule
water	2 hydrogen, 1 oxygen
alumina	1 aluminium, 3 oxygen
quartz	1 silicon, 2 oxygen
ammonia	1 nitrogen, 3 hydrogen
methane	1 carbon, 4 hydrogen
marble	1 calcium, 1 carbon, 3 oxygen
glucose	6 carbon, 12 hydrogen, 6 oxygen

Q2 Write down the number of atoms of each element found in one molecule of: cane sugar, $C_{12}H_{22}O_{11}$; sodium thiosulphate, $Na_2S_2O_3$; ethanamide, C_2H_5NO.

Fig. 2 Carbon dioxide, a compound with the formula CO_2: one carbon atom and two oxygen atoms in every molecule.

Many chemical formulae not only show which atoms are present in a compound, but also how they are linked together. The formula for potassium nitrate is KNO_3, and this means that the three oxygen atoms are linked to the nitrogen atom (not to the potassium). The formula for copper sulphate crystals is $CuSO_4.5H_2O$. This shows that the four oxygen atoms are linked to the sulphur atom, and that the five water molecules have some separate links of their own.

In more complicated formulae you sometimes find brackets. For example, the formula of copper nitrate is $Cu(NO_3)_2$. The nitrogen and oxygen atoms are linked together to make a cluster with the formula NO_3^- (the nitrate ion). Two of these nitrate ions are linked with each copper ion. This means that the substance contains copper, nitrogen and oxygen atoms in the ratio 1Cu:2N:6O. The full formula would be drawn as shown in Fig. 5.

Valency

When atoms combine with one another they can only form chemical bonds with a limited number of other atoms. The usual number of bonds which an atom can form is known as its **valency**. This number is usually the same as the oxidation number (see 4.6). The reason for this is connected with the filling up of electron shells (see 1.6), but a simple picture of valency uses hooks or links.

Figure 4 shows the idea of how valencies can be used in working out a chemical formula.

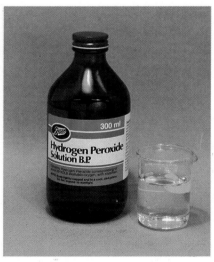

Fig. 3 Hydrogen peroxide, a compound with the formula H_2O_2: two hydrogen atoms and two oxygen atoms in every molecule.

Some valencies

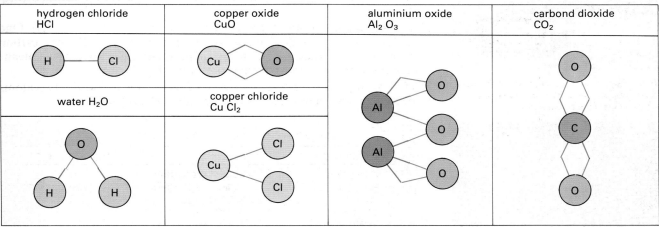

valency 1	valency 2	valency 3	valency 4
hydrogen H chlorine Cl	copper Cu oxygen O	aluminium Al	carbon C

Some formulae

hydrogen chloride HCl	copper oxide CuO	aluminium oxide Al_2O_3	carbond dioxide CO_2
H — Cl	Cu O		O C O
water H_2O O H H	copper chloride $CuCl_2$ Cu Cl Cl	Al Al O O O	

Fig. 4 This is how the idea of valencies is used to build up some simple formulae. Look at these examples, and then show how the formula of hydrogen peroxide, H_2O_2, fits the valencies of hydrogen and oxygen.

Rules for writing the formula of a compound

☐ The chemical formula of a compound represents the smallest particle present. This may be a cluster of ions, or a molecule. Special rules apply to giant structures.

For example, the smallest particle in hydrogen chloride gas is a molecule containing 1 hydrogen atom (H) and 1 chlorine atom (Cl), so its formula is HCl.

☐ The formula shows the symbol of each atom present, and a small number below the line is used where there is more than one atom of the same kind.

For example, the smallest particle in methane is a molecule containing 1 carbon atom (C) linked to 4 hydrogen atoms (H), so its formula is CH_4.

☐ Where possible, the symbols are written in order, so that those atoms which are linked together are placed next to one another.

For example, in calcium sulphate, which has the formula $CaSO_4$, the oxygen atoms (O) are linked to the sulphur atom (S) – and not directly to the calcium (Ca).

☐ The formula of a compound containing a metal atom is usually written with the metal atom first.

For example, lead oxide has the formula PbO, *not* OPb.

☐ Brackets are used to show when the same group of atoms is found more than once in the formula, as in Fig. 5.

The formula of copper nitrate is made up from one copper ion, Cu^{2+} and two nitrate ions, NO_3^-

so the formula of copper nitrate is $Cu(NO_3)_2$

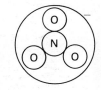

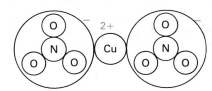

Fig. 5 In copper nitrate there is one copper ion for every two nitrate ions. The nitrate ion contains four atoms.

Radioactivity

Fig. 1 This instrument, known as a Geiger counter, is used for detecting radioactivity.

In most kinds of atom the particles in the nucleus hold together very strongly. The nucleus is **stable**, and will not come apart without powerful battering! There are some kinds of atom, however, which have nuclei that are unstable. In some of these cases the neutrons and protons in the nucleus do not hold together very strongly. In other cases the neutrons themselves have a tendency to break down. Atoms with unstable nuclei are **radioactive**, and they are known as **radio-isotopes**. Most elements have both stable isotopes and radioactive isotopes:

Stable and radioactive isotopes of hydrogen and carbon

Element	Symbol	Atomic Number	Mass Number	Radioactive/stable?
hydrogen				
hydrogen	H	1	1	stable
deuterium	D	1	2	stable
*tritium	T	1	3	radioactive
carbon				
carbon-12	C	6	12	stable
*carbon-14	C	6	14	radioactive

There are radio-isotopes which are naturally occurring, such as those marked with a star (*) above. There are also a number of artificial radio-isotopes which are formed in nuclear reactors. Some of these isotopes have medical and industrial uses. Others are 'nuclear waste' and must be stored away very carefully.

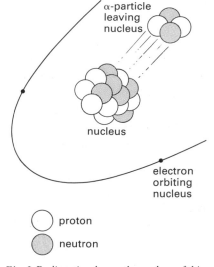

Fig. 2 There is a low level of natural radioactivity everywhere. A higher level exists in some places, especially where the main local rock is granite, such as here at Land's End, Cornwall.

What is 'radioactive decay'?

When radioactive atoms break down they are said to **disintegrate** or **decay**. The result of radioactive decay is that energy is released in two ways: heat is evolved and **radiation** is emitted from the nucleus. For example:

A	*carbon-14	→	nitrogen-14 + beta-radiation
B	*radium-226	→	*radon-222 + alpha-radiation
C	*polonium-210	→	lead-206 + alpha-radiation

Example A is a process which is taking place around us all the time. It allows the method of **radiocarbon dating** to be used. This is explained in 1.15. Example C is the reaction studied by Marie Curie during the early years of this century. In Fig. 3 you can see the nucleus of a radioactive atom represented by a cluster of several particles – protons and neutrons. A smaller group of particles, containing 2 protons and 2 neutrons, has just left the nucleus. This small cluster is an alpha-particle. It is given the chemical formula ^4_2He, because it has the same structure as the nucleus of a helium atom. The nucleus left behind now has 2 fewer protons that it had before, so it has become a different element. If this new element is stable, no further particles will leave its nucleus. If it is radioactive, it will disintegrate further, and yet another new element will be formed.

Fig. 3 Radioactive decay: the nucleus of this atom is disintegrating. An alpha-particle – two protons and two neutrons – are leaving the nucleus.

Q1 Marie Curie (Fig. 4) shared the Nobel prize for physics in 1903, and won the chemistry prize alone in 1911. Use reference books to find out all you can about her life.

Fig. 4 Marie Curie, the discoverer of radium, photographed in her laboratory in about 1910.

Alpha and Beta emission

Alpha-radiation is given out when the nucleus of a radioactive atom breaks up and loses a cluster of 2 protons and 2 neutrons. A new element (called the **daughter isotope**) is formed. The decay of polonium-210 can be represented as:

$$\underset{\text{polonium-210}}{^{210}_{84}\text{Po}} \quad \rightarrow \quad \underset{\text{lead-206}}{^{206}_{82}\text{Pb}} \quad + \quad \underset{\text{alpha-particle}}{^{4}_{2}\text{He}}$$

☐ The cluster of 2 protons and 2 neutrons is the **alpha-particle**, and it is the nucleus of a helium atom.

☐ **Beta-particles** are electrons which have been emitted from the *nucleus* of a radioactive atom. They arise when a neutron disintegrates into a proton and an electron:

$$1 \text{ neutron} \quad \rightarrow \quad 1 \text{ proton} + 1 \text{ electron (beta-particle)}$$

This happens in the radioactive decay of carbon-14:

$$\underset{\text{carbon-14}}{^{14}_{6}\text{C}} \quad \rightarrow \quad \underset{\text{nitrogen-14}}{^{14}_{7}\text{N}} \quad + \quad \underset{\text{beta-particle}}{^{\;0}_{-1}\text{e}}$$

Again, a new element (nitrogen-14) is formed.

☐ An **alpha-emitter** decays to a product with a *mass number 4 less* and an *atomic number 2 less* than the original atom (Fig. 5).

☐ A **beta-emitter** decays to a product with an *unchanged mass number* and an *atomic number 1 more* than the original atom (Fig. 6).

Q2 Use the information on *Datapage H* to write balanced equations to show what happens when the following radio-isotopes decay.
  (a) **alpha-emitters**: radon-220, uranium-238, plutonium-239, californium-248.
  (b) **beta-emitters**: hydrogen-3 (tritium); phosphorus-32; sulphur-35; potassium-40; strontium-90; iodine-131.

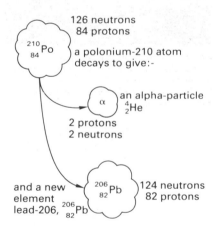

Fig. 5 Alpha-emission: the radioactive decay of polonium-210 (see text).

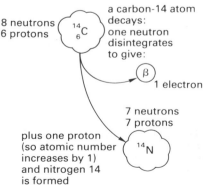

Fig. 6 Beta-emission: the radioactive decay of carbon-14.

37

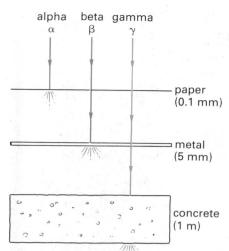

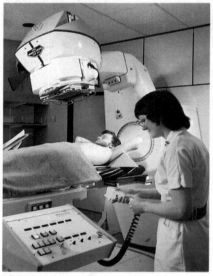

Fig. 1 Comparing the penetrating powers of
alpha-, beta- and gamma-radiation.

Fig. 2 Gamma radiation is used to treat some
types of cancer. This kills the malignant cells,
and for many patients has proved an effective
cure.

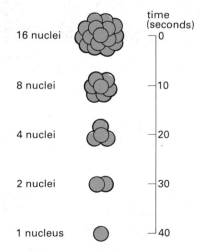

Fig. 3 Radioactive disintegration: what is the
half-life of this isotope?

More about radioactivity

Three kinds of radiation

Alpha-particles are helium nuclei and so are positively charged. They are emitted with fairly small amounts of energy. They will not penetrate a sheet of paper. In air, alpha-particles will travel only a few centimetres before capturing electrons from nearby molecules, and becoming helium atoms.

Beta-particles are electrons and so are negatively charged. They generally have rather more energy than alpha-particles. They will pass through paper, but through only very thin metal. Even a powerful beam of beta-particles will be stopped by a sheet of lead a few millimetres thick.

Some radioactive nuclei disintegrate in a different way similar to X-rays but even more 'powerful'. The particles in the nucleus merely rearrange themselves, and **gamma-radiation** is emitted. Cobalt-60 is one radio-isotope which is a gamma-emitter. Gamma-radiation is a very penetrating form of energy. It will pass through several metres of earth or concrete, and even through several centimetres of lead.

Radioactive half-life

The nuclei in different radioactive substances disintegrate at different rates. Some radio-isotopes decay to new elements in a small fraction of a second. Others take many thousands of years to decay completely. The time taken for one half of all the nuclei in a radio-isotope to decay is known as its **half-life** (Fig. 3).

The half-life depends only on which isotope is decaying, not upon the quantity present. This is because the process of radioactive decay is a matter of chance. For example, suppose you have 16 coins and place them on the table. The chances are greatest that 8 of them would show 'heads' and the other 8 'tails'. If you remove the first 8, and then spin the remaining coins, you could expect 4 'heads' and 4 'tails' next time. If you repeat the process, there are most likely to be 2 'heads' and 2 'tails' in the remaining 4. Each spin of the coins represents one 'half-life' period. There is a 50% chance during this time that any particular coin will show 'heads'.

In one half-life period, half of all the nuclei in a radio-isotope will disintegrate. In the next half-life period, half of those remaining will disintegrate, and so on. In any radio-isotope sample the number of nuclei is so enormous that the half-life has a steady value.

Carbon-14 is a radioactive isotope which emits beta-particles. It is constantly being formed in the atmosphere from nitrogen which is bombarded by cosmic radiation. Animals and plants continuously absorb this 'radio-carbon'. They also exchange carbon with their surroundings, for example by eating carbon-containing substances, and then breathing out carbon dioxide. While they are alive this keeps their level of carbon-14 steady. When they *die*, the carbon exchange ceases. The carbon-14 which is present at death simply disintegrates without replacement.

Since the half-life of carbon-14 is 5568 years, something which died 5568 years ago now contains *half* as much carbon-14 as when it died. Archaeologists can measure the amount of carbon-14 left in objects made from once living materials, such as wood, leather, cloth and bones, and so work out their age. The method is known as **radiocarbon dating** (Fig. 4).

Q1 The half-life of the hydrogen isotope 'tritium' is about 13 years. Show how many radioactive nuclei will be left after 52 years from an original sample which contained 16 million nuclei.

Fig. 4 *Radiocarbon dating is being used to find the age of these fossil bones.*

Some uses of radioactivity

Even tiny amounts of radioactivity are very easy to detect, so **radioactive tracers** can be used to follow the movement of substances carried along in a liquid. This is done by adding a suitable radioactive substance, and making measurements at different points. The method can be used for following the movement of sediment in rivers, and even for tracing substances carried in the bloodstream.

Fixed radioactive sources are often found in factories for use in **thickness gauges**. Many items, from steel to wallpaper, are manufactured as continuous strips. A radioactive source mounted on one side, with a detector on the other (Fig. 5), can be linked to mechanisms which adjust the machinery as necessary.

Fig. 5 *A fixed radioactive source is being used to check the thickness of the metal strip.*

Gamma-radiation is lethal to living organisms. This makes it highly dangerous, but it is possible to **preserve foodstuffs** by 'irradiating' them in sealed containers. Once the micro-organisms inside have been killed, the food will keep without spoiling until the container is opened. However, there is still some argument about the complete safety of food which has been treated in this way.

The heat generated by nuclear reactions can be used to raise steam in **power stations**. About a fifth of the electricity in the UK is now generated in this way.

The use of radioactive materials produces **radioactive waste**. Some of this can simply be buried, so long as suitable sites can be found, but some is extremely dangerous and will remain so for centuries to come. Methods for sealing up dangerous waste are being developed, but we still have a great responsibility to future generations not to leave problems behind us.

Fig. 6 *A radioactive 'tracer': some radioactive 'mud' is poured into the river. Samples taken from different places downstream will show how it has spread.*

Questions

A. What can you remember?

** **1.** Write down the names of the three states of matter. What words are used for the changes of state which take place when different kinds of matter are heated and cooled?

** **2.** Iodine is a substance which sublimes. What does this mean?

** **3.** What is diffusion? Why doesn't diffusion take place in solid substances?

** **4.** What is the difference between an atom and a molecule?

** **5.** Write down the meaning of the following terms: atom, proton, electron, neutron, atomic number, mass number, isotope.

** **6.** Make a carefully labelled drawing which shows an atom containing 2 protons, 2 electrons and 2 neutrons. Find out from *Datapage H* the name of this atom, and write out its full chemical symbol.

** **7.** Make a list of all the fragments which make up a complete atom of $^{12}_{6}C$, and for each fragment state: its electrical charge (if any), its mass (in comparison to other fragments), and where it is found in the atom.

** **8.** There are two kinds of single substance: elements and compounds. Explain the difference between an element and a compound.

* **9.** Write down the symbols for the following elements: carbon, hydrogen, argon, gold, sodium, potassium, titanium, zinc. Check your answers on *Datapage H*.

* **10.** Which elements are represented by the following symbols: C, Ca, Cl, Co, Cr, Cu?

** **11.** The formula for hydrogen gas is H_2, not just H. What does this tell you about hydrogen gas?

B. What have you understood

*** **12.** In 1.2, Q2, changes of state were described as being like a rugby match. Try to describe sublimation in the same way.

** **13.** Imagine that you have a gold coin and a copy made from brass (an alloy of copper and zinc). You have been provided with a magical microscope which allows you to see the individual atoms in each coin. Explain how you would tell which was which.

** **14.** We cannot actually see the atoms in a sheet of metal, yet we know that they are there through indirect evidence. Explain what is meant by indirect evidence.

** **15.** Draw out, or list the full structures of the following atoms: $^{7}_{3}Li$, $^{9}_{4}Be$, $^{14}_{7}N$, $^{16}_{8}O$, $^{20}_{10}Ne$.

** **16.** Hydrogen has an atomic number of 1. It has three isotopes, with mass numbers 1, 2 and 3. Explain clearly what this means, and draw structures for the three different atoms.

** **17.** Explain why the numbers of protons and electrons in an atom are the same, and what holds them together.

*** **18.** It is sometimes said that the nucleus of an atom determines its physics, but that the chemistry of an atom depends upon its electrons. Explain what you think this means.

C. Can you use this information?

* **19.** Plot a cooling curve for the substance 'Salol', using the following figures:

Time (min)	0	1	2	3	4	5	6	7	8	9
Temp. (°C)	50	47	45	44	43	43	43	42	41	40

Use the curve to find out the melting point of Salol.

** **20.** Chlorine consists of two stable isotopes, chlorine-35 and chlorine-37. Use the information in 1.6 to draw a diagram of each.

* **21.** Prepare a chart illustrating the structures of the first 20 elements, which could be used for display in your school laboratory.

** **22.** Make a poster which would explain the meaning of the term *isotope* to someone who had never heard it before.

* **23.** Make a drawing in your notebook, using any atom you want to as an example, to show exactly what is meant by the terms *mass number* and *atomic number*.

* **24.** Make a drawing to show what happens to the particles in ice when it is first melted, and then the water is boiled.

*** **25.** Look again at 1.6, Q1. Plot this graph if you have not already done so. Explain carefully why there are two 'steps' in the curve you have plotted.

* **26.** Use *Datapage T* to find out how the following elements got their names: aluminium; argon; calcium; chlorine; helium; silicon.

* **27.** Use *Datapage T* to find out how these symbols came to be given to the following elements: Cu, copper; K, potassium; W, tungsten; Ag, silver; Hg, mercury.

*** **28.** The following radioactive isotopes are alpha-emitters. Write balanced equations to show what happens when they disintegrate: radon-222; radium-226; americium-241; einsteinium-253. Further information you will need is on *Datapage H*.

*** **29.** The following radioactive isotopes are beta-emitters. Write balanced equations to show what happens when they disintegrate: sodium-24; chromium-55; selenium-83; caesium-134. Further information you will need is on *Datapage H*.

** **30.** Make simple drawings to show how you could use a radioactive isotope to discover (a) whether or not an underground sewage pipe is leaking; (b) the position of a weak point in a steel girder.

D. Taking it further

*** **31.** Suppose that a returning visitor from the moon had brought back some rock which appeared to contain a new element. Explain what evidence you would need to convince you that the element concerned was indeed a new one.

*** **32.** The best balance you have in school can probably record a change in mass of 0.001g. If you breathe on the metal pan, and some water condenses, the increase in mass will be at least this much. Water molecules 'weigh' about 3×10^{-23}g. In 0.001g, how many have condensed?

*** **33.** Electrons are all around us and inside us all the time. They are constantly moving. 'An electric current is a flow of electrons', says a well known text book. Why aren't we continually receiving electric shocks?

*** **34.** There are 92 different elements which occur naturally on the earth. Between them they have nearly 700 different kinds of atom. Explain this.

*** **35.** Try working out this example to give yourself an idea of how small atoms are. A pin-head contains about 0.1g of iron. 56g of iron contain 6×10^{23} atoms of iron.
(a) How many atoms are there in the pin-head?
Now imagine that each of these atoms becomes as large as a grain of sand, with a volume of 1 cubic millimetre. A large lorry will carry 10 cubic metres of sand. [1 cubic metre = 10^9 cubic millimetres]
(b) How many lorry loads would be needed to carry all this sand?
(c) Imagine that these lorries were passing your house every second of the day and night. How long would it take for them all to pass by?

Quick questions

1. Give an everyday example of
   (a) a solid, (b) a liquid, (c) a gas, (d) something melting, (e) something (not ice!) freezing, (f) something evaporating, (g) something diffusing.

2. Give the name and symbol for the atoms which contain: 1 proton; 3 protons; 5 protons; 7 protons.

3. Arrange the following into three lists, headed *elements*, *compounds*, and *mixtures*: sand, sugar, salt, sodium, soap powder, sulphur, silver nitrate, strontium, sunflower oil, soup.

4. Write chemical formulae for water, hydrogen chloride, sulphuric acid, sodium chloride, nitrogen gas.

Solvents and solutions

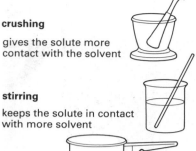

crushing

gives the solute more contact with the solvent

stirring

keeps the solute in contact with more solvent

heating

will make the solute particles bump into solvent particles more often.
it also helps the solvent to "accept" more solute particles

Fig. 1 Better dissolving: three ways to make substances dissolve more quickly.

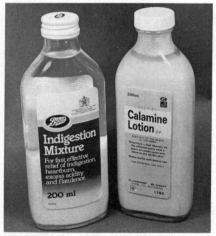

Fig. 2 These medicines are suspensions.

Every time you make a cup of coffee you are making a **solution**.

coffee grains + hot water → cup of coffee
(solute)   (solvent)   (solution)

A solution is a special kind of mixture which contains one substance dissolved in another. Here are some solutions which you know well:

☐ sea water (water with salts dissolved in it).
☐ perfume (alcohol with flower extracts dissolved in it).
☐ model-making cement (a hydrocarbon with plastic dissolved in it).
☐ 'correcting fluid' (water or trichloroethane with plastic dissolved in it).

Making solutions: solvents and solutes

The liquid you use when making a solution is called the **solvent**. The solvent is the substance which does the dissolving. The substance which is actually dissolved is called the **solute**.

There are three things you can do to make the solute dissolve better (Fig. 1):

☐ stirring it in will make it dissolve more quickly.
☐ crushing it to a powder first of all will also help.
☐ heating the solution will speed up the dissolving, *and* it will allow more to dissolve.

Saturated solutions

However much stirring or crushing you do, you will not alter the amount of solute which will dissolve at any particular temperature. There is a limit when no more will dissolve, and at this point the solution is **saturated**. A saturated solution is one in which no more solute will dissolve unless you change the temperature. To be certain that the solution is saturated, there must always be some undissolved solute present.

Soluble and insoluble substances

Substances which dissolve in a particular solvent are **soluble** in that solvent. Those which do not are **insoluble**. For instance, salt is soluble in water, but wax is insoluble in water. On the other hand, salt is insoluble in petrol, whereas wax is soluble.

When you shake up a solid with a liquid in which it is insoluble, you get a **suspension**. The bits of solid remain 'suspended' in the liquid, until they settle to the bottom. Some medicines and lotions are like this (Fig. 2). Calamine lotion, for itchy spots (like chicken pox), and Kaolin medicine, for a bad stomach, are both suspensions. You must shake the bottle well before use.

Q1 Write a note for a friend who has missed the lesson, explaining fully the differences between a 'solution' and a 'suspension'.

Fig. 3 Some common household solutes.

Fig. 4 The carbon dioxide gas dissolved in this drink gives it a sharper taste.

Fig. 5 Some shampoos are immiscible, and have to be shaken well before use.

Dissolving gases and liquids

Fizzy drinks, swimming pool water, and even the water from the tap are all solutions which contain **dissolved gases** (Fig. 4). Small amounts of chlorine gas are dissolved in swimming pool water to help kill germs. The gas dissolved in fizzy drinks is carbon dioxide, and it is put in under high pressure so that as much as possible will dissolve. When you take the top off the bottle, some of that pressure is released. You notice two things: a puff of gas from the mouth of the bottle; and bubbles rising out of the liquid. Releasing the pressure of the gas above the liquid has an effect on the amount of gas which can be held in solution. The lower the pressure, the less gas will remain dissolved.

Dissolved gases will also come out of solution if you raise the temperature. The 'singing' sound made by a kettle as it starts to boil is made by air bubbles which can no longer remain dissolved in water at this temperature. You notice the difference in taste if you drink water that has been boiled. It seems 'flat', just as old lemonade does, when it has lost its dissolved gas. There is not a great deal of air dissolved in tap water, but it is enough to keep fish alive.

When you put washing-up liquid into a bowl of water you are dissolving one liquid in another. Liquids which dissolve in one another are called **miscible liquids**. Those which don't mix, like oil and water, are **immiscible**.

Q2 In the above paragraphs there is quite a lot of evidence that gases do dissolve in liquids. List these pieces of evidence.

Q3 Describe how each of the items shown in Fig. 3 is used to make a solution at home. Be sure to use the words 'solvent' and 'solute' correctly, and to explain what the solution is for.

More about solvents

Fig. 1 Non-aqueous solvents at work: nail polish and the solvent used to remove it.

Fig. 2 Non-aqueous solvents at work: some paint strippers dissolve the paint away.

Fig. 3 Non-aqueous solvents at work: a safe alternative to dangerous solvents.

The best known solvent of all is water. It dissolves a remarkable number of other substances – gases, liquids and solids. Solutions in which water is the solvent are known as **aqueous solutions**. Most of the bottles on the laboratory shelves contain aqueous solutions. Lots of liquids besides water are useful solvents, however. Sometimes these are called **non-aqueous solvents**.

Here are some widely used non-aqueous solvents: dry-cleaning fluid; methylated spirits; nail-polish remover; garage-floor cleaner; and paint stripper. A number of glues, paints and varnishes, and many aerosol sprays, are solutions where the solvent has a strong smell.

Some people seem to like these smells, and there has been a lot of worry about 'glue-sniffing'. **Solvent-abuse**, to give it its proper name, is actually a very serious problem. Many non-aqueous solvents are extremely poisonous. Even tiny amounts can cause permanent damage to the lungs, liver and other parts of the body. Some of them are also flammable, and form explosive mixtures with the air. This is why you should always use strongly smelling glues and paints in a well-ventilated place, or out of doors. Solvents in the laboratory are kept in a special cupboard, and disposed of safely after use.

Solubility

You can dissolve more sugar than salt in a cup of water. Sugar is more soluble in water than salt at the same temperature. It has a greater **solubility**. The solubility of a solute is usually given as the number of grams which will dissolve in 100 grams of solvent at a stated temperature. There is more information on *Datapage E*.

The solubilities of most solids in water and in other solvents increase as the temperature is raised. Boiling water will dissolve nearly ten times as much potassium nitrate, for example, as the same amount of water at room temperature. Here are the figures:

Temperature (°C)	0	10	20	40	60	80	100
Solubility (g/100 g water)	13	21	32	64	110	169	246

This information is shown in the graph (Fig. 4). The points have been joined together to make a curve, because there is a gradual change of solubility with every small change in temperature. A graph like this is known as a **solubility curve**.

> **Q1** Read from the curve the temperatures at which the solubility of potassium nitrate is (a) 50 g (b) 100 g (c) 200 g per 100 g water.

Crystallisation

☐ Crystals will form when a saturated solution **cools**. This happens because more substances become less soluble at lower temperatures. The more slowly the solution cools, the larger the crystals become. In Fig. 5 you can see some large sugar crystals, sometimes known as 'misray'.

☐ Crystals form when a saturated solution **evaporates**. Lake Magadi (Fig. 6) evaporates quickly in a hot dry climate. So much material has crystallised that parts of the Lake are covered with a crust which is thick enough to support a person's weight.

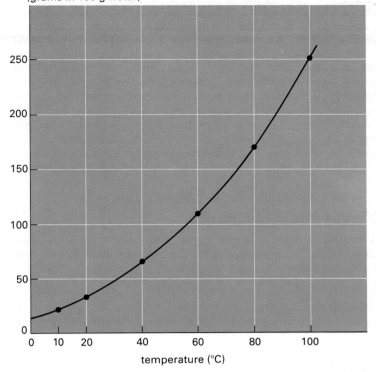

solubility of potassium nitrate
(grams in 100 g water)

Fig. 4 A solubility curve for potassium nitrate in water.

Using a solubility curve

A solubility curve provides information for making decisions and predictions. Potassium nitrate is used by fireworks manufacturers for making the blue 'touch paper'. Graphs like Fig. 4 help in the work of the factory.

Problem: How much potassium nitrate will dissolve in 100 litres of water at 20°C? (100 litres of water weigh 100 kg.)

Answer: The table of figures tells you that, at 20°C, 32 g of potassium nitrate dissolve in 100 g of water. 100 kg of water is 1000 times as much as 100 g, so 1000 times 32 g (= 32 kg) of potassium nitrate will dissolve.

> **Q2** Use the solubility curve to work out how much *extra* potassium nitrate would dissolve, if the temperature of the water is raised to 26°C.

Problem: What happens if a solution containing 50 g of potassium nitrate per 100 g of water is allowed to cool down from 40°C to 20°C?

Answer: The curve shows that nothing happens at first, until the temperature drops to 32°C. This is the temperature at which 50 g of potassium nitrate is just enough to **saturate** 100 g of water. As soon as the temperature falls a little more, there is more solute present than can remain dissolved, so **crystallisation** begins. Crystals of potassium nitrate begin to appear in the solution. At 20°C the amount of potassium nitrate needed to saturate 100 g of water is just 32 g, so the mass of crystals which appears is 50 g − 32 g, which is 18 g.

Fig. 5 These large sugar crystals were formed from a saturated solution as it cooled.

Fig. 6 Evaporated salts at the side of Lake Magadi in Kenya. The same process of crystallisation from a saturated solution has taken place here.

Single substances and mixtures

Fig. 1 Granite, a mixture of three solids: quartz, felspar and mica.

There are some common things – like copper, lead and a number of other metals – which are elements. Others – like water, sugar and salt – are compounds. These are **single substances** – every *particle* is the same, since each has the same atoms to make it up.

However, the great majority of everyday substances are **mixtures**. They consist of two or more elements or compounds mixed together in some way. There are some very well-known mixtures: cake mixture, concrete, liquorice allsorts, and so on.

Different kinds of mixture

Since there are three different states of matter (solid, liquid and gas) you could in theory find mixtures containing any pair of these – or, of course, all three. Here are some possibilities:

☐ **Solid/solid** mixtures, for example many rocks, soils, foodstuffs
☐ **Solid/liquid** mixtures, for example muddy water, and the suspensions mentioned in 2.1, together with all the solutions made by dissolving substances in water and other solvents
☐ **Liquid/liquid** mixtures, for example oil, milk, petrol
☐ **Liquid/gas** mixtures, such as fizzy drinks, and the other solutions of gases in liquids mentioned in 2.1
☐ **Gas/gas** mixtures, usually called **gaseous** mixtures, for example the air.

Fig. 2 The ground itself is a mixture of solids. (These miners in Gloucestershire, photographed about 80 years ago, were digging out lumps of strontium.)

Petrol – a familiar mixture

All the fuels on sale at a filling station are mixtures. Each one is slightly different, and is made to suit different engines. The most popular fuel for cars is 4-star petrol (see *Datapage P2*), but more and more cars now have engines which can use 2-star fuel. Many filling stations have now stopped selling 3-star petrol, which was yet another mixture, made by mixing 2-star and 4-star grades.

☐ Petrol and other motor fuels are some of the many products made from one of the most valuable mixtures ever discovered – crude oil. There is more about this in Chapter 6.

Fig. 3 Another familiar mixture: milk is a mixture of liquids.

Q1 Choose a household product with the word 'mixture' in its name, and find out from the label what substances it contains.

Q2 Make a large copy of this table, and write in the appropriate square as many examples of mixtures as you can. Start with the ones given on this page.

Mixtures	Solid	Liquid	Gas
Solid			
Liquid			
Gas			

Q3 The differences between a single substance and a mixture are sometimes obvious, but not always. Explain what steps you could take if you were asked to find out if an unknown substance was a mixture or a single substance.

Fig. 4 *Each of these cans contains a single drink, but every one is a mixture made from gases, liquids and solids.*

Pure substances

The 'opposite' of a mixture is a completely pure substance – just one single substance without a trace of other substances in it. There are various ways of telling whether a substance is completely pure or not. For example:

☐ The same pure substance always has the same **melting point** and **boiling point**. Pure water melts (and freezes) at exactly 0°C, and boils at exactly 100°C. Even a tiny amount of impurity will affect both these figures.

   Surprisingly enough, the effect is different for the two temperatures. The freezing point of some water with a little salt dissolved in it, is **lower** than 0°C. The boiling point of the same 'impure' water is **higher** than 100°C.

☐ Pure substances have a sharp melting point, whereas mixtures often melt gradually as the temperature is raised.

☐ Separation methods, like careful filtering, evaporation, chromatography, and distillation will all give clues about the presence of an impurity. These methods are all used for making things pure, and also for checking afterwards to find out whether the purification has been successful.

Q4 Using information from this page, explain carefully why putting salt on icy roads causes the ice to melt.

Q5 Wax is not a pure substance. What evidence is there to support this statement?

CERTIFICATION TRADE MARK
PURE NEW WOOL

Fig. 5 *'Pure new wool' is described as a 'pure' substance, because it contains wool alone – and no other fibres.*

Separating mixtures

Many mixtures contain a useful substance mixed with unwanted material. If the useful substance is to be obtained on its own, a suitable method for separating the mixture must be found. The choice of method depends entirely on what substances are in the mixture. It must make use of the *differences* between the different substances which are present. Mixtures of **liquids** with **solids** are the easiest to think about.

Liquid/solid mixtures

☐ Every time you use a tea strainer, a chip pan, a sieve, or even a fishing net, you are separating something solid from a liquid! In ᴀ laboratory it is usual to separate a solid from a liquid by **filtering**.

☐ At home you may use a spin drier to remove the liquid (water) from a solid (clothes). A laboratory instrument called a **centrifuge** does much the same thing. For example, by spinning a tube of muddy water in a centrifuge, you can make the solid sink to the bottom, and then pour the liquid off (Fig. 1).

Solid/solid mixtures

Perhaps the most important **solid/solid** mixtures are the metal ores and other minerals.

☐ The prospector panning for gold (Fig. 2) knows that gold is more dense than the other substances in the river sediment. After some careful swishing, the gold particles are left behind in the pan. Today, metals are often extracted from their ores by using a chemical method which affects the metal required, but not the rest of the material present.

☐ Scrap iron can be separated from other metals by using a **magnet** like the one in Fig. 3. This method works because of the difference between iron and the other metals. Iron is magnetic, and the other metals are not.

☐ Salt is obtained from 'rock salt' – a mixture of salt, clay and other impurities – simply by using water. The salt will dissolve in the water, but the other substances in rock salt will not.

Liquid/liquid mixtures

Ways of dealing with **liquid/liquid** mixtures also depend on what is there.

☐ Some liquid/liquid mixtures can be separated by using the fact that the liquids they contain have different boiling points. The method is known as **distillation** and it is used in industries as widely different as the oil business and drinks manufacture.

Gaseous mixtures

You might think that it would be almost impossible to separate one gas from another in a **gaseous mixture**, but this is not so.

☐ A common problem is that a gas may become contaminated with water vapour, and so need 'drying'. This is easily solved by passing the gaseous mixture through a chemical which will absorb water. Two suitable chemicals for doing this are anhydrous calcium chloride and silica gel.

☐ The principle behind the gas mask is the same. If the air you are breathing contains a poisonous gas, this can be taken out by absorbing it in a suitable substance such as charcoal.

Fig. 1 A laboratory centrifuge which works like a small spin drier in separating a liquid from a solid.

Fig. 2 'Panning for gold' is a method for separating different solids with different densities. Unwanted material is washed away as the heavier gold is left behind.

Fig. 3 Magnetic materials can be separated from others like this.

Fig. 4 *The three grades of petrol you can get from this pump are different mixtures. They have been made at an oil refinery from an even more complicated mixture, crude oil.*

Chromatography

Chromatography is an important method for finding out more about mixtures. You have probably used it to separate the dyes in inks.

Chromatography is used in hospitals, in health laboratories, and in helping to solve crimes. Even the mixtures in the rocks brought back from the moon were sorted out with the aid of chromatography.

Substances in a mixture can be separated by chromatography if you can find a solvent which has different effects on each of the substances in the mixture. Here are some examples:

☐ The inks in water-based pens can be separated by using water.
☐ The inks in spirit-markers can be separated by using non-aqueous solvents.
☐ The pigments in grass are separated with a mixture of alcohol and water.
☐ Many food colourings are best separated with mixed solvents, although water works quite well for some colours.

Q1 Figure 5 shows a **chromatogram** produced by an analyst looking at fruit drinks. Look at brand A. How many different colourings have been used in it? Just one – but what about brand B? There are two different colours here, and one of them is the same as the one used in brand B.
(a) How do you know this? (b) What about brand C?
Explain what information this chromatogram gives. You should say how many colourings have been used in brand C, and whether any of them are the same as the ones used in brands A and B.

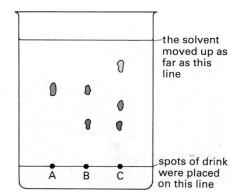

the solvent moved up as far as this line

spots of drink were placed on this line

A B C

Fig. 5 *Chromatogram of colourings found in three fruit drinks.*

Fig. 1 Each of these cars is travelling at a different speed, or 'rate'.

Fig. 2 A rapid reaction calls for rapid reactions!

Fig. 3 Some reactions are very slow. These are Roman pruning knives.

2.5

How fast is a chemical reaction?

Imagine a motor race in progress. The winner will be the car which takes the shortest time to cover a fixed distance. In some races, such as the Le Mans '24 hours', the winner is the car which covers the greatest distance in a fixed time. The **rate** at which a car is travelling, usually called its **speed**, can be worked out by dividing the number of miles travelled by the number of hours spent going round the track, that is:

$$\textbf{Rate} = \text{speed (in miles per hour)} = \frac{\text{distance (in miles)}}{\text{time (in hours)}}$$

It is possible to think about the rate of a chemical reaction in the same way. The fastest chemical reactions are those which are over in the shortest time. Here are some examples:

Very fast: explosions, flames, car engines
Moderate: cooking, metals dissolving in acids
Very slow: metals tarnishing, rusting

> **Q1** Write down two more examples for each category in the list above.

How can the rate of a reaction be measured?

As with moving cars, there are two possible questions:

☐ How long does it take to cover a fixed distance?
☐ How far can it go in a fixed time?

When hydrogen peroxide solution decomposes, it gives off oxygen:

$$\text{hydrogen peroxide} \rightarrow \text{water} + \text{oxygen}$$

The rate of this reaction can be judged by measuring either

☐ how long it takes to produce a fixed amount of oxygen, *or*
☐ how much oxygen is produced in a fixed period of time.

> **Q2** Two solutions of hydrogen peroxide are marked A and B. Solution A produces $20\,cm^3$ of oxygen gas in 20 seconds. Under the same conditions, Solution B produces $30\,cm^3$ in 20 seconds.
> (a) Which solution is reacting more rapidly?
> (b) Which solution would give $50\,cm^3$ of gas in the shorter time?
> (c) Which reaction has the greater rate?
> (d) Write a set of numbered instructions for someone who has to carry out this experiment again, to check the figures given.

How does the idea of 'distance' apply to a chemical reaction? One answer is to think of it as 'the amount of new substance formed'. Another method is to consider 'the amount of starting material used up'. Depending on the reaction you choose, it may be possible to measure either or both of these quantities. Sometimes there is a change in mass which can be recorded while the reaction is going on. In other cases you can measure the volume of a gas which is being given off.

52

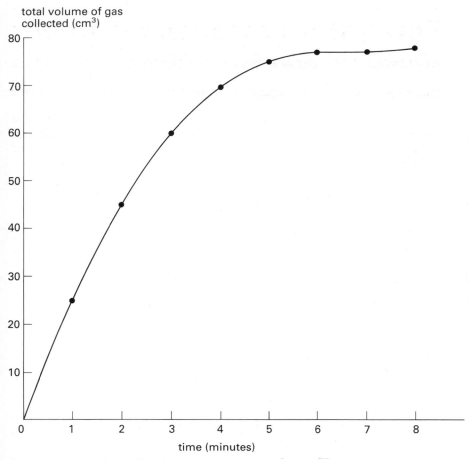

total volume of gas collected (cm³)

Fig. 4 *The volume of gas collected as magnesium reacts with an acid.*

Plotting graphs of reaction rates

Magnesium ribbon is reacting with an acid, giving off hydrogen. Here are some figures for the volume of gas collected at one-minute intervals during this reaction. *All* the magnesium has dissolved at the end of the experiment, but not all the acid has been used up.

Volume of gas collected as magnesium reacts with an acid

Time (minutes)	0	1	2	3	4	5	6	7	8
Total volume of gas collected (cm³)	0	25	45	60	70	75	77	77	78

A graph of these figures is shown in Fig. 4.

Q3 (a) After how many minutes has the reaction come to an end?
   (b) How many cubic centimetres of hydrogen gas have been collected at the end of the reaction?
   (c) How many minutes does it take to collect (i) the *first* 35 cm³ of hydrogen, and (ii) the *second* 35 cm³ of hydrogen?

Q4 Think of what happens as the reaction progresses. Does it speed up, slow down, or proceed at a constant rate?

Q5 Make a sketch copy of the graph, and on it draw an extension to the curve, showing what would happen if you went on adding magnesium until no more would dissolve.

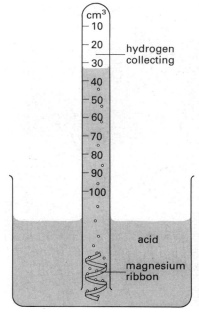

Fig. 5 *This is what you see when magnesium reacts with the acid.*

What makes a chemical reaction speed up and slow down?

Cooking a Christmas pudding is a good example of a chemical reaction! If you put it into a steamer it takes several hours. Baking it takes a shorter time, and putting it into a microwave oven is even quicker. By changing the conditions you can change the rate of the reaction. The five main 'factors' which influence the rate of a reaction are:

☐ the **temperature** at which the reaction takes place.
   Reactions generally go faster when the temperature is raised.
☐ the **concentration** of the reacting substances.
   Increases in concentration usually increase reaction rates.
☐ the use of **catalysts** and **inhibitors**.
   Catalysts speed up chemical reactions. Inhibitors slow them down.
☐ the presence of **light**.
   Ultraviolet light, especially, may speed up a chemical reaction.
☐ the **size of the particles** which are reacting.
   Reactions involving small particles of solid are often very fast.

Making use of changes in reaction rates

The effects of changing temperature and concentration are well known in laboratory reactions. In industry these factors are used to control reaction rates, and also the amount of product which can be obtained from a manufacturing process.

Catalysts influence the rates of an enormous range of reactions, both in living organisms and in laboratories, homes and factories. Biological catalysts, called enzymes, help to digest food, clean your laundry, and manufacture foodstuffs like bread, yoghurt, and even soft-centred chocolates. Some precious metals, particularly platinum and rhodium, are very useful catalysts. They have been used to cut down the pollution from motor vehicle exhausts, for example. Another metal, nickel, is used as a catalyst in the manufacture of margarine. **Chlorophyll**, the green substance in plants, is the vital catalyst for the chemical reaction which plants use to capture the sun's energy – photosynthesis (see 3.1).

There are also 'negative catalysts' or 'inhibitors', which slow chemical reactions down. Many foods would go stale or turn an unpleasant colour more quickly without the use of inhibitors called 'anti-oxidants'. Food additives with an E-number between 300 and 321 are all anti-oxidants (see 7.11 and *Datapage M*).

Light is essential for photosynthesis to occur. Sometimes you see greenhouses with powerful lighting on at night, so that this process does not stop. A quite different chemical reaction, which also depends on light, is the one which takes place on photographic film.

Changing the particle size can help a reaction, but can also be dangerous. Very finely powdered substances can react so rapidly that they may burn, or even explode. Coal dust in mines is always kept wet, not only to cut down the amount of dust which the miners may breathe, but also to prevent explosions of coal dust with air.

Fig. 1 Reactions generally go faster when the temperature is raised!

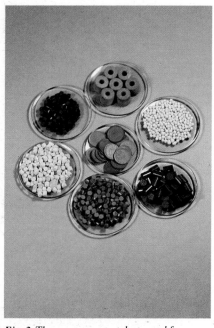

Fig. 2 These are some catalysts used for processes in the fertilizer industry. The pennies in the centre give you an idea of their size.

> **Q1** Write a letter to a friend who has missed the lesson, describing an experiment you have done or seen which shows the effect of one of these 'factors' on the rate of a chemical reaction.

Fig. 3 Coal dust can react explosively with air. Spraying water in coal mines helps to cut down this risk.

Why do changes in conditions affect the rate of a chemical reaction?

Chemical reactions take place when the reacting particles collide with one another. Changing the conditions affects these collisions.

☐ An increase in temperature makes the particles move faster. This means that they will hit one another harder and more often. Both these effects will increase the chance of a chemical reaction.

☐ An increase in concentration (or pressure in the case of gases) means that the particles will be more crowded together, so they will collide more often, and the chances of a reaction taking place are greater.

☐ Catalysts work in a number of ways, but a common one is for the catalyst to act as a kind of framework which holds the reacting particles together for just a little longer than would happen during a normal collision. This provides extra time for the chemical reaction to take place.

☐ Light has a different effect. Most frequently it breaks up a particle like a molecule or an ion into smaller particles, which are more reactive than the particles originally present.

☐ The *smaller* the *particles* in a given amount of substance, the *greater* the area of *surface* exposed for chemical reaction.

Fig. 4 This block of flats collapsed because of an explosion caused by a gas leak, but the gas itself was ignited by another explosion: someone dropped a bag of flour! It was this small explosion which led to the disaster.

Q2 The drawing (Fig 5) shows two blocks of the same size and mass.
  (a) One is a single 'particle', measuring 10cm x 10cm x 10cm. Work out the total area of its surface.
  (b) The other is made of one thousand 'small particles', each measuring 1cm x 1cm x 1cm. Work out the total area of surface which is exposed when these are set free.
  (c) Complete this statement: "When the large block is broken up into 1000 tiny blocks the surface area is .... times greater".

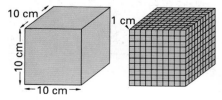

Fig. 5 This should help you with Q2.

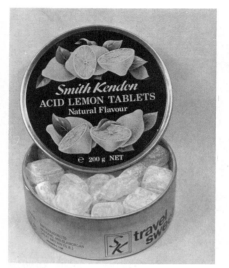

Fig. 1 Many sweets contain fruit acids.

Fig. 2 Litmus is made from lichens like this which grow in warm climates on clifftops and trees.

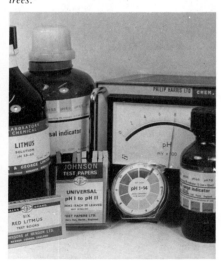

Fig. 3 These are used for measuring pH in the lab.

56

2.7

Acids, alkalis and the pH scale

Vinegar is the acid which most people know best. They put it on meals, like fish and chips, or use it for preserving pickled foods. You don't have to look far to find a number of other acids. Many fruit juices contain acids, and an acid is used in car batteries. All these acids are very different. Some can be eaten, but others would kill you. Some are found in nature, but others are manufactured. What do they have in common? The word **acid** means sharp or sour. The sharp taste of lemon juice and the sour taste of milk which has 'gone off' are both due to acids. The name 'acid' was originally given to things which tasted like this.

Q1 Collect labels and pictures of all the acids you can think of. Make a chart showing where they are found or how they are used.

Later it was discovered that acids had something else in common: they all had the same effect on certain coloured substances which could be extracted from plants. There is a blue substance called **litmus**, which is obtained from some kinds of lichen (Fig. 2). It goes red when acids are put with it. The blue colour comes back if you add another chemical which can 'cancel out' the effect of the acid. Substances which change colour when acids are added to them, and which change back if the acid is chemically removed, are called **indicators**. Litmus is an indicator which has been known for more than 400 years. There are other natural indicators which you can make from plants: the juices from elderberries, blackberries and red cabbage all work well.

Turning back the colour of an indicator is not just a question of taking the acid away. The acid has a chemical effect on the indicator, and actually alters its molecules. Changing the molecules back to what they were restores the original colour. This has to be done by substances which have the opposite chemical effect to acids – and these are called **alkalis**. Baking soda and lime are well-known alkalis. They will both turn reddened litmus back to blue.

Q2 Write a note for someone who has missed the lesson, explaining carefully what is meant by the words 'acid' and 'indicator'.

Litmus is still used in many laboratories, especially in the form of litmus paper, an absorbent paper which has been soaked in litmus solution and dried. However, there are some better indicators today. Many of these are mixtures, like **universal indicator** or **full-range indicator**, which give a whole variety of bright colours, depending upon the strength of the acid or alkali which is added to them.

Acids and alkalis at home

Acids		Alkalis	
Where found	Name of acid	Where found	Name of alkali
fruit juice	citric acid	garden lime	calcium hydroxide
vinegar	ethanoic acid	household ammonia	ammonia solution
rust remover	phosphoric acid	baking soda	sodium hydrogencarbonate
TCP, Dettol	various phenols	washing soda	sodium carbonate
battery acid	sulphuric acid	oven cleaner	potassium hydroxide
soda water	carbonic acid	milk of magnesia	magnesium hydroxide

			Universal Indicator Colour											
	red		orange		yellow	green				blue		purple	
pH	1	2	3	4	5	6	7	8	9	10	11	12	13	14

all these are acids	neutral	all these are alkalis
acids have pH numbers **lower** than 7		alkalis have pH numbers **higher** than 7

The stronger the **acid**, the lower the pH

The stronger the alkali, the higher the pH

Fig. 4 The pH scale is a range of numbers to describe how acidic or alkaline a substance is.

The pH scale

As soon as you use one of the universal indicators you can see that some acids are 'more acid' than others. Battery acid turns universal indicator bright red, but vinegar will only turn it orangey–yellow. Different substances give a whole range of different colours. The most acidic ones produce a strong red colour, and the most alkaline ones give a dark purple.

There is a scale of numbers from 1 to 14 for describing how acidic or alkaline a substance is. This scale is known as the **pH scale** (note: small 'p', big 'H'), and the numbers are called pH numbers. The strong acids have a pH number of 1 and the strong alkalis have a pH number of 14. The pH number 7 is the mid-way point on the scale, and represents substances which are neither acidic nor alkaline. Pure water has a pH of 7. It is not an acid or an alkali; it is **neutral**.

> **Q3** Draw a diagram showing the pH scale. Put in the colours of universal indicator alongside the corresponding pH values. Label the diagram fully and keep it for future reference.

Measuring pH values

Figure 3 shows several items which can be used for measuring the pH of a solution. One possibility is to use test papers which are sensitive over a wide range of values. Another way, if you already know the approximate pH value of a solution, is to use a more accurate test paper which covers a narrower range. The instrument in the background is called a pH meter. It is a voltmeter connected to an electrical device which is affected by the pH value of the solution.

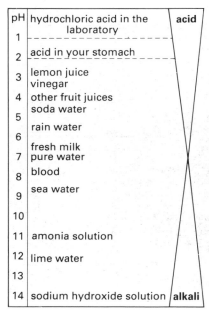

pH		
	hydrochloric acid in the laboratory	**acid**
1		
2	acid in your stomach	
3	lemon juice vinegar	
4	other fruit juices soda water	
5		
6	rain water	
7	fresh milk pure water	
8	blood	
9	sea water	
10		
11	amonia solution	
12	lime water	
13		
14	sodium hydroxide solution	**alkali**

Fig. 5 The pH values of some well known substances.

Neutralisation

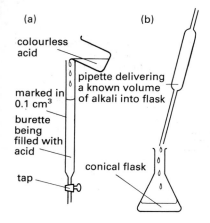

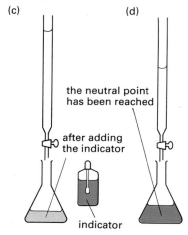

Fig. 1 *Carrying out a titration.*

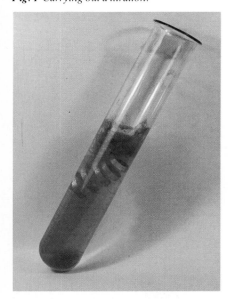

Fig. 2 *Hydrogen is given off as magnesium starts to react with an acid.*

When you add an alkali to an acid, it 'cancels out' the acidity. If an indicator is present while this is happening, you can see the colour changing. As you keep adding alkali the pH of the mixture rises. At pH 7 you reach the **neutral** point on the scale. The acid has been **neutralised**. This process is called **neutralisation**.

Q1 Suppose you had spilled some battery acid on the garage floor. Look at the list of 'Acids and alkalis at home' (see 2.7) and decide what to do. Write a clear explanation of how you would deal with the spillage.

Accurate neutralisation requires special apparatus. You need to be able to approach the neutral point very gradually. This is because it is very easy to 'overshoot' by adding a tiny bit too much of the neutralising chemical. The name given to the method is **titration** (Fig. 1).

To carry out a titration you need a **burette** and a **pipette**. A burette is a tall tube, marked in $0.1cm^3$ divisions, and fitted with a tap at the bottom. A pipette is usually shaped like the one shown in Fig. 1. First you fill a burette with acid. Then you use a pipette to put a known volume of alkali into a flask. A pipette is used for this, because it is designed to *deliver* a precisely known volume of liquid. After adding a few drops of indicator to the alkali, you run acid carefully from the burette into the flask. Neutralisation is complete when the changing colour of the indicator shows that the pH value is 7.

What happens during neutralisation?

When an acid and an alkali have reacted together in exactly the amounts needed to neutralise one another, *two new substances* have been formed. These are **water** and **a salt**. We can say:

$$\text{acid} + \text{alkali} \xrightarrow{\text{neutralisation}} \text{salt} + \text{water}$$

You can't see the water or the salt when you neutralise an acid by titrating it. There is a lot of water there anyway, from the solutions you have been mixing, and the salt is dissolved in it. To obtain the salt alone, you would have to evaporate the solution from the conical flask. There is a small problem here: at the end of a titration the flask contains indicator.

Q2 Explain how you could obtain the pure salt in solid form. (Hint: titration is still used.)

Seeing the salt and water

To see the salt and water forming directly during a neutralisation you need to start with dry materials, not solutions. One way of doing this is to pass an acid which is a *gas* over something *solid* which will neutralise it. In Fig. 4 hydrogen chloride (hydrochloric acid gas) is being passed over heated iron oxide. Even when the acid gas and the iron oxide are completely dried at the start, some *water* can be seen forming during the neutralisation. The other substance formed is a *salt* called iron(III) chloride.

Labels from Fig. 1:
(a) colourless acid; marked in 0.1 cm³; burette being filled with acid; tap
(b) pipette delivering a known volume of alkali into flask; conical flask
(c) after adding the indicator; indicator
(d) the neutral point has been reached

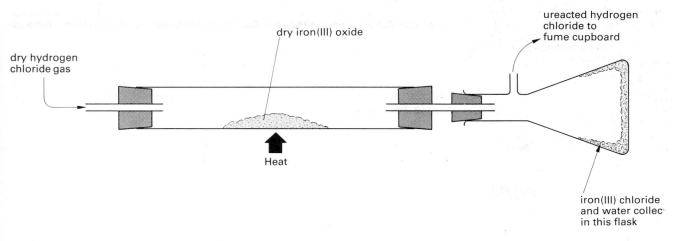

Fig. 3 Perfectly dry iron (III) oxide reacts with dry hydrogen chloride gas, forming a solution of iron(III) chloride. The water for dissolving the iron(III) chloride is produced by the neutralisation reaction itself.

Forming new substances from acids

You already know that:

☐ acids taste sharp or sour
☐ acids have a pH number less than 7
☐ acids will neutralise alkalis

But all acids have something else in common:
☐ acids contain **replaceable hydrogen**.

This means that, in one way or another, hydrogen can be released from all acids. For example, if you put a piece of magnesium ribbon into almost any acid which has been dissolved in water, you see bubbles of hydrogen forming (Fig. 2). The magnesium dissolves in the acid. As it does so, it forms a new substance with whatever is left of the acid, once the hydrogen has been released:

magnesium + acid   →   new substance + hydrogen

The new substance is a *salt*, and the magnesium is reacting with the acid as it dissolves. If you go on adding magnesium until no more will react (Fig. 4), you complete the process:

magnesium + acid   →   salt + hydrogen

The kind of salt you get depends upon the acid you use. With hydrochloric acid the salt is magnesium chloride, so

magnesium + hydrochloric acid   →   magnesium chloride + hydrogen

Q3 Write word equations for the neutralisation reactions which are taking place in Fig. 1 and Fig. 3.

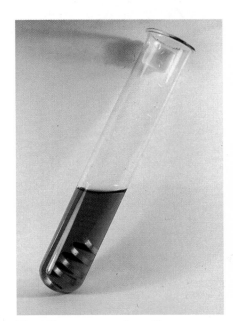

Fig. 4 No more magnesium will react, because the acid has been neutralised. What is the pH of the solution now?

Fig. 1 Sea salt evaporating at Guerande in Brittany, France.

Fig. 2 Some well-known salts.

Salts

Table salt, bath salts, sea salt, rock salt – they all mean something different. The salt we know best is the chemical compound sodium chloride, but the word 'salt' has a wider meaning in chemistry as well. *Any* substance which has been formed by replacing (some or all) of the hydrogen in an acid is known as a **salt**. You will find a list of some salts on *Datapage E2*.

Salts from alkalis and bases

You already know that

☐ alkalis will neutralise acids, forming salts
☐ alkalis have a pH number greater than 7.

It is also true that:

☐ all alkalis are soluble in water

There are other substances – not necessarily alkalis – which will neutralise acids and form salts. These substances are called bases.

☐ A **base** is a substance which will react with an acid to form a salt and water only.
☐ An **alkali** is a base which is soluble in water.

So you can write the neutralisation process as:

$$\text{acid} + \text{base (or alkali)} \rightarrow \text{salt} + \text{water}$$

Making soluble salts

Soluble salts can be made by the reactions between:

(1) an *acid* and an *alkali* (for example, sodium chloride)
(2) an *insoluble base* and an *acid* (for example, copper sulphate)
(3) a *carbonate* and an *acid* (for example, lead nitrate)
(4) a fairly reactive *metal* and an *acid* (for example, zinc sulphate).

Method 1 is carried out by titration, as described in 2.8. The other methods all require the same apparatus, and you need to follow the procedure shown in Fig. 3. First, you add the solid substance to the acid, and stir it in until no more will dissolve. Then you remove the undissolved solid by filtering, and collect the filtered solution in an evaporating basin. This solution, which contains the salt, should be evaporated until only a small amount of liquid remains. Then you put it aside to cool and crystallise.

Q1 Using the four pictures in Fig. 3 as a guide, write instructions for someone who has to make *either* copper sulphate (by method 2), *or* zinc sulphate (by method 4).

Did you know?

What pure chemical is sold in the largest quantity by British shops?

No, not salt but sugar! (= sucrose)

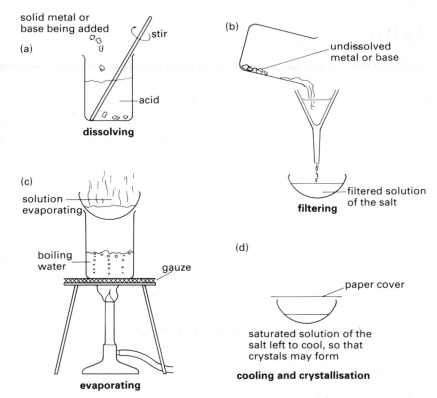

Fig. 3 *Making a soluble salt.*

Making other salts

Insoluble salts are made by the **precipitation** method (sometimes called 'double decomposition'). You need two soluble salts which will supply the parts of the salt you want to make. Lead sulphate is an insoluble salt, so to make it you mix solutions of lead nitrate and zinc sulphate. A white solid appears, which can be filtered off. This is a **precipitate** of lead sulphate:

lead nitrate + zinc **sulphate** → zinc nitrate + **lead sulphate**
(solution) + (solution)   →   (solution) + (solution)

A few salts can be made by combining two elements together. This method is called **direct combination** or **synthesis**. A metal and a non-metal may react to form a salt, for example:

copper (s) + chlorine (g) → copper chloride (s)

Naming salts

The name of each salt begins with the name of a metal (sodium, magnesium etc.). This is because the salt always takes its name from the acid and the base or metal which is used to make it, for example:

sodium hydroxide + hydro**chloric** acid → **sodium chloride** + water
copper oxide + **sulph**uric acid   →   **copper sulphate** + water

Three helpful **rules for naming a salt** are:

☐ the name of the metal always comes first
☐ if the salt contains only two elements, the name ends in **-ide**
☐ if the salt contains three or more elements, one of which is oxygen, the name ends in **-ate**.

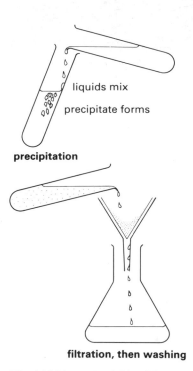

Fig. 4 *Making an insoluble salt by precipitation.*

Acids, alkalis and ions

Fig. 1 The word 'ion' was coined by Michael Faraday in 1834 during the course of some electrical experiments in this laboratory.

Acids and ions

All acids contain hydrogen. This hydrogen can be replaced during chemical reactions because it is present in the acid as **hydrogen ions**. Acids also contain one other type of ion: **salt-forming ions**.

Ions are charged particles (see 1.11).

☐ On the *hydrogen ion* (H^+) the charge is *positive*.
☐ On the *salt-forming ion* from an acid, the charge is *negative*.

Hydrochloric acid is a simple example. The gas hydrogen chloride, HCl, consists of covalently bonded molecules of the type explained in 1.10. When it dissolves in water it forms an acid solution, because the hydrogen ions become free to move about in the solution:

hydrogen chloride + water → hydrogen ions + chloride ions
(gas)   (liquid)   (in solution)   (in solution)

Water molecules pull away ions from the hydrogen chloride molecules and surround them, as in Fig. 2. Ions in an aqueous solution are often written with the symbol (aq) after them, to show that this has happened. The equation then becomes:

$$HCl(g) + aq \rightarrow H^+(aq) + Cl^-(aq)$$

Q1 Make drawings and write similar equations to show the reactions of hydrobromic acid (HBr), nitric acid (HNO_3) and sulphuric acid (H_2SO_4) with water.

A molecule of water, H_2O, and . . .

. . . a molecule of hydrogen chloride, H Cl . . .

. . . react to become . . .

. . . a hydrated hydrogen ion, H^+ (aq), and . . .

. . . a chloride ion, Cl^-.

Fig. 2 Hydrogen chloride molecules reacting with water to form ions.

Alkalis and ions

Like acids, the alkalis contain two kinds of ion.

☐ There is a *positive ion*, usually a *metal ion*.
☐ There is a *negative ion*, usually a *hydroxide ion* (OH^-).

Sodium hydroxide is one example of an alkali. Solid sodium hydroxide consists of a lattice of ions which is pulled apart by water molecules as the substance dissolves. As with acids, the water molecules attach themselves to the ions, and remain there when the solid has dissolved (Fig. 3):

sodium hydroxide + water → sodium ions + hydroxide ions
(solid)   (liquid)   (in solution)   (in solution)

$$NaOH(s) + aq \rightarrow Na^+(aq) + OH^-(aq)$$

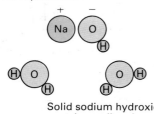

Solid sodium hydroxide contains sodium ions, Na^+, and hydroxyl ions, OH^-, which link up with water molecules, H_2O . .

. . . and form . . .

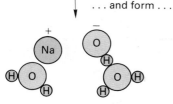

. . . two hydrated ions Na^+ (aq) and OH^- (aq) in solution.

Fig. 3 Water molecules attaching themselves to the ions of sodium hydroxide.

The ions in some acids and alkalis

Name of substance	Ions present
Acids	
Hydrochloric acid	H^+(aq) and Cl^-(aq)
Nitric acid	H^+(aq) and NO_3^-(aq)
Sulphuric acid	H^+(aq) and SO_4^{2-}(aq)
Alkalis	
Calcium hydroxide	Ca^{2+}(aq) and OH^-(aq)
Sodium carbonate	Na^+(aq) and CO_3^{2-}(aq)
Sodium hydroxide	Na^+(aq) and OH^-(aq)

Fig. 4 Neutralisation at work: lime is being added to the soil to neutralise some of the acids. This raises the pH to a suitable value for growing next year's crop.

What happens to the ions during neutralisation?

There are several ways of writing equations for the neutralisation of hydrochloric acid by sodium hydroxide.

The **word equation** is:

$$\text{sodium hydroxide(aq)} + \text{hydrochloric acid(aq)} \rightarrow \text{sodium chloride(aq)} + \text{water(l)}$$

The full **formula equation** is:

$$NaOH(aq) + HCl(aq) \rightarrow NaCl(aq) + H_2O(l)$$

If all the ions are fully written out, you get:

$$Na^+(aq) + OH^-(aq) + H^+(aq) + Cl^-(aq) \rightarrow Na^+(aq) + Cl^-(aq) + H_2O(l)$$

You can now see that there is some repetition here. The $Na^+(aq)$ ions and the $Cl^-(aq)$ ions have not taken part in any chemical change at all. They have been present unchanged throughout. Because of this they are sometimes called **spectator ions**. Usually the spectator ions are left out of the **ionic equation**, which is written:

$$\underset{\text{(from the acid)}}{H^+(aq)} + \underset{\text{(from the alkali)}}{OH^-(aq)} \rightarrow H_2O(l)$$

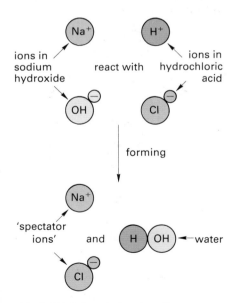

Fig. 5 This is how the ions in sodium hydroxide solution react with the ions in hydrochloric acid during a neutralisation reaction.

Q2 Write (a) a word equation, (b) a formula equation, and (c) an ionic equation for the reactions which take place when hydrochloric acid is neutralised by:
   (i) potassium hydroxide, KOH
   (ii) calcium hydroxide, $Ca(OH)_2$
   (iii) sodium carbonate, Na_2CO_3.

63

Questions

A. What can you remember?

** 1. Give one example of each of the following, and say when it is used: a solvent, a solution, a solute, a suspension.

* 2. Give three everyday examples of a solution which contains a gas (or gases) dissolved in a liquid.

** 3. Explain, with a labelled sketch, what is meant by a solubility curve.

** 4. What is meant by a *pure substance*? How does a pure substance differ from a mixture?

** 5. List four ways of separating mixtures, and give an example of how each one might be used.

* 6. Give two examples of fast chemical reactions. Explain how you know that the reaction is a fast one.

** 7. State what is meant by the *rate* of a chemical reaction.

* 8. What is a catalyst? Give two examples of how a catalyst is used.

** 9. What is the pH scale? Explain as fully as you can.

** 10. What new substances are formed during a neutralisation reaction? What does the word *neutral* mean here?

* 11. Explain the difference between a base and an alkali, and give one example of each.

** 12. Give names to the salts formed during the following reactions:
(a) copper oxide reacting with hydrochloric acid
(b) lead oxide reacting with nitric acid
(c) sodium carbonate reacting with sulphuric acid
(d) magnesium reacting with hydrochloric acid.

*** 13. Give the names and formulae of the ions present in
(a) a solution of hydrogen chloride in water,
(b) dilute sulphuric acid,
(c) sodium nitrate solution,
(d) water.

B. What have you understood?

** 14. Explain carefully how you would make a saturated solution of salt in water.

* 15. Your friend is finding it difficult to dissolve some salt in water. What advice would you give?

** 16. Fish in a tank can sometimes be seen gasping near the surface. How could you supply them with more air?

*** 17. The solubility of magnesium chloride is 54.2g per 100g water at 20°C. Given a supply of magnesium chloride and water, how could you check this statement?

** 18. Explain the principle of chromatography. Give one example of how it can be used.

** 19. Explain how a gas mask works.

** 20. Copper oxide, raw meat and celery all contain substances which will catalyse the reaction:

hydrogen peroxide → oxygen + water

Suggest a method for finding out which is the best catalyst.

** 21. An anti-oxidant, used in foods to stop them spoiling, is sometimes called a negative catalyst. What do you think this means? Can you think of any other examples of negative catalysts?

X ** **22.** Chemical reactions affected by light are quite common. Give two examples, and explain what effect you think the light has.

* **23.** The pH scale is used to measure acidity. Explain what this means, and give an example.

** **24.** The reaction between an acid and an alkali produces water. How could you prove this?

*** **25.** Look again at 2.10, and then write a letter to a friend who is away from school without a book, explaining what is meant by spectator ions.

C Can you use this information?

X ** **26.** Oxygen is about twice as soluble as nitrogen in water. Suppose you could collect some of the air which comes out of the spout of a boiling kettle. Suggest what gases it would contain, and in what proportion.

** **27.** The solubilities of some common substances are given in *Datapage E*. Study this table and write down some general rules. Here is one to help you: 'All the sodium salts listed here are soluble in water.'

* **28.** Look at *Datapage E2*, and write down:
   (a) the name of the salt on this list which is most soluble at 10°C,
   (b) the name of the salt on this list which is least soluble at 10°C,
   (c) the name of the salt on this list which is most soluble at 90°C,
   (d) the name of the salt on this list which becomes less soluble as the temperature is increased,
   (e) the name of the salt on this list for which the solubility increases least as you raise the temperature.

** **29.** Use information from *Datapage E2* to plot solubility curves for the *chlorides* listed. All curves should be drawn on the same axes. Find out from the curves
   (a) the temperature at which sodium chloride and potassium chloride have the same solubility value,
   (b) the solubility values for all four salts at 75°C.

** **30.** Use information from *Datapage E2* to plot solubility curves for the three potassium salts listed.
   All three curves should be drawn on the same axes. Find out from the curves
   (a) the temperature at which potassium chloride and potassium nitrate have the same solubility value,
   (b) the three different temperatures at which these salts have a solubility of exactly 50g per 100g water.

** **31.** Use information from *Datapage L5* to estimate roughly:
   (a) how much acid is present in a 200cm can of ginger beer,
   (b) how much sugar you would expect in the same can,
   (c) what volume of carbon dioxide gas you might collect by boiling the contents of the can!

D. Taking it further

*** **32.** Raising the temperature by just 10 degrees will double the rate of many chemical reactions.
   (a) Suggest an example where this is put to use.
   (b) Why do you think this large increase in rate happens?

* **33.** You are required to produce a new solvent for sale as a paint stripper. Write down a list of the properties which you would require this product to have.

** **34.** Draw a labelled piece of apparatus which would be suitable for drying a gas (see 2.4).

** **35.** Many flowers and soft fruits grow best on acid soils (pH 4–6), but most vegetables prefer alkaline soils (pH > 7).
   (a) How would you try to measure the pH of garden soil?
   (b) How would you raise the pH value of an acid soil in order to grow vegetables?

Quick questions

1. What are the dissolved gases in (a) a swimming pool, (b) a fizzy drink, (c) a goldfish tank?

2. Why does stirring a cup of coffee help to dissolve the sugar?

3. List some non-aqueous solvents you could find in the kitchen or garage.

4. List as many different kinds of filter in everyday use as you can.

5. The pH of some oven cleaners is 14. What kind of substances are these?

Some non-metals and their compounds

Gases of the air

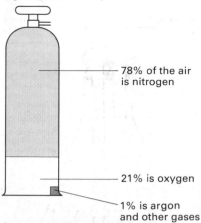

a gas cylinder of dry air

— 78% of the air is nitrogen

— 21% is oxygen

— 1% is argon and other gases

Fig. 1 Dry air contains these gases.

You really notice the air only when you leave a window open, or when the wind is blowing hard. Every breath contains more molecules than you can possibly imagine, but for most of the time we take the air completely for granted. The main gases in the air are shown in Fig. 1. The full list is given on *Datapage 12*.

Finding out how much oxygen is in the air

Two gas syringes are arranged as shown in Fig. 2. One contains 100 cm^3 of the air sample. The other contains no air. The connecting tube contains something which will react with oxygen – in this case the metal copper. The copper is heated, and air from the left-hand syringe is slowly passed over the hot copper and into the other syringe. The copper goes black, as copper oxide forms on its surface, and the air decreases in volume as the oxygen is taken out of it. The process is continued, passing the air backwards and forwards, until nothing more happens. Then, when the apparatus is cool, the volume of the remaining air is measured.

Q1 If you begin this experiment with 100 cm^3 of air, how many cubic centimetres of 'remaining air' would you expect to find left at the end? What gas(es) are present in the 'remaining air'?

Q2 It is obviously important that the apparatus should be airtight for this experiment. How would you check this before starting?

Q3 Explain why it is necessary to allow the apparatus to cool before measuring the volume of the 'remaining air'.

Q4 Copper is chosen here to react with oxygen from the air.
(a) Would magnesium or iron be suitable? Explain your answers.
(b) The experiment will only be accurate if there is some unreacted copper left at the end. Explain why.

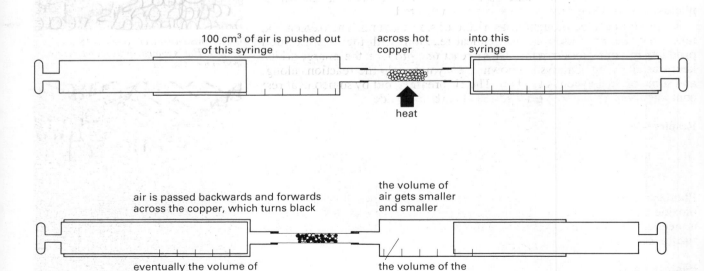

100 cm^3 of air is pushed out of this syringe

across hot copper

into this syringe

heat

air is passed backwards and forwards across the copper, which turns black

the volume of air gets smaller and smaller

eventually the volume of air stops getting smaller

the volume of the remaining air is measured

Fig. 2 Finding out how much oxygen is in the air. The volume of a sample of air is measured before and after the oxygen has been removed.

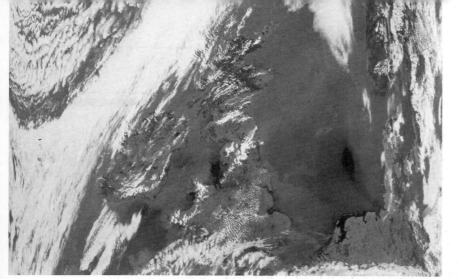

Fig. 3 *Water evaporates into the air from the sea and land. These white clouds over Britain are made of tiny droplets of condensed water vapour.*

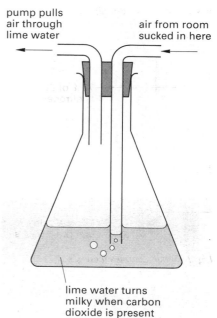

Fig. 4 *Pumping air through lime water, to detect carbon dioxide.*

Carbon dioxide and water vapour in the air

Although the amount of **carbon dioxide** in the air is very small (around 0.3%), it is possible to show quite easily that it is there. A pump arranged as shown in Fig. 3 will draw a large quantity of air through a small amount of lime water.

> **Q5** What would you see forming in the lime water tube after a while?

Even when it is not raining, there is moisture in the air. It is there in the form of a gas known as **water vapour**. The amount of water vapour in air varies with the weather, and is affected by temperature.

Respiration and photosynthesis

Animals and plants 'exchange gases' with the air around them. Animals breathe in air and use some of its oxygen to 'burn the fuel' which they take in as food. This process is called **respiration**. Plants take in air and use some of its carbon dioxide to make stored food. This process is known as **photosynthesis**. Both processes are very complicated.

Respiration can be thought of as a kind of slow burning. The oxygen you take from the air is used up in chemical reactions with the digested food products in your bloodstream. These reactions produce the energy which keeps us all going. Catalysts, known as enzymes, help the reactions along, and some of the oxygen is used up. The air breathed out by someone at rest contains about 16% of oxygen and 4% of carbon dioxide.

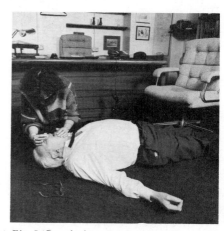

Fig. 5 *'Breathed out air' contains 16% oxygen. This is enough to give someone else artificial respiration.*

Respiration:

$$\text{nutrients} + \text{oxygen} \xrightarrow{\text{enzymes}} \text{waste products} + \text{carbon dioxide}$$

energy is released

Photosynthesis is effectively the opposite process. Plants take in carbon dioxide and water, and use it to make foodstuffs (carbohydrates). Sunlight is needed for this to happen, and the catalyst in this case is the green substance chlorophyll.

Photosynthesis:

$$\text{carbon dioxide} + \text{water} \xrightarrow{\text{sunlight and chlorophyll}} \text{carbohydrates}$$

energy is absorbed

Fig. 6 *Light energy is essential for photosynthesis to take place.*

Oxygen

Fig. 1 Joseph Priestley (1733–1804) is usually credited with the discovery of oxygen.

In 1774 an English minister named Joseph Priestley (Fig. 1) obtained a gas which he thought of as a kind of 'super-air'. On breathing it he "felt peculiarly light and easy". "In time", he wrote, "this pure air may become a fashionable article in luxury. Hitherto only two mice and myself have had the privilege of breathing it." This was **oxygen** – "the breath of life".

Q1 Priestley made his oxygen by heating mercury oxide with a burning glass. Find out more about this, and either (a) write a short illustrated article, as for a newspaper of the time, explaining what he did; or (b) imagine you were Priestley and write a letter to a friend describing your experiments.

In the same year, the Swedish scientist Scheele recognised that air is a mixture of gases. He realised that there is one part which allows things to burn and breathe in it, and another part which does not. He called these two parts 'fire air' and 'foul air'.

The name 'nitrogen' was soon given to the 'foul air'. For more than 100 years no-one realised that there were still more gases in the air to be discovered. There is more about the discovery of these gases in 3.3 and more about nitrogen in 3.4.

Fig. 2 Sulphur burning in oxygen. In the air it would burn less brightly.

How is oxygen used today?

Oxygen can combine with some elements to form solid compounds. Many of these compounds are present in the earth. In fact oxygen makes up about 47% of the earth's crust (see *Datapage II*). Oxygen gas makes up almost 21% by volume of the air. Oxygen is extracted from the air, and used in many ways, for example:

- ☐ in life-support systems of all kinds (in hospitals, in aeroplanes and spacecraft, for diving and mountaineering); it can even be supplied to the homes of people with breathing difficulties.
- ☐ in rockets, where liquid oxygen is used to burn the fuel.
- ☐ in many kinds of welding and cutting apparatus which rely on the high temperatures achieved by 'oxy-gas' flames.
- ☐ in steel manufacture which requires oxygen to 'burn out' impurities in the molten iron (Fig. 5).

Fig. 3 This diver working on a wreck carries the oxygen he needs to breathe in a cylinder on his back.

Q2 To make 12 tonnes of steel, about 1 tonne of oxygen is needed. How many cubic metres of air must be processed to obtain 1 tonne of oxygen? (Assume that 20% of the air is oxygen. Its density at 20°C is 1.33 kilograms per cubic metre. 1 tonne = 1000 kg.)

Q3 Collect illustrations from magazines, and use them to make a poster which explains the uses of oxygen.

The chemical behaviour of oxygen

Priestley noticed that a glowing piece of wood sparkled in oxygen, and that a candle burned more brightly in it. You will remember that the test for oxygen still used is that it 're-lights a glowing splint'. Since then it has been found that anything which burns at all will burn better in oxygen.

Fig. 4 Hospitals need a ready supply of oxygen for many patients.

Fig. 5 The largest industrial use of oxygen is for making steel. Here molten iron is being poured into a converter. Oxygen will then be blown in to remove the impurities.

Many elements react directly with oxygen to form their oxides, usually when heated. The oxides of *non-metals* are generally *acidic*, while the oxides of *metals* are usually *basic* or alkaline. A few oxides are neutral: water is the best known example. Others may behave both as acidic oxides in the presence of a base *and* as basic oxides in the presence of an acid. Oxides of this type are known as **amphoteric**.

Some reactions between elements and oxygen

Element	Effect of burning in oxygen	Oxide formed	Notes
sulphur	bright blue flame	$SO_2(g)$	acidic
carbon	glows brightly	$CO_2(g)$	weakly acidic
hydrogen	blue flame	$H_2O(g)$	neutral
zinc	bright bluish flame	$ZnO(g)$	amphoteric
iron (wool)	sparkles brightly	$Fe_2O_3(s)$	basic
magnesium	dazzling white flame	$MgO(s)$	basic
sodium	bright yellow flame	$Na_2O(s)$	alkaline

Q4 Use the above information to predict how the following elements would react with oxygen: lithium, calcium, aluminium, silicon, phosphorus. If possible, check your predictions with a reference book.

Fig. 6 Some rockets used to launch spacecraft carry as much as 80 tonnes of liquid oxygen.

71

Extracting useful gases from the air

Fig. 1 An air distillation plant like this takes in 3 tonnes of air per minute!

The oxygen needed for hospitals, steelworks, diving and space travel is taken from the air. So is the nitrogen used for making fertilisers. So, too, is the argon for filling light bulbs. To extract these gases it is first necessary to turn the air to a liquid. The process is shown in Fig. 4, and works like this:

(1) Dust, water vapour and carbon dioxide are removed from the air.
(2) The clean dry air is compressed and passed to the **heat exchanger**. Here it is cooled by very cold nitrogen, piped from the **distillation column**.
(3) The cold, compressed air is allowed to expand rapidly. This causes it to cool still further, and become a liquid.
(4) The liquid air is fractionally distilled, giving nitrogen, oxygen and the noble gases.

Q1 Look up the boiling points of nitrogen, oxygen and argon (*Datapage I2*). Below what temperature would *all three* of these gases become liquids?

Q2 Find out what happens when carbon dioxide is cooled (see 3.6). Explain how this would affect the process for liquefying the air, and suggest what could be done about it.

Q3 Using your answer to Q1, list the gases of the air in the order they would be produced when liquid air at $-200\,°C$ is warmed.

Fig. 2 The argon used to fill this light bulb prevents the filament from burning.

Noble gas	Arrangement of electrons
helium	2
neon	2.8
argon	2.8.8
krypton	2.8.18.8
xenon	2.8.18.18.8

Fig. 3 The noble gases are unreactive because their atoms have full outer shells of electrons.

The noble gases

The unreactive gases in the atmosphere are known as the **noble gases**. All except argon are present in tiny quantities. This table tells you more about the noble gases:

Noble gas	Symbol	Atomic no.	% in atmosphere	B.P. (°C)
helium	He	2	0.0005	−269
neon	Ne	10	0.0018	−246
argon	Ar	18	0.93	−186
krypton	Kr	36	0.0001	−152
xenon	Xe	54	0.00001	−107
radon	Rn	86	variable*	−62

* Radon is produced by the breakdown of radioactive elements in the earth. Its concentration varies according to the nature of the ground, and how quickly it spreads on reaching the surface.

The atoms of the noble gases have no 'vacancies' for electrons in the outer shell. For this reason they are very unreactive. A few noble gas compounds do exist, but special conditions are needed to make them.

How the noble gases were discovered

The noble gases were completely unsuspected until about a century ago. Then in 1892 it was pointed out that nitrogen from the air appeared to be slightly more dense than nitrogen which had been prepared chemically.

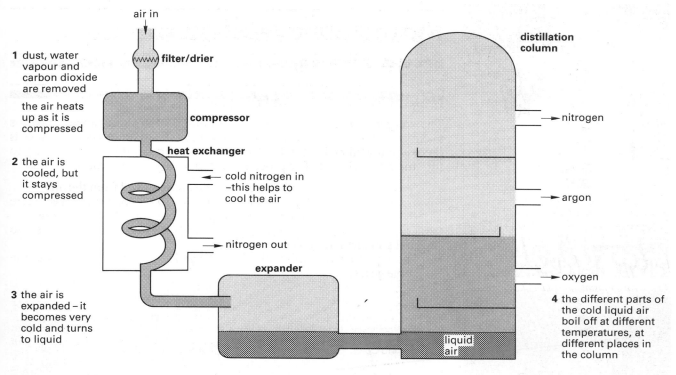

1 dust, water vapour and carbon dioxide are removed

the air heats up as it is compressed

2 the air is cooled, but it stays compressed

3 the air is expanded – it becomes very cold and turns to liquid

air in

filter/drier

compressor

heat exchanger

cold nitrogen in –this helps to cool the air

nitrogen out

expander

liquid air

distillation column

nitrogen

argon

oxygen

4 the different parts of the cold liquid air boil off at different temperatures, at different places in the column

Fig. 4 Fractional distillation is used to extract useful gases from liquid air.

William Ramsay, working at University College, London, arranged for 'pure nitrogen' from the air to be passed repeatedly over heated magnesium. He knew that magnesium and nitrogen reacted together to form a solid compound, so in theory there should have been no gas left at the end. In fact, about 1% of the so-called 'nitrogen' remained, showing that other gases must have been present all the time. These came to be known as the noble gases, and today they are very useful:

Uses of the noble gases

Noble gas	Everyday use	Reason
helium	filling balloons	very light, non-flammable
	as a mixture with oxygen for divers working under pressure	helium is not very soluble in the blood, avoids "bends"
neon	neon signs, lasers	gives right kind of light
argon	filling household lamps	prevents filaments from burning
	welding	provides an unreactive atmosphere
krypton	filling low-power lamps	helps good light output
xenon	lasers, specialised lamps, e.g. for lighthouses	it is a bad conductor of heat
radon	radiotherapy	it is radioactive

Q4 Collect suitable pictures and use information from this section to make an illustrated chart: 'Noble Gases and their uses'.

Fig. 5 Some powerful lamps are filled with xenon gas – a bad conductor of heat.

Fig. 6 Airships are filled with helium because it is light and unreactive.

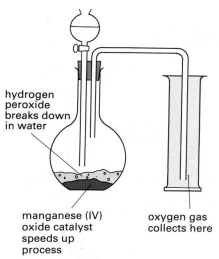

hydrogen
peroxide
breaks down
in water

manganese (IV)
oxide catalyst
speeds up
process

oxygen gas
collects here

Fig. 1 Oxygen can be made in the lab from hydrogen peroxide.

Fig. 2 Pouring liquid oxygen.

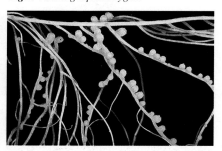

Fig. 3 Bacteria in these root nodules enable the pea plant to absorb nitrogen directly.

More about gases in the air

Making oxygen in the laboratory

Oxygen is easy to obtain in the laboratory. A safe and simple way for making it is shown in Fig. 1. The flask contains a solution of hydrogen peroxide, H_2O_2, a substance which breaks down easily:

$$\text{hydrogen peroxide} \rightarrow \text{water} + \text{oxygen}$$

$$2H_2O_2(aq) \rightarrow 2H_2O(l) + O_2(g)$$

The production of oxygen is speeded up by adding a catalyst, such as manganese(IV) oxide, to the hydrogen peroxide.

> **Q1** Copy Fig. 1 and write step-by-step instructions for someone who has been asked to make and collect a few tubes of oxygen.

If oxygen gas is cooled below $-183°C$ it forms a blue liquid. In Fig. 2 you can see that at this temperature it freezes the water vapour in the air as soon as it comes into contact with it. The main use of liquid oxygen is in the rockets used for space research. Many of these rockets carry two tanks – one for fuel, and another with the liquid oxygen which is needed for the fuel to burn.

Nitrogen

An early name for nitrogen was 'azote', which means 'without life'. Many of today's uses for nitrogen gas rely on the fact that things cannot live or burn in it. Nitrogen is used

☐ to provide a non-reacting atmosphere for welding, glass-making and many other processes
☐ as liquid nitrogen, for quick freezing of foods
☐ for flushing out oil pipelines and tanks, to remove flammable or explosive vapour, especially on ships
☐ for packaging, so that food is not affected by oxygen in the air
☐ in corn silos, to prevent dust explosions.

> **Q2** Collect pictures from magazines to make an illustrated chart which shows 'The uses of nitrogen'. Use a large sheet of paper and write a short explanation of each picture.

Nitrogen and the fertiliser industry

Nitrogen from the air is used to make ammonia, which is in turn used for making 'nitrogenous fertilisers'. Nitrogen is a vital plant food; it is needed for making the green pigment chlorophyll and all proteins. Very few plants can take nitrogen directly from the air. Only those with special 'nodules' on the roots (Fig. 3) can do this.

Nitrogen must be absorbed, usually as ammonium or nitrate ions from the soil. So a nitrogenous fertiliser must supply nitrogen in one of these forms. Ammonium nitrate is the nitrogen compound most widely used as a fertiliser. It contains nearly 35% of nitrogen. Ammonia itself and a substance called urea (NH_2CONH_2) are also used.

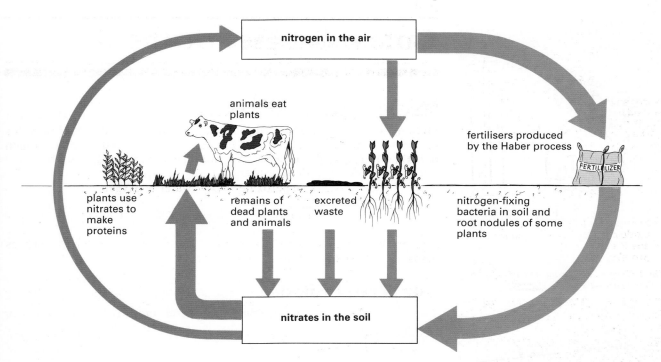

Fig. 4 *The nitrogen cycle.*

The nitrogen cycle

Until people learned the skills of farming, the main source of new nitrogen compounds in the soil was dead plant and animal material which had decayed. Later, the value of using animal manure as a fertiliser was recognised. In the present century the growth of manufactured fertilisers has been immense. Today, the main 'input' of nitrogen to the soil comes from air which has first been turned into ammonia, using the Haber process.

Nitrogen compounds pass from the soil to plants, and from there to animals and back to the soil (Fig. 4). This circulating process is known as the **nitrogen cycle**. New nitrogen compounds must constantly be added because of 'losses' from the cycle. Some are removed as proteins in the food we eat. Others are washed from the soil into streams, or pass away as sewage.

Pollutants in the air

The atmosphere is made up of more than the gases found in pure air. It also contains other substances which have got there naturally, or through the activities of people. Where these are potentially harmful they are known as **pollutants**. The main pollutants of the air are the solid particles from smoke and dust, and the gases from vehicle exhausts and chimneys. Some of these are responsible for 'acid rain'. You can find more details in 6.13.

> **Q3** The dangers of air pollution are now well recognised. Prepare a short talk for the rest of your class on one of the following: the Alkali Acts of the 19th Century; smoke-controlled zones; smokeless fuels; electrostatic precipitators on chimneys; the 'lean burn' car engine.

Fig. 5 *Mexico City suffers from air pollution problems. The lower picture was taken on a bad day.*

Fig. 1 All these drinks contain carbon dioxide.

Fig. 2 This fire extinguisher contains carbon dioxide under pressure.

Fig. 3 Dry ice in water: how to make a 'mist effect'.

3.5

Carbon dioxide

Carbon dioxide is found in small but very important amounts in the air. One litre of air contains about $3\,cm^3$ of carbon dioxide. This is 300 parts per million (ppm). This figure has been reasonably constant for many thousands of years, because there has been a balance between the carbon dioxide added to the atmosphere by burning and breathing, and that taken out by plants during photosynthesis.

> **Q1** There is evidence that the concentration of carbon dioxide in the atmosphere has risen from 0.300% (300 ppm) in 1958 to 0.345% (345 ppm) in 1985. What reasons can you suggest for this?

Uses of carbon dioxide

Carbon dioxide is a by-product of several industrial processes. For example, it is formed when limestone is heated to produce lime, and also when hydrogen is made from natural gas. This is how carbon dioxide is used:

☐ In fire extinguishers, which use the gas to smother the flames.
(It is a dense, non-flammable gas.)
☐ In fizzy drinks, to give a sharp tingling taste.
(It dissolves in water, especially under pressure.)
☐ In stage and television shows to produce mist effects.
(It freezes at $-78°C$, forming a solid called 'dry ice'. Putting lumps of dry ice into warm water causes cold, wet carbon dioxide gas to be released, carrying with it clouds of condensed water vapour.)
☐ In cold boxes, where dry ice may be used as a refrigerant.

The chemical behaviour of carbon dioxide

Carbon dioxide dissolves in water to form a weak acid, called carbonic acid. This process can be reversed, and when the solution is warmed (or the cap is taken off a bottle of fizzy drink) the carbon dioxide is released. Carbonic acid breaks down completely when it is heated.

$$\text{carbon dioxide} + \text{water} \rightleftharpoons \text{carbonic acid}$$
$$CO_2(g) + H_2O(l) \rightleftharpoons H_2CO_3(aq)$$

> **Q2** What would you expect to see if you added a few drops of universal indicator to some distilled water, and then
> (a) bubbled carbon dioxide through it,
> (b) gently warmed the solution until it was boiling?

Carbon dioxide does not burn, and other substances will not normally burn in it. However, if the burning substance is already at a high temperature, the carbon dioxide molecule may be split – supplying oxygen for the burning to continue. For example, a piece of burning magnesium does not stop burning in carbon dioxide:

$$\text{magnesium} + \text{carbon dioxide} \rightarrow \text{magnesium oxide} + \text{carbon}$$
$$2Mg(s) + CO_2(g) \rightarrow 2MgO(s) + C(s)$$

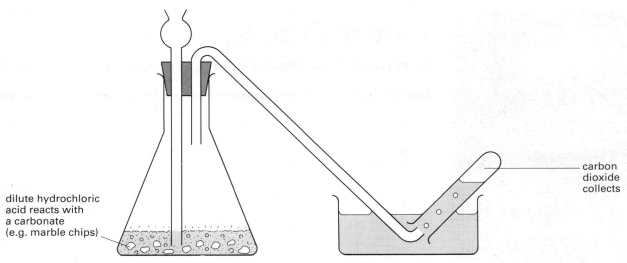

Fig. 4 *Carbon dioxide can be made in the lab by reacting a carbonate with an acid.*

dilute hydrochloric acid reacts with a carbonate (e.g. marble chips)

carbon dioxide collects

Making carbon dioxide in the laboratory

Carbon dioxide is made in the laboratory by the reaction between a carbonate and an acid, for example:

$$\text{calcium carbonate} + \text{hydrochloric acid} \rightarrow \text{calcium chloride} + \text{water} + \text{carbon dioxide}$$

$$CaCO_3(s) + 2HCl(aq) \rightarrow CaCl_2(aq) + H_2O(l) + CO_2(g)$$

This reaction between hydrochloric acid and carbonates is used by geologists. If a rock fizzes when tested with dilute hydrochloric acid, it is sure to contain a carbonate mineral (see 6.10).

The lime water test for carbon dioxide

Because carbon dioxide is acidic it will react with bases and alkalis to form salts. The best known reaction of this kind is the **lime water test** for carbon dioxide:

$$\text{carbon dioxide} + \text{lime water} \rightarrow \text{cloudy lime water}$$

$$CO_2(g) + Ca(OH)_2(aq) \rightarrow CaCO_3(s) + H_2O(l)$$

Lime water is calcium hydroxide solution, and cloudy lime water is a suspension of calcium carbonate, $CaCO_3$, in water. If more carbon dioxide is allowed to react with cloudy lime water, the solution goes clear again, because a soluble substance is formed:

$$\text{carbon dioxide} + \text{cloudy lime water} \rightleftharpoons \text{solution of calcium hydrogencarbonate}$$

$$CO_2(g) + CaCO_3(s) + H_2O(l) \rightleftharpoons Ca(HCO_3)_2(aq)$$

Q3 This reaction is reversible. Describe what you would see if the clear solution of calcium hydrogencarbonate was heated.

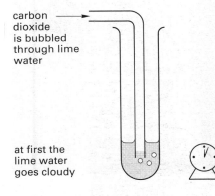

carbon dioxide is bubbled through lime water

at first the lime water goes cloudy

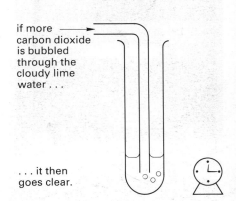

if more carbon dioxide is bubbled through the cloudy lime water . . .

. . . it then goes clear.

Fig. 5 *Two stages in the lime water test for carbon dioxide.*

Sodium carbonate and sodium hydrogencarbonate

Fig. 1 Washing soda crystals are hydrated sodium carbonate. They contain water of crystallisation.

Fig. 2 Soda ash is anhydrous sodium carbonate. Anhydrous salts do not contain water.

Fig. 3 Carbon dioxide is released when these tablets are put into water.

Carbonic acid, H_2CO_3, is a **dibasic** acid. This means that it contains two replaceable hydrogen atoms, and so it can form *two* kinds of salt:

☐ **Normal salts**, which are carbonates, for example sodium carbonate, Na_2CO_3 (where both hydrogens have been replaced by a metal ion)

☐ **Acid salts**, which are hydrogencarbonates, for example sodium hydrogencarbonate, $NaHCO_3$ (where just one hydrogen has been replaced by a metal ion).

These salts are formed when carbon dioxide reacts with a solution of sodium hydroxide:

carbon dioxide + sodium hydroxide → sodium carbonate + water

$$CO_2(g) + 2NaOH(aq) \rightarrow Na_2CO_3(aq) + H_2O(l)$$

followed by:

sodium carbonate + carbon dioxide + water → sodium hydrogencarbonate

$$Na_2CO_3(aq) + CO_2(g) + H_2O(l) \rightarrow 2NaHCO_3(s)$$

Because it is not very soluble in water the sodium hydrogencarbonate may be produced as a solid in this reaction.

Washing soda and baking soda

Sodium carbonate crystals, $Na_2CO_3.10H_2O$, are best known to the public as **washing soda**. They are sold for cleaning floors and drains. Washing soda is also added to some washing powders to 'soften' the water. Washing soda crystals contain water as well as sodium carbonate. This is why the chemical formula includes $10H_2O$. The water in the crystals is called water of crystallisation. Salts which contain water of crytallisation are called hydrated salts or **hydrates**. Anhydrous sodium carbonate, Na_2CO_3, does not contain water. It is used in large quantities to make glass, alkalis and detergents.

Sodium hydrogencarbonate, $NaHCO_3$, is known as **baking soda**, or 'bicarbonate of soda'. It is widely used in cooking. For example, it is this substance which turns 'plain flour' into 'self-raising flour'. The substance sold as baking powder is a mixture of 'baking soda' with a solid acid. When heated, the two react together:

baking soda + acid → a salt + water + carbon dioxide

The carbon dioxide produced in this way is the 'raising agent', which gives the cake a nice spongy texture. Effervescent tablets, such as 'Alka-Seltzer', work in a similar way. They, too, contain a mixture of sodium hydrogencarbonate with an acid. The reaction which produces carbon dioxide takes place when the tablet is put into water.

Q1 Make a chart showing the uses of sodium hydrogencarbonate and sodium carbonate. Where possible, include labels from actual products containing these substances.

Fig. 4 *Self-raising flour, or baking powder is needed to make these crumpets rise. Carbon dioxide released during cooking also makes the holes.*

Heating sodium hydrogencarbonate

Sodium hydrogencarbonate breaks down when it is heated, releasing carbon dioxide:

sodium hydrogencarbonate $\rightarrow$ sodium carbonate + water + carbon dioxide

$$2NaHCO_3(s) \rightarrow Na_2CO_3(s) + H_2O(g) + CO_2(g)$$

Q2 Further heating produces no more reaction, because sodium carbonate is *not* affected by heat. Suggest a reason for this.

The effect of acids

Both sodium carbonate and sodium hydrogencarbonate react with acids. The sodium salt of the acid is formed, together with carbon dioxide:

$$Na_2CO_3(s) + 2HCl(aq) \rightarrow 2NaCl(aq) + H_2O(l) + CO_2(g)$$

$$NaHCO_3(s) + HCl(aq) \rightarrow NaCl(aq) + H_2O(l) + CO_2(g)$$

Unlike most other carbonates, sodium carbonate is soluble in water. A solution of sodium carbonate will precipitate other carbonates from solution. The precipitation reaction for calcium carbonate is:

$$Ca^{2+}(aq) + CO_3^{2-}(aq) \rightarrow CaCO_3(s)$$

Q3 Other insoluble carbonates which can be made in this way include zinc carbonate, iron carbonate, copper carbonate and lead carbonate. Write word equations and formula equations for these reactions.

Q4 Figure 5 shows one method for testing a rock sample to see whether or not it is a carbonate. Describe how you would carry out this test on malachite (Fig. 6), and say what you would expect to see.

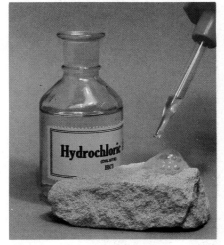

Fig. 5 *This piece of Cotswold limestone is calcium carbonate. It reacts with hydrochloric acid and gives off carbon dioxide.*

Fig. 6 *Malachite, a beautiful mineral form of copper carbonate.*

Hydrogen

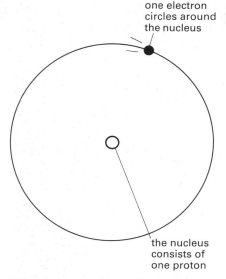

one electron circles around the nucleus

the nucleus consists of one proton

Fig. 1 The hydrogen atom is the simplest atom of all.

Hydrogen is the simplest element of all. Its atom contains just one proton and one electron. Hydrogen gas has a lower density than any other substance.

How can hydrogen be produced?

☐ Hydrogen is produced when reactive metals dissolve in water. Potassium, sodium, lithium and calcium will all react with cold water, releasing hydrogen, for example:

$$\text{sodium} + \text{water} \rightarrow \text{sodium hydroxide} + \text{hydrogen}$$

$$2Na(s) + 2H_2O(l) \rightarrow 2NaOH(aq) + H_2(g)$$

☐ Less reactive metals, such as magnesium, zinc and iron, react with steam in a similar way, for example:

$$\text{zinc} + \text{steam} \rightarrow \text{zinc oxide} + \text{hydrogen}$$

$$Zn(s) + H_2O(g) \rightarrow ZnO(s) + H_2(g)$$

☐ A dilute solution of an electrolyte in water will almost always give hydrogen at the cathode during electrolysis.

Recognising hydrogen

A mixture of hydrogen and air burns with a 'squeaky pop' when you apply a light to the end of the test tube. This reaction is often used as a **test for hydrogen**.

How is hydrogen manufactured?

Hydrogen is manufactured from hydrocarbons, such as natural gas or oil. This is not a simple process, but it can be summed up as:

$$\text{hydrocarbon} + \text{steam} \xrightarrow[\text{catalyst}]{\text{heat}} \text{carbon dioxide} + \text{hydrogen}$$

This process is used on a very large scale. The hydrogen is often combined with nitrogen to make ammonia for the fertiliser industry. This is also how carbon dioxide is made in large quantities.

Q1 Suggest why the other reactions mentioned on this page may not be suitable for manufacturing hydrogen on a large scale.

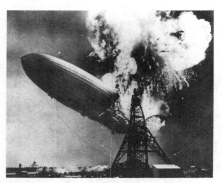

Fig. 2 The Hindenburg disaster, 1937. Hydrogen begins to burn at the tail end.

Fig. 3 As the tail falls to the ground, hydrogen burns like a flare from the top.

How has hydrogen been made and used?

Hydrogen is present in all acids. Metals which are not too low in the Reactivity Series will dissolve in acids, releasing hydrogen. For example:

$$\text{zinc} + \text{hydrochloric acid} \rightarrow \text{zinc chloride} + \text{hydrogen}$$

$$Zn(s) + 2HCl(aq) \rightarrow ZnCl_2(aq) + H_2(g)$$

This reaction is generally used for making hydrogen in the laboratory.

Fig. 4 J. A. C. Charles coming back down to earth after the first manned ascent in a hydrogen-filled balloon on 1st December 1783.

The similar reaction:

$$\text{iron} + \text{sulphuric acid} \rightarrow \text{iron sulphate} + \text{hydrogen}$$

was used to make the gas for the first hydrogen balloon. More than 2 tonnes of acid and more than 4 tonnes of iron were used to fill an enormous hydrogen balloon which took off from Paris in 1783. It travelled about 15 miles before falling back to earth in a village where the locals attacked it with scythes and pitchforks, believing that it was an unwelcome visitor from space! Later in the same year a duck, a cockerel and a sheep made the first experimental passenger-carrying flight. This was soon followed by the first manned flight.

Because of its low density, hydrogen was widely used in the early part of the present century for filling airships. It fell out of use for the reason which will be obvious from Figs 2 and 3. The 'Hindenburg' caught fire as it came in to land after crossing the Atlantic. Amazingly, 62 of the 97 people on board survived this disaster.

Fig. 5 Vincenzo Lunardi's balloon (1784) was the first in England to use hydrogen for a manned flight. Iron nails and sulphuric acid were used in this apparatus to make the hydrogen for Lunardi's balloon.

> **Q2** Write a letter to an absent friend, explaining how you could make and test a few tubes of hydrogen. The apparatus shown in 3.5, Fig. 4 could be adapted for the purpose.

81

The chemical behaviour of hydrogen

Hydrogen burns in air, producing water:

$$\text{hydrogen} + \text{oxygen} \quad \rightarrow \quad \text{steam}$$

$$2H_2(g) + O_2(g) \quad \rightarrow \quad 2H_2O(g)$$

This reaction can be a quiet flame, a gentle 'squeaky pop', or a devastating explosion and fire. It all depends on how it happens. A jet of hydrogen gas from a cylinder will burn quietly in air. The flame is almost invisible – it is blue, tinged with yellow by the water particles which are formed.

A mixture of hydrogen and air (or oxygen) will explode if the two gases are there in the right proportions. A 2:1 mixture of hydrogen with oxygen fits the balance of the chemical equation, but it is not necessary for these exact quantities to be present for an explosion to occur. Hydrogen's very low density causes it to diffuse very quickly, so even a small leak can cause a very rapid escape of gas. For this reason it is *very important to treat hydrogen with great respect*.

Fig. 1 The blue flame of hydrogen burning quietly.

Fig. 2 Hydrogen cylinders are normally painted red as a safety warning.

Q1 Design a safety poster which could be displayed in your laboratory whenever hydrogen is being used.

Q2 The burning of hydrogen releases great amounts of energy. This, together with its low density, makes it very suitable as a rocket fuel. Liquid hydrogen is used. Write an equation for this process, remembering to include the correct state symbols.

Hydrogen as a reducing agent

A **reducing agent** is a substance that will remove oxygen from a compound such as an oxide. (There is more about this in 4.5.) Hydrogen is a powerful reducing agent. It will remove oxygen from most metal oxides on heating (Fig. 4). For example:

$$\text{copper oxide} + \text{hydrogen} \quad \rightarrow \quad \text{copper} + \text{steam}$$

$$CuO(s) + H_2(g) \quad \rightarrow \quad Cu(s) + H_2O(g)$$

Q3 A textbook says that 'the ease with which hydrogen is able to reduce a metal oxide depends on the position of the metal in the Reactivity Series.' Explain what is meant by this statement. You can find more information in 4.3 and 4.4.

Hydrogen will reduce natural oils to fats, which are more solid substances. It is used in this way to make margarine from vegetable oils.

Fuel cells

When a fuel burns, the energy is given out as *heat* during the chemical reaction. This is not always the form of energy you want. If only you could take it out as *electrical* energy, the process would be twice as efficient. In theory, many reactions are capable of giving out electrical energy, but to harness it in practice is usually difficult.

Fig. 3 The energy used to power this rocket comes from the reaction between hydrogen and oxygen. These are carried as liquids in the fuel tanks.

In a power station you have to burn the fuel, and then generate electrical energy from the heat. Imagine the benefits of getting electricity directly from coal and air! This has been done, but only on a small scale, and the process is slow. A device in which a fuel reacts with the oxygen of the air, to produce electrical energy directly, is known as a **fuel cell**.

Fuel cells using hydrogen as the fuel have been used in manned spacecraft. Oxygen is required, and the product of the fuel cell reaction is water:

$$2H_2(g) + O_2(g) \rightarrow 2H_2O(l)$$

Large fuel cells producing enough electricity as a source of power require large amounts of fuel. However, there are some quite tiny cells which have unexpected uses. One is used in the latest type of breathalyser: alcohol and air in the drinker's breath react on the catalyst inside the cell to produce a voltage. Another is being used to predict earthquakes, because it has been found that a few days before an earthquake, small puffs of hydrogen begin to issue from the ground. Small fuel cells left in the area will show a voltage when the hydrogen begins to emerge.

Q4 Give three reasons why this reaction might be a good choice for use on spacecraft.

Q5 Figure 5 shows how a fuel cell works. Design a simple piece of apparatus which you could build in the laboratory for testing out the idea of a fuel cell. What precautions should be taken while the fuel cell is in use?

Q6 Collect information for either a wall chart or a short talk on the subject of 'Fuel Cells'.

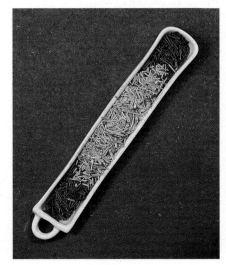

Fig. 4 Most metal oxides can be reduced to the metal using hydrogen. Here some copper oxide (black) has been reduced to copper (pink).

Carbon

The element carbon is found in many forms which are very familiar. Soot, pencil 'lead', diamonds and charcoal are just a few. So it is surprising to find that there are just two ways in which carbon atoms can link together to form larger structures. These structures, sometimes called 'giant molecules', are known to us as **graphite** and **diamond**.

Comparing graphite with diamond

	Graphite	Diamond
Structure of giant molecule	atoms linked in sheets (Fig. 1)	atoms linked in tetrahedral structure (Fig. 2)
Density (g/cm^3)	2.25	3.5
Hardness	very soft	extremely hard
Conducts electricity	yes	no
Uses	nuclear reactors crucibles electrodes pencil leads	gemstones cutting tools wire-drawing tools grinding tools

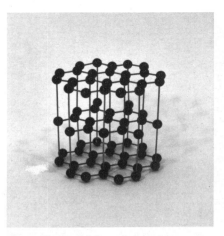

Fig. 1 This model shows how carbon atoms in graphite are arranged in sheets. The links between 'atoms' represent bonds.

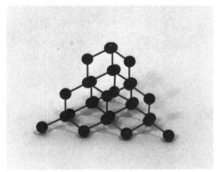

Fig. 2 Carbon atoms in diamond are arranged in tetrahedral structure – each atom is bonded to four others.

Fig. 3 Diamond is much tougher than glass. Here diamond coated wheels are being used to grind spectacle lenses.

Q1 In which substance, graphite or diamond, would you expect to find the atoms more closely packed? Explain your answer.

Q2 Both graphite and diamond have very high melting points. Explain which substance you would expect to have the higher melting point.

Q3 Explain why graphite conducts electricity and diamond does not.

Q4 Find out more about some of the uses of diamond and graphite and write a few lines about each.

Allotropes

A few elements have atoms which are able to link together in more than one way when they become a solid. These solid forms of an element which have different structures are called **allotropes**. Graphite and diamond are the two allotropes of carbon. Sulphur is another element which forms allotropes.

Why are diamond and graphite so different?

Both diamond and graphite are pure carbon. They are formed entirely from carbon atoms. All the differences between them are due to the different ways in which these carbon atoms are linked together.

In graphite the carbon atoms are covalently bonded in sheets, as you can see in Fig. 1. The sheets themselves are strongly held together. The link between one sheet and the next is weak, however, and contains electrons which can move between the sheets. The sheets can slide over one another quite easily, and this is why graphite is so soft and slippery.

In diamond (Fig. 2) the carbon atoms are covalently bonded together in what is called a 'tetrahedral' structure. This means that the four bonds from each carbon atom point towards the corners of a tetrahedron. You can only break a diamond by breaking some covalent bonds, and these are very strong. Diamond is therefore very hard.

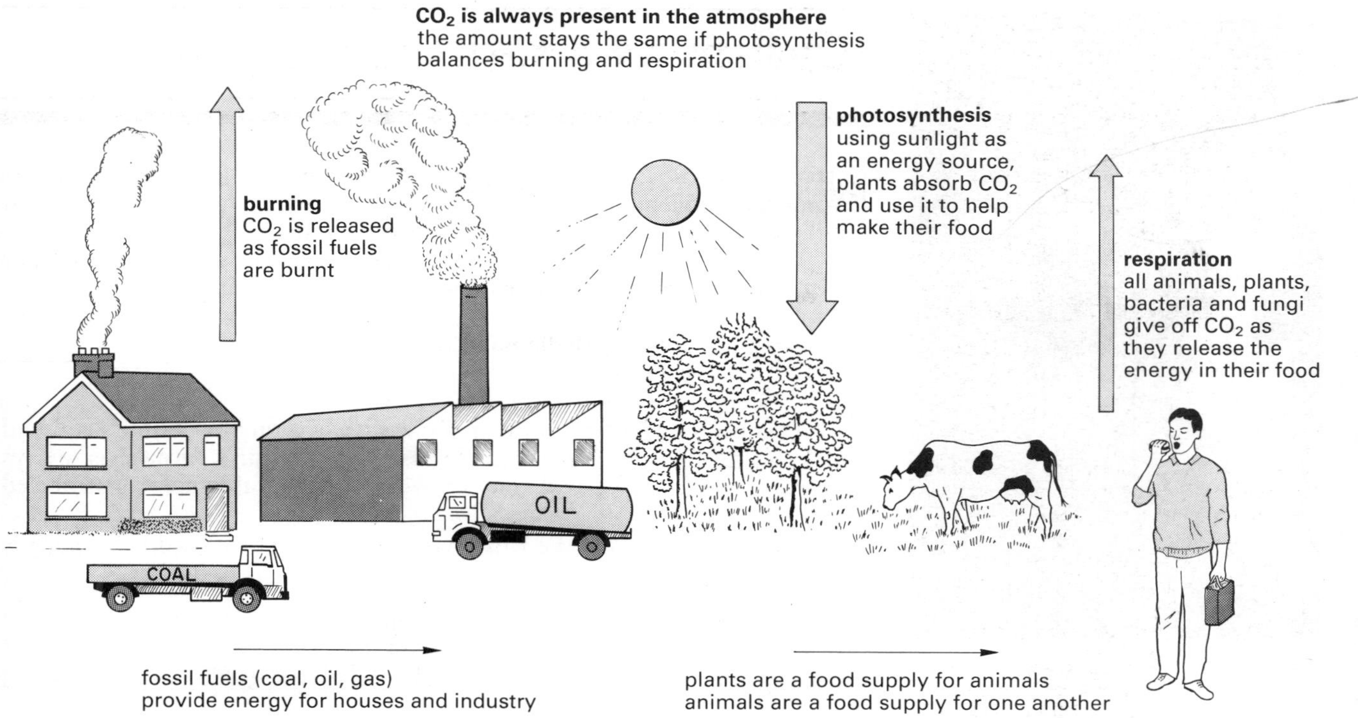

CO2 is always present in the atmosphere
the amount stays the same if photosynthesis
balances burning and respiration

burning
CO_2 is released
as fossil fuels
are burnt

photosynthesis
using sunlight as
an energy source,
plants absorb CO_2
and use it to help
make their food

respiration
all animals, plants,
bacteria and fungi
give off CO_2 as
they release the
energy in their food

OIL

COAL

fossil fuels (coal, oil, gas)
provide energy for houses and industry

plants are a food supply for animals
animals are a food supply for one another

Fig. 4 The carbon cycle.

Carbon in the natural world

Carbon is an essential element in substances like carbohydrates, proteins
and fats, which make up living things. It is also vital to the processes of
respiration and photosynthesis. This carbon is constantly being 're-cycled'
between living things and their surroundings, in a series of processes called
the **carbon cycle**.

Carbon dioxide is the key substance in the carbon cycle (Fig. 4). It gets
into the atmosphere when fossil fuels are burned, and as a result of
respiration. It leaves the atmosphere because of photosynthesis, and by
dissolving into sea water.

The chemical behaviour of carbon

When pure carbon burns in a good supply of oxygen, it forms carbon
dioxide:

$$\text{carbon} + \text{oxygen} \quad \rightarrow \quad \text{carbon dioxide}$$

$$C(s) + O_2(g) \quad \rightarrow \quad CO_2(g)$$

In practice, however, carbon is usually burned in heaps with air flowing
through it – in coke fires or furnaces, for example. Here the process is a
little different (Fig. 5). The first coke does indeed burn to carbon dioxide,
but this carbon dioxide meets some more hot coke, and is reduced to
carbon monoxide:

$$CO_2(g) + C(s) \quad \rightarrow \quad 2CO(g)$$

Carbon monoxide itself burns with a clear blue flame, forming more carbon
dioxide:

$$2CO(g) + O_2(g) \quad \rightarrow \quad 2CO_2(g)$$

*Fig. 5 The blue flames at the top of a coke fire
are carbon monoxide burning. The carbon
dioxide formed in this process goes up the
chimney.*

85

Carbon as a reducing agent

Carbon is a reducing agent. It will remove oxygen from metal oxides, leaving behind the metal. For example:

$$\text{zinc oxide} + \text{carbon} \xrightarrow{\text{heat}} \text{carbon monoxide} + \text{zinc}$$

$$ZnO(s) + C(s) \xrightarrow{\text{heat}} CO(g) + Zn(g)$$

This reaction is important in the manufacture of a number of metals. Lead and iron are made by similar processes. The heat of a furnace is always necessary, and in the case of zinc you will notice that the metal is produced as a gas!

The lower the metal in the Reactivity Series, the more readily its oxide is reduced.

Q1 Describe and explain all you would expect to see when some black copper oxide is mixed with powdered carbon and heated.

Powdered carbon is one of the components of gunpowder. It is mixed with an oxidising agent, and other substances, to give a mixture which will react very rapidly and produce a large volume of gases in a short time. The rapid expansion of the hot gases gives force to the explosion.

Some other forms of carbon

Carbon in the form of charcoal has been used as a fuel for centuries. It is made by heating wood in a restricted supply of air. The traditional method of 'charcoal burning' (Fig. 2) is an ancient forest craft which supplied the iron-making and gunpowder industries with charcoal until the present century. Charcoal is still an important fuel in some parts of the world, and the transportable kiln shown in Fig. 3 is a modern adaptation of a traditional method. In Britain, the growing popularity of barbecues has led to modern methods of charcoal production, using electrically heated kilns.

The spongy or powdery forms of carbon can 'soak up' other substances. Carbon will remove the colouring matter from a solution of brown sugar, so it is used in sugar-refining. Specially absorbent forms of carbon will also take in gases. They have been used in gas masks and in filter hoods for cookers.

Q2 The beach scene in Fig. 4 includes a variety of natural and man-made things which contain carbon. Find as many of these things as you can and write down the part carbon plays in each one.

Q3 Choose *one* of the uses of carbon you have found and find out more about it. Write an illustrated account, suitable for display in your laboratory.

Carbon monoxide

Carbon monoxide, CO, is a poisonous gas. It is produced whenever carbon-containing compounds burn in a limited supply of air. This is why carbon monoxide is found in motor exhaust fumes.

Fig. 1 Carbon is used in this furnace to reduce a mixture of lead and zinc ores. In this way zinc and lead are obtained from a single process

Fig. 2 Charcoal-burning: these logs are covered with turf, then lit. they burn slowly and turn into charcoal.

Fig. 3 This kiln for making charcoal is easily taken down and moved from place to place in the forest.

Fig. 4 *Carbon is present in living and man-made things.*

Carbon monoxide poisoning

Carbon monoxide is colourless and has no smell. Its action on the body is simple, but devastating. It prevents the blood from carrying the oxygen you need to where it is required. Oxygen normally diffuses from the lungs into the blood, where it becomes attached to molecules of haemoglobin:

$$\text{oxygen} + \text{haemoglobin} \rightleftharpoons \text{oxy-haemoglobin}$$

This process is reversible, and the oxygen is released when it is needed as a fuel for the 'slow-burning' process known as 'respiration'. Unfortunately, carbon monoxide is also able to attach itself to haemoglobin:

$$\text{carbon monoxide} + \text{haemoglobin} \rightarrow \text{carboxy-haemoglobin}$$

This process is much less easily reversed, so the carbon monoxide tends to stick to the haemoglobin. This means that the body's method of transporting oxygen is blocked. The chemistry of life soon comes to a halt! If only 10% of your haemoglobin is converted to carboxy-haemoglobin, you will have a nasty headache. More than this can be fatal. Just 0.1% of carbon monoxide in the air is almost certain to cause dangerous poisoning.

Fig. 5 *Exhaust fumes contain carbon monoxide. Many cars release 10 g of this gas for every mile they cover.*

Carbon monoxide is a reducing agent

It is formed in a blast furnace during the smelting of iron ore. The reduction of the iron oxide ore to molten iron is brought about by this carbon monoxide:

$$\text{iron ore (iron oxide)} + \text{carbon monoxide} \rightarrow \text{iron} + \text{carbon dioxide}$$

$$Fe_2O_3(s) + 3CO(g) \rightarrow 2Fe(l) + 3CO_2(g)$$

Fig. 6 *Barbecues are for use **out of doors!** (Why?)*

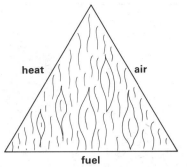

Fig. 1 This fire triangle shows the three things needed to keep a fire burning.

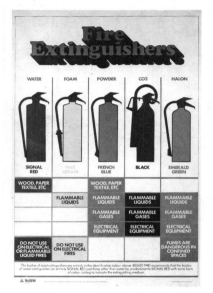

Fig. 2 Different types of fires require different fire extinguishers.

Fig. 3 Vehicles carrying this sign have flammable liquids on board.

Fire!

Fire has fascinated people from the earliest times. Yet only in the last 200 years have we begun to understand it as a chemical process. Burning is a rapid chemical reaction. Something burnable, a **fuel**, reacts with oxygen from the **air**, giving out **heat**.

The fire triangle

Firefighters learn that fuel, air and heat are needed for a fire to keep burning. Often these three are shown in a diagram known as the **fire triangle**.

When fighting a fire you have to decide which side of the fire triangle to 'attack'. Sometimes it is best to remove the fuel: often the only way to deal with a raging forest fire is to cut down a strip of trees ahead of the path of the fire. Smaller fires are often best put out by cutting off the supply of air, for example by covering a burning chip pan. Buildings on fire may need a lot of cooling before the fire will go out, so water from a powerful hose is used to remove heat – and also to soak things which might otherwise continue to burn.

Q1 Suggest how you would use the 'fire triangle' idea to tackle the following fires: person with burning coat; fire in waste bin; curtains on fire; cigarette fallen on sofa; car engine on fire.

Fire extinguishers

Water may be used for tackling both large and small fires, but *never* on oil or fat, or if there is danger from electricity. Water-filled fire extinguishers usually contain a small canister of pressurised carbon dioxide which forces the water out in a powerful jet, once the seal is broken. Sometimes a foaming material is added to the water, so that a layer of carbon dioxide **foam** rests on top of the fire as the extinguisher is used. Large foam extinguishers are used for aircraft fires.

Carbon dioxide is a dense gas which can be used to smother fires and keep out the air. It will not burn, or allow burning to continue. In fire extinguishers the carbon dioxide is kept under pressure in a metal cylinder, which is usually painted black.

Dry powder fire extinguishers contain solid sodium hydrogencarbonate, in the form of a fine powder. This too is expelled by carbon dioxide, and settles on the burning material, preventing air from reaching it.

Among the older fire extinguishers is the **soda-acid** type, which uses the reaction between sodium carbonate and an acid to generate carbon dioxide when the two are mixed.

Burning liquids

A liquid which catches fire easily is called a **flammable liquid**. Many flammable liquids are used as fuels. They must be handled very carefully because they all give off flammable vapour into the air. The temperature at which a mixture of the vapour and air will catch fire if it comes into contact with a small flame is known as the **flash point**. The flash point of most flammable liquids is well below normal room temperature.

At a higher temperature, no flame is needed to ignite a flammable vapour. It catches fire in air by itself, for example when a chip pan

Fig. 4 Water being used to remove heat from a fire.

Fig. 5 To tackle this fire turn off the heat, protect your hands, cover the flames and leave the pan to cool.

overheats and flames appear. This temperature is known as the **self-ignition temperature**. You should fry chips at about 190°C. The self-ignition temperature of most cooking oils is over 300°C. As cooking oil is repeatedly used its self-ignition temperature becomes lower, so be especially careful if the oil is not fresh.

Danger from fire

Nearly 1000 people die in the UK each year as a result of fire. Some of these fires occur at work, or after road accidents. Many happen at home or where leisure activities take place. At home the main dangers are matches, smoking (especially in bed!), faulty room heaters and unguarded fires. Some kinds of foam upholstery produce extremely poisonous smoke if they catch fire. All soft furniture should now be treated and should carry a ticket to show that it will not catch fire easily.

Q2 On average, someone in the UK dies every day in their own home because of fire. Use the information on this page – and anything else you can find out – to write a short booklet of advice, suitable for giving away to people living near you.

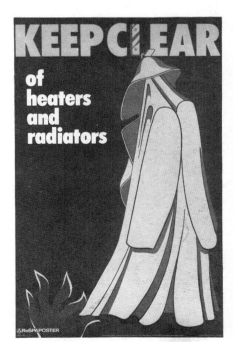
Fig. 6 This poster warns you to watch out for fire risks.

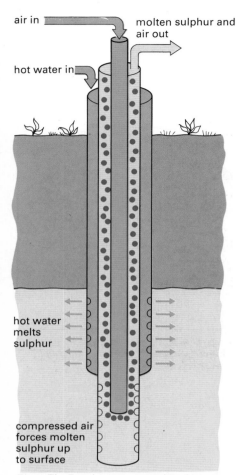

air in

molten sulphur and air out

hot water in

hot water melts sulphur

compressed air forces molten sulphur up to surface

Fig. 1 The Frasch process is used to obtain sulphr from underground deposits.

Fig. 2 Stocks of sulphur are often stored in these enormous solid blocks, known as 'vats'.

Sulphur

Using sulphur

The main use of sulphur is for making sulphuric acid. You can find out more about sulphuric acid in 7.6. This in turn is mostly converted into fertilisers, so although sulphur is used in huge quantities, many of its products are not immediately recognisable. Other uses for sulphur include:

☐ making sodium thiosulphate, a chemical used in photography

☐ making carbon disulphide, a solvent used in making rayon and plastic film

☐ 'vulcanising' rubber, a process in which natural rubber is made harder and tougher by heating it with sulphur.

☐ making sprays for killing insects and fungi on fruit trees.

☐ making calcium hydrogensulphite, a chemical used to bleach wood pulp for paper-making.

☐ making matches: safety match-heads contain sulphur, ordinary matches phosphorus sulphide.

Sources of sulphur

Sulphur is one of the few elements found 'native' in the earth's crust. The word 'native' means 'not combined with any other element'. There are also many naturally occurring compounds of sulphur.

Native sulphur is found in volcanic regions, past and present. Commercial quantities of sulphur are found today in the southern States of the USA, and in Mexico, Poland and the USSR.

Natural gas and **oil** contain sulphur compounds which must be removed before they can be used as fuels. Otherwise there would be damage to both the burners and to the environment. This sulphur, known as 'recovered sulphur', is now the single most important source of all: it accounted for 60% of world sulphur production in 1984.

Some important **metal ores**, notably those of zinc and lead, are sulphides. During the extraction of the metal the ore must be roasted in air, and sulphur is released as sulphur dioxide. This is nearly always converted directly to sulphuric acid.

Extracting sulphur by the Frasch process

Native sulphur is found as solid deposits, often about 200 metres below the ground. It is removed either by mining or by the Frasch process. Hermann Frasch was a German engineer who moved to work in the USA in the 1890s. Sulphur had been found beneath a layer of quicksand. Mining was impossible, so he developed a process which relies on the fact that sulphur has a fairly low melting point.

☐ Superheated water is first pumped down to the sulphur layer. This melts the sulphur.

☐ The molten sulphur is forced to the surface by compressed air.

The equipment for doing this consists of three pipes running inside one another (Fig. 1). The outer one carries the hot water, the inner one is used for the compressed air, and the sulphur comes up the one in between. Once the sulphur has been brought to the surface it may be allowed to solidify, or it may be kept hot enough to be stored and transported as a liquid. A store of solid sulphur, built up as a large block, is known as a 'vat' (Fig. 2).

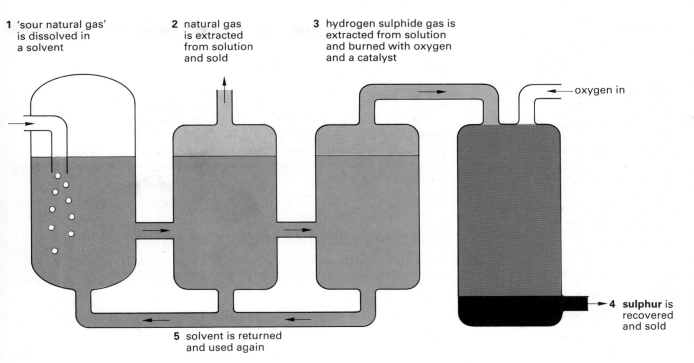

1 'sour natural gas' is dissolved in a solvent

2 natural gas is extracted from solution and sold

3 hydrogen sulphide gas is extracted from solution and burned with oxygen and a catalyst

oxygen in

4 **sulphur** is recovered and sold

5 solvent is returned and used again

Fig. 3 Recovering sulphur from 'sour natural gas'.

Recovering sulphur from fossil fuels

The sulphur in natural gas and crude oil is present in the form of hydrogen sulphide. It is 'recovered' by the method shown in Fig. 3.

☐ The hydrogen sulphide is first dissolved out of the natural gas with a suitable solvent.

☐ Then it is released from the solution.

☐ Finally, it is burned in a controlled way, using a catalyst and just the right amount of oxygen, to convert it to sulphur.

One of the first sources of recovered sulphur was the 'sour' natural gas, discovered at Lacq in southern France in 1951. The gas is described as sour because of the awful smell of hydrogen sulphide. Other 'sour natural gas' supplies, which have since been harnessed for the production of sulphur, include major deposits in Alberta (Canada) and Astrakhan (USSR). Sulphur production is now closely linked to the fortunes of the oil and gas industries.

Most of the natural gas found in the earth contains sulphur compounds. When the gas is burned these sulphur compounds also burn, and form sulphur dioxide, a dangerous gas which pollutes the air. This means that natural gas which is to be used as a fuel should have its sulphur removed, not only because sulphur is a valuable substance, but also because it is harmful to leave it in.

Q1 Make an illustrated chart showing how sulphur is used in agriculture and in industry.

1 one molecule of sulphur contains 8 atoms joined in a ring like this.

2 From the side the molecule looks like this.

3 In a crystal of sulphur the rings pack together like this.

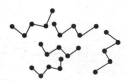

4 When sulphur is melted the rings are 'unpacked'.

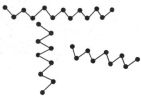

5 As the temperature is increased, the rings break open and link together

6 They reach their greatest length and tangle up with one another most at about 160°C

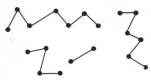

7 At higher temperature still, the tangled chains break up. At 444°C, when sulphur boils, a gas containing S_2 molecules is formed.

Fig. 1 Molecules of sulphur are greatly affected by changes in temperature.

What is sulphur like?

Sulphur is a brittle yellow solid, with almost no smell. It does not dissolve in water, and it is not harmful. Its properties are those of a typical non-metal.

> **Q1** Make a list of 'the properties of a typical non-metal'.

Sulphur does not conduct electricity when solid, molten or dissolved. It has low melting and boiling points. Sulphur crystals are made up of molecules with the formula S_8.

What happens when sulphur is heated?

Unlike most elements, sulphur does not have a sharp melting point. It begins to melt at about 112°C; melting is complete by about 118°C.

> **Q2** What does this tell you about the structure of solid sulphur?

Sulphur which has just melted is a runny, pale yellow liquid. As the temperature is raised, however, it soon begins to darken to a reddish-brown colour, and it becomes much less runny. At about 160°C it becomes suddenly very viscous, so sticky that it will not run out of an upturned test tube. Then, as the temperature is raised still further, it becomes less viscous again, but darker and darker in colour. At 444°C it boils.

All these changes are due to changes in the structure of the sulphur as it is heated. Solid sulphur consists of molecules which are eight-membered zig-zag rings, neatly stacked together (Fig. 2). Heating begins to destroy the stack, so that the molecules move about independently. Further heating causes the rings to open up, so that the molecules become chain-like, and can tangle together. At the temperature where the viscosity is very high, the short chains link together to form much longer chains which tangle together much more. At higher temperatures still, these chains begin to break, and the liquid becomes more runny. To sum up:

Changes which occur when sulphur is heated

Temperature (°C)	Appearance of sulphur	Explanation
below 112	yellow solid	molecules regularly packed
112–118	melting occurs	crystals 'un-packed'
118–160	viscosity increases	ring molecules opening up
160	maximum viscosity	molecules large, very tangled
160–444	viscosity falling	molecules breaking up

Sulphur on the move

Much of the sulphur today is kept in a molten state until it reaches its destination. This means that its temperature must be carefully controlled: too cool and it solidifies, too hot and it becomes viscous. The tanker in Fig. 2 has been built like a giant 'thermos flask' for carrying liquid sulphur to customers, such as sulphuric acid manufacturers, who can use it in this form.

Fig. 2 Poland exports about 4 million tonnes of sulphur every year. Much of it is melted underground, brought straight to the dockside while still a liquid, and loaded into tankers like this one.

The crystal forms of sulphur

Solid sulphur has two crystalline forms, or **allotropes**, which are named according to their shape: rhombic and monoclinic. Both consist entirely of sulphur. Both contain the same S_8 molecules. The difference is in the way these molecules are packed to form the crystal. This means that there are no differences in chemical behaviour between the two forms of solid sulphur, but there are slight differences in physical properties:

Comparing rhombic sulphur with monoclinic sulphur

Property	Rhombic sulphur	Monoclinic sulphur
crystal shape	rhombohedral	prismatic needles
M.P. (°C)	115	120
density (g/cm^3)	2.07	1.96
soluble in	carbon disulphide	xylene

Rhombic sulphur crystals can be made by dissolving sulphur in carbon disulphide, and allowing the solution to evaporate in a fume cupboard. (**Care:** This is a dangerously flammable and poisonous solvent!)

Monoclinic sulphur crystals are easily made by pouring some molten sulphur into a folded filter paper. As soon as a skin forms on the surface of the liquid, crystals may be found beneath. They are stable above 95 °C, but slowly turn to powdery rhombic crystals when cool.

Fig. 3 Sulphur for laboratory use is sold as a powder, or in the form of these pale yellow sticks.

Sulphur dioxide and sulphur trioxide

Fig. 1 Sulphur dioxide is a gas which becomes a liquid under pressure at room temperature.

When sulphur is burned in air it forms a colourless gas with a strong sharp smell. This is **sulphur dioxide**:

$$S(l) + O_2(g) \rightarrow SO_2(g)$$

There is also another oxide of sulphur, called **sulphur trioxide**. This is a white solid at room temperature. Both sulphur dioxide, SO_2, and sulphur trioxide, SO_3, are harmful acidic substances.

Sulphur dioxide is produced when almost any substance containing sulphur is burned in air. Sadly, most of the substances we burn *do* contain sulphur! The fossil fuels – coal, oil and natural gas – all contain sulphur. Some of this can be removed for use as 'recovered sulphur'. The method is described in 3.12. The sulphur in coal, however, cannot easily be taken out before it is burned. Unless fitted with special equipment, coal-fired power stations release large amounts of sulphur dioxide into the atmosphere. Some of this later returns in 'acid rain'. More details are given in 6.13.

Fig. 2 Sulphur dioxide is a serious pollutant. Building taller chimneys helps carry it away, but where does it go?

Uses of sulphur dioxide

It is important to realise that, despite its bad reputation, sulphur dioxide has beneficial uses:

☐ Most importantly, it is made into **sulphuric acid**, which is used in many parts of the chemical industry.

☐ Sulphur dioxide is a widely used food **preservative**, which you will find in many fruit and drink products. It works in several ways – by killing bacteria, by lowering the pH, and by preventing oxidation. In some foodstuffs, such as flour, its bleaching action 'improves' the appearance. A litre bottle of cider may contain 0.2 g of sulphur dioxide.

☐ Sulphur dioxide is also used in paper manufacture. It is made into substances which **bleach** wood pulp.

> **Q1** Look for some food labels with the additive number E220. This is sulphur dioxide. Make a list of products containing E220 (see *Datapage M*), and arrange them in groups to show which kinds of foodstuff contain this preservative.
>
> **Q2** Make an illustrated chart showing 'the two faces of sulphur dioxide' – good and bad.

Fig. 3 Sulphur dioxide (substance E220) is used as a preservative in some foods and drinks.

The chemical behaviour of sulphur dioxide

Sulphur dioxide is a gas at room temperature, but may be condensed to a liquid by increasing the pressure. You may have seen yellow canisters of sulphur dioxide for laboratory use (Fig. 1). These contain compressed liquid sulphur dioxide. It is an irritant poison, and is especially bad for people suffering from wheeziness or asthma.

As a typical non-metal oxide, sulphur dioxide dissolves in water and reacts with it to form an acid solution:

$$SO_2(g) + H_2O(l) \rightarrow H_2SO_3(aq)$$

This acid is commonly called 'sulphurous acid', but its more correct name is 'sulphuric(IV) acid'.

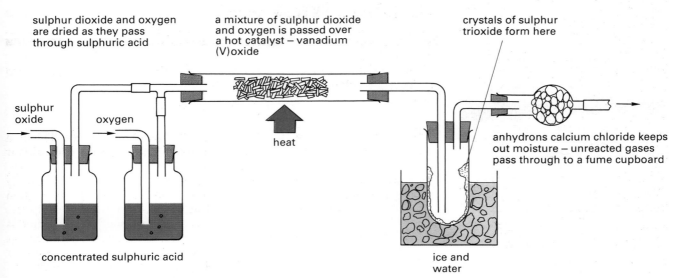

sulphur dioxide and oxygen are dried as they pass through sulphuric acid

a mixture of sulphur dioxide and oxygen is passed over a hot catalyst – vanadium (V)oxide

crystals of sulphur trioxide form here

sulphur oxide

oxygen

heat

anhydrons calcium chloride keeps out moisture – unreacted gases pass through to a fume cupboard

concentrated sulphuric acid

ice and water

Fig. 4 *Sulphur trioxide crystals can be made in the lab like this. This is the essential step in the Contact process, used on an industrial scale to make sulphuric acid.*

Sulphur dioxide gas and its solution in water are reducing agents. They have a bleaching action on many dyestuffs and natural colourings.

Q3 Describe two effects which you would expect sulphur dioxide to have on moistened indicator paper.

Sulphur dioxide is easily oxidised by acidified solutions of potassium manganate(VII) and potassium dichromate(VI). These reactions are used as **tests for sulphur dioxide**. When sulphur dioxide is bubbled in:

□ potassium manganate(VII) solution loses its purple colour and goes colourless; and

□ potassium dichromate(VI) solution goes from orange to green.

Here, too, sulphur dioxide is acting as a reducing agent.

Sulphur trioxide

Sulphur trioxide, SO_3, is a white crystalline substance (Fig. 5), made by reacting sulphur dioxide with oxygen:

$$2SO_2(g) + O_2(g) \rightarrow 2SO_3(s)$$

In industry this reaction is the basis of the Contact process for making sulphuric acid. This is described in 7.6. Figure 4 shows a method for making sulphur trioxide in the laboratory.

Did you know?

When was the first book about air pollution in London published?

1661. It was by John Evelyn, and called "Fumifugium; or the inconveniences of the aer and smoak of London dissipated".

Fig. 5 *Sulphur trioxide is a white crystalline solid which looks like this.*

The halogens

Group		
VI	**VII**	**0**
O 8	F 9	Ne 10
S 16	Cl 17	Ar 18
Se 34	Br 35	Kr 36
Te 52	I 53	Xe 54
Po 84	At 85	Rn 86

The halogens

Fig. 1 The halogens are in Group VII of the Periodic Table.

Fig. 2 Bromine is obtained from sea water. This pipe brings sea water to a bromine factory in Anglesey.

The elements in Group VII of the Periodic Table (Fig. 1) are called the **halogens**. The name comes from Greek words meaning 'salt formers'. Common salt contains the best known halogen – chlorine.

Similarities among the halogens

☐ The halogens all have strong smells. Bromine even takes its name from a Greek word meaning 'stink'! In fact, it is dangerous to breathe any of the halogens, because they cause severe damage to the nose and lungs. Chlorine was used as a war gas, and bromine is extremely irritating to the eyes. There is more about chlorine in 7.8.

☐ All the halogens **dissolve in water**:

$$\text{halogen} + \text{water} \longleftrightarrow \text{halide ion} + \text{'hypohalite' ion}$$

$$X_2(g) + H_2O(l) \longleftrightarrow X^-(aq) + OX^-(aq)$$

In other words, a laboratory solution called 'bromine water' contains bromine and water, and *also* the two ions Br^- and OBr^-.

☐ The halogens all react readily with a number of other elements to form **'halides'**, for example:

$$\text{chlorine} + \text{iron} \rightarrow \text{iron(III) chloride}$$

$$3Cl_2(g) + 2Fe(s) \rightarrow 2FeCl_3(s)$$

Exactly similar reactions take place with other metals (for example aluminium, zinc, copper, tin, sodium, magnesium) and with some non-metals (for example sulphur, phosphorus, silicon).

☐ The halogens are all **oxidising agents**. Fluorine is the most strongly oxidising element of all. Chlorine is used to oxidise the bromide ions in sea water, to manufacture bromine. The sea does not contain a very high concentration of bromide ions, so huge quantities of sea water are needed (Fig. 2). The process may be summarised as:

$$Cl_2(g) + 2NaBr(aq) \rightarrow 2NaCl(aq) + Br_2(l)$$

☐ When a halogen atom becomes a halide ion it gains an electron. In other words it oxidises something. The oxidising reaction may be represented:

$$\text{halogen} + \text{electrons} \longleftrightarrow \text{halide ions}$$

$$X_2 + 2e \longleftrightarrow 2X^-$$

Q1 Look at the information in the table on page 97 and write down as many 'similarities' between the halogens as you can.

Q2 The two *ions* present in 'bromine water' are both colourless. Explain why a solution of bromine in water is brown.

Fig. 3 *Chlorine and bromine are two halogens used to kill bacteria in swimming pool water.*

Differences between the halogens

The similarities among the halogens arise because they all have 7 electrons in the outer shell. Within the general pattern there are important differences and trends, however.

Comparing the halogens

Halogen	fluorine	chlorine	bromine	iodine
State at room temperature	gas	gas	liquid	solid
Colour	colourless	green	brown	black
B.P. °C	−188	−35	59	184
Symbol	F	Cl	Br	I
Formula of molecule	F_2	Cl_2	Br_2	I_2
Atomic number	9	17	35	35
No. of outer shell electrons	7	7	7	7
Name of halide ion	fluoride	chloride	bromide	iodide
Formula of halide ion	F^-	Cl^-	Br^-	I^-

Q3 Write down all the 'differences' between the halogens you can find in the table above.

Many of the differences between the halogens are due to the different sizes of the halogen atoms. An iodine atom, for instance, is almost twice as large as a fluorine atom. This means that electrons from other particles colliding with an iodine atom do not get very close to its nucleus. Collision with a fluorine atom would bring them much closer to a nucleus, and the attachment would be stronger. Fluorine is a stronger oxidising agent than iodine because fluorine atoms have a stronger pull on electrons.

The oxidising power of the halogens therefore decreases in the order $F_2 > Cl_2 > Br_2 > I_2$. There is a sort of 'reactivity series', with fluorine, the most reactive halogen, at the top. This is most easily seen in reactions like:

chlorine + sodium bromide solution $\rightarrow$ sodium chloride + bromine

$$Cl_2(g) + 2NaBr(aq) \rightarrow 2NaCl(aq) + Br_2(l)$$

In other words, when chlorine gas is passed into a solution of sodium bromide a brown colour is seen as bromine is produced. The chlorine has oxidised the bromide ions:

$$Cl_2(g) + 2Br^-(aq) \rightarrow 2Cl^-(aq) + Br_2(l)$$

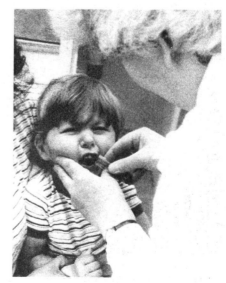

Fig. 4 *Iodine treatment being given after the Chernobyl accident. The non-radioactive iodine mixes with any radioactive iodine in the body. This 'diluting' effect reduces the harm suffered by the victim.*

Questions

A. What can you remember?

    *   **1.** Rearrange these letters to list the four main gases in the air:

              GO COAXING TORN REINDEER ON BOXING DAY

   **   **2.** Write simple word equations which summarise the processes of (a) respiration, and (b) photosynthesis.

    *   **3.** List *four* ways in which oxygen is used. In each case give a *reason* why oxygen is used in this way.

   *   **4.** Complete the following statement: 'Oxides of metals are usually . . ., but oxides of non-metals are usually . . .' Give examples to show the meaning of this statement.

   **   **5.** What is a *noble gas*? Name three noble gases, and give one example of how each is used.

   **   **6.** Draw a fully labelled diagram to show how you could *make* and *collect* some oxygen in the laboratory.

   *   **7.** Name *three* substances which are common air pollutants. Explain how each of these substances gets into the atmosphere.

   **   **8.** Write down *three* uses of nitrogen, and explain why it is used in these ways.

   *   **9.** How would you test a gas which you think is probably carbon dioxide? What will you expect to see if you are right?

  *   **10.** Give *three* important uses of carbon dioxide, and explain why it is used in these ways.

  **   **11.** Draw a fully labelled diagram to show how you could *make* and *collect* some carbon dioxide in the laboratory.

  **   **12.** Write down what you would see when
       (a) sodium carbonate crystals are heated,
       (b) sodium carbonate reacts with hydrochloric acid,
       (c) sodium hydrogencarbonate is heated.
       Name the new substances formed in each case.

  *   **13.** Give the names and formulae of the following gases:
       (a) the lightest gas,
       (b) the gas which makes up about 80% of the air,
       (c) the gas formed when an acid is added to a carbonate,
       (d) the gas which is essential for breathing and burning,
       (e) a noble gas used for filling light bulbs.

  *   **14.** Write down what you would see when
       (a) sodium reacts with cold water,
       (b) zinc reacts with steam,
       (c) hydrogen gas burns.
       Name the new substances formed in each case.

  **   **15.** Draw diagrams to show the difference between the two allotropes of carbon – graphite and diamond.

  *   **16.** Write down the main uses of diamonds and explain why they are used in these ways.

  **   **17.** Explain the meaning of the term *allotrope*, and give two examples of its use.

  **   **18.** What is carbon monoxide, and why is it dangerous?

  *   **19.** Draw a diagram showing the 'fire triangle', and explain what it means.

  *   **20.** Draw a labelled diagram of a carbon dioxide fire extinguisher.

  **   **21.** Describe what you would see as sulphur is heated from room temperature until it is boiling.

** **22.** Write down *two* ways in which sulphur dioxide may be formed. How is sulphur dioxide used?

* **23.** Explain why sulphur dioxide is such a serious pollutant.

** **24.** Describe how you would carry out a chemical test for recognising sulphur dioxide, and say what you would see.

** **25.** Write down the names and formulae of the halogens. Explain why this is an important group of elements.

B. What have you understood?

** **26.** Explain why hydrogen is such a dangerous gas.

** **27.** Hydrogen is sometimes used as a rocket fuel. Explain the reasons for this.

*** **28.** Draw a diagram to show how the processes of *respiration* and *photosynthesis* depend on one another.

* **29.** Explain why oxygen is necessary for a fire to burn.

*** **30.** Zinc oxide is amphoteric. Explain how you would show that this statement is true.

** **31.** Oxygen is obtained by fractional distillation of liquid air. Draw a diagram which explains this.

** **32.** Explain why noble gases are used for filling light bulbs. What other gases might be suitable, and why?

** **33.** Nitrogen gas can only be absorbed by a very few plants, yet the main use of nitrogen is in the fertiliser industry. Explain why this is so.

** **34.** Look back at 3.4 Fig. 4, and then draw your own detailed diagram of the Nitrogen Cycle which explains all that is going on.

** **35.** Re-read the final paragraph in 3.5, and then explain exactly what happens when carbon dioxide reacts with lime water.

** **36.** You could not distinguish between sodium carbonate and sodium hydrogencarbonate simply by adding an acid. Why not?

* **37.** Explain why hydrogen was once chosen for filling balloons, but is no longer used in this way.

** **38.** Draw a labelled diagram to explain why graphite conducts electricity.

* **39.** Explain why wood must be heated very carefully if it is to be made into charcoal.

* **40.** Explain why it is so dangerous to try to put out a chip pan fire with water.

** **41.** Sulphur is often transported as a liquid. Explain the advantages and likely problems of this.

*** **42.** Natural gas is now a major world source of sulphur. Explain why, and show how the sulphur is extracted.

** **43.** In 3.15 the halogens are represented by the symbol X. Write equations for the reactions between a halogen and (a) water, (b) magnesium and (c) sodium.

C. Can you use this information?

** **44.** Use 3.15 and *Datapage C* to make a table which lists the *halogens*, and gives as much information as possible about them.

** **45.** Look at *Datapage I2* and list the gases of the air in order of their boiling points.
 (a) Which gas (other than radon) would appear first as a liquid when air is cooled?
 (b) Is there any parallel between the boiling points of these gases and their relative molecular masses?

** **46.** Find out from *Datapage T* how the halogen elements got their names.

47. A pupil took a chemical from the shelf and heated it strongly in a test tube. A glowing wood splint re-lit when placed in the mouth of the tube. The substance left in the tube at the end had changed colour. What conclusions can you draw from this?

D. Taking it further

** **48.** Helium is occasionally found in the earth as an impurity in Natural Gas (methane). Using information from 3.3 and 6.7, suggest how the helium might be separated from the methane.

* **49.** A newly discovered gas is thought to be harmful to plant life. Describe a simple experiment which would allow you to test this theory safely.

** **50.** Draw an apparatus which would be suitable for measuring the percentage of oxygen in the air breathed out by a hamster. Include the animal in your diagram, and remember that it must be humanely treated!

*** **51.** Suggest a safe method for collecting the gas from a light bulb, and then finding out whether it is nitrogen or argon.

Quick questions

1. Which English minister is often credited with the discovery of oxygen?

2. Give the formulae for the following gases: oxygen, nitrogen, carbon dioxide, argon, hydrogen, carbon monoxide, steam.

3. What simple test is used for carbonate minerals?

4. What is the difference between baking soda and baking powder? (See 3.6)

5. Which element has been used for absorbing gases in gas masks?

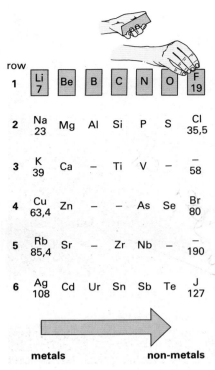

row							
1	Li 7	Be	B	C	N	O	F 19
2	Na 23	Mg	Al	Si	P	S	Cl 35,5
3	K 39	Ca	–	Ti	V	–	– 58
4	Cu 63,4	Zn	–	–	As	Se	Br 80
5	Rb 85,4	Sr	–	Zr	Nb	–	– 190
6	Ag 108	Cd	Ur	Sn	Sb	Te	J 127

metals → non-metals

Fig. 1 Part of Mendeleyev's original Periodic Table (1869). What does 35,5 mean? And what is the element with the symbol J?

The Periodic Table

In most chemistry books and laboratories you will find a chart, known as the **Periodic Table**, showing all the elements. Altogether, 107 elements are now known. Ninety-two of these occur naturally. The other 15 have been made since the first artificial element, neptunium, was recognised in 1940. Sorting out this long list was a puzzle for many years, especially before anything was known about the structure of atoms, and when some elements were still undiscovered.

Mendeleyev and the Periodic Table

The Periodic Table was devised by the Russian scientist D.I. Mendeleyev in 1869. At that time 63 elements were known. He wrote down what he knew about each element on a separate card, and then sorted the cards into piles, bringing together elements which had features in common. Then he laid the cards out in rows, in order of what we now call 'relative atomic mass'. Every time he returned to the first pile of cards he started a new row.

The beginning of his layout looked like Fig. 1. He noticed that he needed to start a new row with every eighth element. In each row there was a pattern in the properties of the elements, from metal to non-metal. Mendeleyev called it a **periodic variation** in the properties, and this is how the Table got its name.

> **Q1** Mendeleyev's inspiration was to leave gaps for elements which, he guessed, had still to be discovered. Using *Datapage B*, list some elements which would have been unknown to Mendeleyev.

Mendeleyev was born in 1834 in Siberia, the youngest of 17 children. While he was a professor at St. Petersburg (now Leningrad) he proposed his 'periodic system of the elements'. He lived until 1907. By then, many of the gaps which he left in the Table had been filled by elements with the properties that he had predicted.

The modern Periodic Table

The basic arrangement of the Periodic Table in use today (Fig. 2) is not very different from Mendeleyev's.

☐ the horizontal rows are called **periods**
☐ the vertical columns are called **groups**
☐ **metals** appear on the *left* of the Table
☐ **non-metals** appear on the *right*.

Groups are numbered according to the *number of outer shell electrons* in the elements which they contain. For example, the metals in Group I have one outer shell electron. Several of the groups also have names:

> Group I   alkali metals
> Group II   alkaline earth metals
> Group VII   halogens
> Group 0   noble gases

The metal elements 21–30, 39–48 and 72–80 are known as the **transition elements**, or transition metals. Elements 57–71, the lanthanides, and 89–103, the actinides, are also regarded as transition elements.

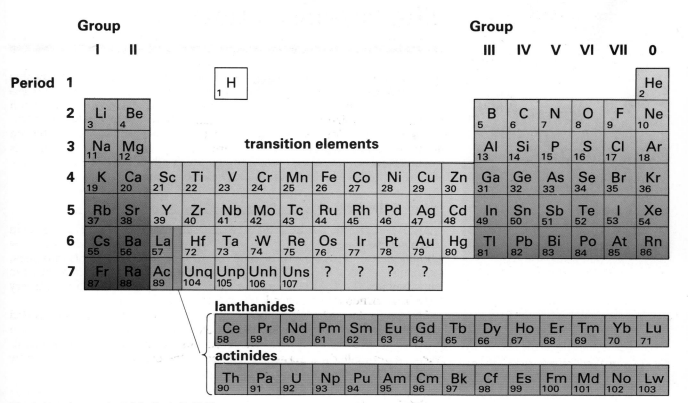

Fig. 2 *A modern version of the Periodic Table.*

Patterns in the Periodic Table

☐ Elements at the left-hand end of a period are metals;
those at the right are non-metals.

☐ The most reactive metal is at the bottom of Group I;
the most reactive non-metal is at the top of Group VII.

☐ Elements at the bottom of a group have larger atoms than those at the
top. The larger the atom, the further the outermost electrons are from
the nucleus, and the easier they are to remove. An element which
readily loses its outer electron(s) is a metal.

☐ Elements in the same group form compounds with similar formulae. For
instance, the chlorides of the alkali metals are all of the form MCl (LiCl,
NaCl, KCl etc.). The chlorides of the Group IV elements are all of the
form MCl_4 (CCl_4 etc.).

☐ For Groups I–IV, the group number is the same as the valency of the
elements in the group. For Groups V–VIII it is 8 *minus* the usual valency
of the elements.

Naming new elements: the problem of Element 104

The choice of name for a new element traditionally goes to the person
discovering it. Element 104 has been given two names. The Russians call it
kurchatovium, and the Americans favour the name rutherfordium. A
recent meeting of the International Union of Pure and Applied Chemistry
has ruled that a systematic name based upon the atomic number of the
element should be used for this and future discoveries. Element 104 now
becomes unnilquadium!

Fig. 3 *Lithium is floating in this beaker of oil.
It is the lightest of all metals.*

Metals and non-metals

If you ask people to tell you what metals are like, they will probably say that metals are bright and shiny. Or else that they are hard, and go 'clang!' if you drop them on the floor. If people think harder, they may realise that metals can be very different: mercury, sodium and copper, for example. The same applies to the non-metals: sulphur, chlorine and helium are completely different.

Nevertheless, there are certain things which all metals have in common, and other things which all non-metals have in common.

Metals and non-metals

Property	Metals	Non-metals
The elements		
physical state	solids (except for mercury)	few solids, many gases
appearance	shiny	usually dull, or gaseous
conduction of electricity and heat	good	poor (except for graphite)
flexibility and strength	usually good	brittle if solid
Their compounds		
oxides	solids which are basic or alkaline or amphoteric	solids or gases which are acidic or neutral
chlorides	solids with ions linked in giant lattices	solids or liquids with covalently bonded molecules

Fig. 1 Ingots of the precious metal platinum, which is solid, shiny and conducts electricity well.

Fig. 2 Strong metals are often used to construct buildings. The roof of London's St. Pancras station is made of iron.

Q1 Imagine that you have been provided with samples of a new solid element, and it is necessary to find out whether it is a metal or a non-metal. Describe *three* experiments you could carry out.

Metals are found on the left-hand side of the Periodic Table, and non-metals on the right. The transition elements, in the centre, are all metals. Part of the Periodic Table is shown in Fig. 3. The groups are numbered 0 to VII.

The oxides of metals and non-metals

The compound formed when an element reacts with oxygen is known as an oxide. The oxides of **metals** are usually solids which are **basic** or alkaline. The oxides of **non-metals** are solids or gases which are usually **acidic**. The commonest non-metal oxide of all is the most unusual: water is a neutral liquid. Some metal oxides are **amphoteric**. This means that they have both acidic and basic properties. There is more about oxides in 3.2.

Q2 Which groups in the Periodic Table contain (a) only metals? (b) only non-metals? (c) both metals and non-metals?

Q3 Would it be possible to draw a line across the Table which separates the metals from the non-metals? If so, copy out the region of the Table where it would lie, and mark it in. Are there any 'borderline cases'?

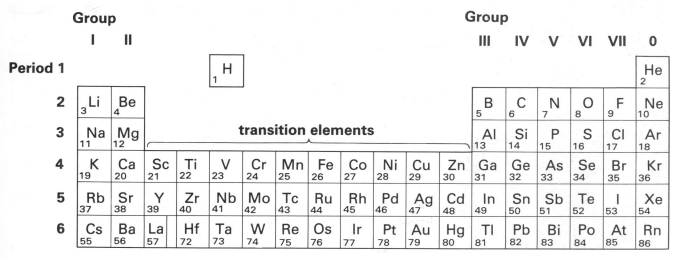

Fig. 3 *Part of the Periodic Table. Is it possible to mark where the metals end and the non-metals begin?*

A 'borderline case' – silicon

Silicon is an element which does not fit conveniently into either category. Here is some information about it:

Some facts about silicon

physical state	solid
appearance	grey, shiny crystals
	also brown powder
conduction of electricity	crystalline form conducts electricity
	brown powder form does not
mechanical properties	hard but brittle

It is almost impossible to decide from this information whether silicon is a metal or not, especially as it has two solid forms. The decision is much easier when you look at some silicon compounds:

Some facts about silicon compounds

silicon oxide	white solid which will react with an alkali to form a salt
silicon hydroxide	usually known as 'silicic acid'; will react with alkalis
silicon chloride	colourless liquid which will react with water

Fig. 4 *These discs are slices of pure silicon which will be used to make 'chips' for computers.*

Silicon forms a whole family of very useful compounds, known as **silicones**. The silicones are colourless, non-poisonous substances with molecules of varying sizes. Some are clean oily liquids, used in cosmetic creams and hair preparations. Others are rubbery solids which can even be shaped into replacement flesh for people who have suffered accidents or undergone surgery. Silicones repel water, and may be used for waterproofing fabrics and building materials. A great advantage of silicones is that the molecules can be 'tailor-made' for the job which the final product has to do.

Q4 Write down the arguments for *or* against regarding silicon as a non-metal.

Fig. 5 *This is silicon oxide in its most beautiful form: quartz crystals.*

The reactivity series

Think of three different metals – let's say sodium, iron and gold. Sodium is soft and reacts violently with water. In the air it corrodes at once. Iron also reacts with water and air, but much more slowly – forming rust. Gold, on the other hand, can even remain on the sea bed for hundreds of years, and still come up bright and shining. Gold is a much less **reactive** metal than iron or sodium.

Q1 Write down the names of two other metals. Explain, giving all the evidence you can, which one is the more reactive of the two.

In Fig. 3 there are some metals listed in order, with the most reactive one first. This list is known as a **Reactivity Series**. It has been drawn up from the results of many experiments.

Reactions of metals with air and oxygen

Many metals react with the oxygen of the air:

☐ Potassium, sodium and lithium react so readily with the air that they must be stored under oil.

☐ These metals, and also calcium and magnesium, burn easily in air.

☐ Aluminium, zinc and iron will burn too, if powdered or shredded into wool. They are used in fireworks to produce sparks and flares.

Oxides of the metals are formed in all these reactions. The more vigorous the reaction, the higher the metal is placed in the Reactivity Series.

Reactions of metals with ice, water and steam

☐ Potassium will catch fire if placed on a piece of ice!

☐ Sodium reacts so rapidly with water that it whizzes around the surface, melts and dissolves very rapidly.

☐ Lithium and calcium react quite quickly with cold water, producing a steady stream of bubbles.

☐ Magnesium does react with cold water, but you have to look quite closely to see that anything is happening.

☐ Magnesium, zinc and iron will react with steam.

In all these reactions, hydrogen is released and the hydroxide or oxide of the metal is formed. The more readily the metal reacts, the higher it is placed in the Reactivity Series.

Q2 Write equations for the reactions between lithium, calcium and zinc and (a) air or oxygen; (b) water or steam.

Did you know?

Napoleon III (Emperor of France from 1848 to 1873) was said to possess a dinner service made from a metal more precious than gold. Only his special guests were allowed to use it. Which metal was it made from?

Aluminium – very costly because it was then so difficult to extract.

Fig. 1 This Viking sword has a gold and silver handle and an iron blade. Which is the most reactive metal?

Fig. 2 This mask from Peru is 900 years old and looks as good as new, because the reactivity of gold is so low.

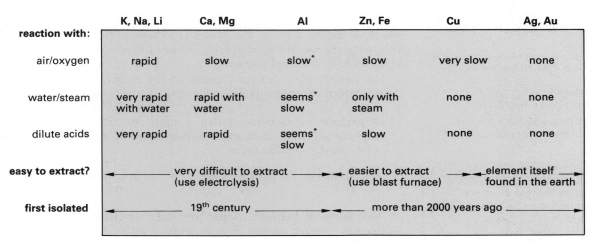

decreasing reactivity

reaction with:	K, Na, Li	Ca, Mg	Al	Zn, Fe	Cu	Ag, Au
air/oxygen	rapid	slow	slow*	slow	very slow	none
water/steam	very rapid with water	rapid with water	seems* slow	only with steam	none	none
dilute acids	very rapid	rapid	seems* slow	slow	none	none
easy to extract?	←——————— very difficult to extract (use electrclysis) ——————→		←— easier to extract (use blast furnace) —→		←— element itself found in the earth —→	
first isolated	←—————— 19th century ——————→		←—————— more than 2000 years ago ——————→			

* Aluminium reacts readily with the air and a tough oxide layer forms on its surface. This often prevents further reaction and disguises aluminium's true reactivity.

Fig. 3 The metals at the top of this chart are listed in order of their reactivity. This list is called a Reactivity Series.

Discovery and isolation of the metals

The first metals to be discovered were those which were easiest to obtain from their ores – metals which are low in the Reactivity Series. There are no written records of these discoveries, but lead, copper and the precious metals were certainly known in ancient times. Zinc was smelted in India and iron was obtained in China, more than 2000 years ago. The metals discovered more recently are the reactive ones. Potassium was not discovered until 1807, by Humphry Davy, inventor of the miners' safety lamp. Within a short time he had also isolated sodium, calcium and magnesium. Aluminium was first obtained in 1827. There is more about this on *Datapage R*.

Methods of extracting metals

☐ Aluminium and other metals high in the Reactivity Series are extracted commercially by electrolysis. The molten metal chloride is often used. For aluminium the raw material is its oxide, bauxite.

☐ Zinc, iron and copper are obtained by reducing their ores with carbon. The raw materials for zinc and copper are usually sulphide ores. The ores of iron are oxides.

☐ Silver and gold occur 'native', that is, in an uncombined state. They can therefore be obtained by a process of mechanical separation – crushing up the rock in which they are found until the fine particles are released. Much silver and some gold are also recovered as by-products from the extraction of other metals.

Q3 Use library books or an encyclopaedia to find out how *one* of the following metals is extracted: tungsten, titanium, uranium.

Fig. 1 Food cans are made of iron protected with a coating of the less reactive metal tin.

zinc metal
(contains zinc atoms, Zn (s))

copper sulphate solution
(contains copper ions, Cu^{2+})

zinc atoms lose electrons and become zinc ions in solution
$Zn(s) \rightarrow Zn^{2+}(aq) + 2e^-$

copper ions **gain** electrons and become copper atoms
$Cu^{2+}(aq) + 2e^- \rightarrow Cu(s)$

copper coating is deposited

Fig. 2 A displacement reaction: zinc and copper compete to be in solution. Zinc is more reactive – it displaces copper from the solution.

Fig. 3 A competition reaction at work: this 'thermit' mixture of aluminium and iron oxide is reacting to produce molten iron just where it is needed for welding a railway line.

Finding places for elements in the Reactivity Series

The iron used for making food cans is protected by a coating of tin – a metal which is below iron in the Reactivity Series. If you can measure the reactivity of a metal you can predict some of its chemical reactions. You can also decide how it might be used.

The correct place for an element in the Reactivity Series is found by doing various experiments. For instance:

☐ **Displacement reactions:** When a piece of zinc is placed in copper sulphate solution, it becomes slowly covered in copper, and the blue colour of the solution fades:

zinc atoms(s) + copper ions(aq) $\rightarrow$ copper atoms(s) + zinc ions(aq)
   grey   blue   red-brown   colourless

This happens because copper *ions* take electrons from zinc atoms to become copper *atoms*. Zinc is more reactive than copper, so zinc is placed higher in the Series. Experiments with other metals and other solutions make it possible for the rest of the Series to be built up.

☐ **Competition reactions:** A similar kind of reaction can be arranged, using a metal and the *oxide* of a different metal. Two mixtures are made. In one there is *zinc* powder mixed with *copper oxide*. In the other, *copper* powder is mixed with *zinc oxide*. When they are heated, one mixture reacts, but the other does not. It is not hard to guess that the reaction which 'goes' is:

$$\text{zinc(s) + copper oxide(s)} \xrightarrow{\text{heat}} \text{zinc oxide(s) + copper(s)}$$

The oxygen is 'won' by zinc – the metal which is higher in the Reactivity Series. Similar reactions can be used to fix the positions of other metals in the Series.

☐ The **'thermit' process** (pronounced therm*ite*) is a very useful competition reaction. Great heat is developed in the competition reaction between aluminium and a metal oxide, for example:

aluminium + iron (III) oxide $\rightarrow$ aluminium oxide + iron
$2Al(s)$ + $Fe_2O_3(s)$ $\rightarrow$ Al_2O_3 + $2Fe(l)$

The iron produced in this reaction is molten. One way of using it is in welding railway lines (Fig. 3), a method still used today where extra metal is needed.

☐ There is an electrical method of measuring the reducing power of a metal. A reactivity list compiled in this way is known as an **Electrochemical Series**. More details are given in 4.5.

Q1 Make a chart, using magazine pictures of metals in use, which shows the metals in their Reactivity Series order.

Q2 Look back at 4.3, Fig. 3, and predict what would happen in the following reactions: magnesium ribbon dipped into copper sulphate solution; iron filings heated with lead oxide. Explain each one as fully as you can.

Fig. 4 The gleaming chrome and paintwork on these old Morris cars protects the reactive metal iron from the air.

Reactions of metals with dilute hydrochloric or sulphuric acids

Metals above magnesium in the Reactivity Series react so violently with acids that special equipment is needed to carry out the reactions safely. Magnesium itself reacts rapidly with dilute acids. Zinc and iron react more slowly. Copper and the metals below it are not affected by dilute hydrochloric or sulphuric acids. Hydrogen is released whenever the metal reacts, and a salt is formed.

> **Q3** Write word and formula equations for the reactions between three metals of your own choice and dilute sulphuric acid.

Finding places for non-metals in the Reactivity Series

Displacement and competition reactions can be carried out with non-metals, such as carbon and hydrogen, as well as with other metals. A place for hydrogen in the Reactivity Series can be found by setting up a reaction in which hydrogen is 'competing' for oxygen with a metal. It is found that hydrogen:

☐ *will* remove the oxygen from copper oxide (when hydrogen gas is passed over heated copper oxide), and

☐ *will not* remove the oxygen from magnesium oxide under the same conditions.

This puts hydrogen above copper, but below magnesium in the list. Further experiments allow the position to be fixed. The position of carbon can be decided in a similar way.

> **Q4** Describe how you would set up experiments to find out whether (a) carbon and (b) hydrogen are above or below lead in the Reactivity Series.

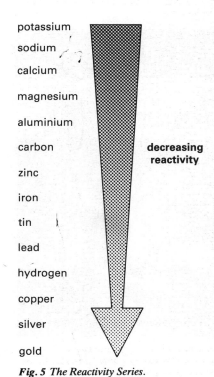

potassium
sodium
calcium
magnesium
aluminium
carbon
zinc
iron
tin
lead
hydrogen
copper
silver
gold

decreasing reactivity

Fig. 5 The Reactivity Series.

Oxidising and reducing

Oxidising

Metal objects, such as buttons or brassware, are sometimes offered for sale in different styles. There are ones with a 'bright finish' and others with a duller 'oxidised finish'. A tarnished coin, a green copper roof, and a rusted piece of iron are all sometimes described as 'oxidised'. The surface of the metal has been affected by oxygen in some way.

When oxygen combines with an element or a compound, converting it to another substance, it **oxidises** it. The process is called **oxidation**. The substance which does the oxidising, in this case oxygen, is known as the **oxidising agent**.

> **Q1** Another word for 'oxidising agent' is **oxidant**. What do you think is meant by 'anti-oxidant'? (These words often appear on food labels.)

Sometimes oxidation happens naturally, for example when the surface of a new sheet of aluminium is exposed to the air:

$$\text{aluminium(s)} + \text{oxygen(g)} \rightarrow \text{aluminium oxide(s)}$$

Sometimes this surface is oxidised on purpose, as in the manufacture of anodised aluminium.

Oxidation doesn't only take place on the surface of a metal, however. When magnesium ribbon is burned, it is completely oxidised to magnesium oxide:

$$\text{magnesium(s)} + \text{oxygen(g)} \rightarrow \text{magnesium oxide(s)}$$

Nor is oxidation confined to metals. When hydrogen is burned, it too is completely oxidised – to hydrogen oxide, or steam:

$$\text{hydrogen(g)} + \text{oxygen(g)} \rightarrow \text{hydrogen oxide(g)}$$

All burning processes are oxidation reactions, whether they are rapid (like fires and explosions) or slow (like rusting and respiration). In all these cases the products include oxides. Carbon dioxide is formed from the oxidation of carbon itself, and by the oxidation of fuels and foodstuffs. Iron oxides are formed during the rusting process.

> **Q2** Suggest three everyday oxidation processes, and explain carefully what is happening in each.

Corrosion Whenever a metal corrodes, an oxidation reaction is taking place. Oxygen from the air is the commonest oxidising agent. The statue in Fig. 1 is made from bronze. This is an alloy of two metals, copper and tin, which are low in the Reactivity Series. Bronze corrodes quite slowly, and the result is pleasant to look at. The steel tank in Fig. 3 must be painted every few years if the iron, a more reactive metal, is to be prevented from rusting. If the corrosion is allowed to continue, the tank will be ruined in just a few years. There is more about rusting in 5.5.

Fig. 1 Slow oxidation has taken place here, producing a lovely green finish on this bronze statue of an ancient Egyptian cat goddess.

Fig. 2 Rapid oxidation of aluminium: the explosion could be heard 10 miles away when this aluminium powder factory blew up in 1983.

Fig. 3 Painting an oil storage tank to stop it oxidising. The paint forms a barrier between the metal tank and the air.

Fig. 4 This racing car engine works by oxidising a fuel (petrol). The air needed to do this is taken in through the gauze-covered intakes.

Reducing

'Reducing' in chemistry has nothing to do with 'getting smaller'. It means, quite simply, the opposite of oxidising. **Oxidising** is about adding oxygen; **reducing** is about taking oxygen away.

A simple way to show a reducing process is to look again at a competition reaction. When zinc reacts with copper oxide, it takes away oxygen:

$$\text{zinc(s)} + \text{copper oxide(s)} \rightarrow \text{zinc oxide(s)} + \text{copper(s)}$$

Fig. 5 The production of metals from their ores is a reduction process.

Zinc has a **reducing** effect on the copper oxide. Copper oxide is reduced to copper. A chemical reaction in which oxygen is removed from one of the reacting substances is known as **reduction**. The substance which does the reducing is known as the **reducing agent** (or **reductant**).

Whenever a metal is obtained from its ore, a reduction process is needed. Iron ore is an oxide; removing the oxygen leaves iron. Zinc ore is converted to an oxide, and then reduced to zinc metal (seen here in Fig. 5).

Oxidation–reduction reactions

Look again at the reaction between zinc and copper oxide. The copper oxide has indeed been reduced, but what has happened to the zinc? Zinc oxide has been formed. The zinc has been oxidised.

The function of a reducing agent, like zinc in this case, is to remove oxygen. In doing so it becomes oxidised itself! This has to happen, or the reducing action would not occur. In other words, *there can be no reduction without a corresponding oxidation*, and vice-versa.

> **Q3** Write an equation for the reaction between zinc and copper oxide. Show which substance has been oxidised, and which reduced.

Fig. 6 Alcohol in the drinker's breath is the reducing agent which affects the Breathalyser.

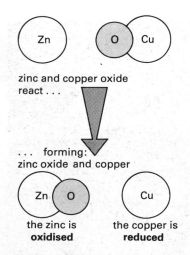

zinc and copper oxide
react . . .

. . . forming:
zinc oxide and copper

the zinc is
oxidised

the copper is
reduced

Fig. 1 The oxidation–reduction reaction between zinc and copper oxide.

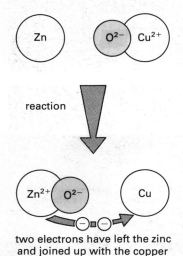

reaction

two electrons have left the zinc
and joined up with the copper

Fig. 2 Another way of looking at the reaction in Fig. 1 – electrons are transferred from the zinc atom to the copper ion.

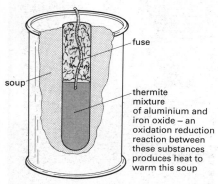

fuse

soup

thermite
mixture
of aluminium and
iron oxide – an
oxidation reduction
reaction between
these substances
produces heat to
warm this soup

Fig. 3 A design for a self-heating soup can for emergency use. The design was a failure! Can you suggest why?

Oxidation–reduction and the gain and loss of electrons

In a competition reaction, like the one between zinc and copper oxide, the zinc is oxidised as the copper oxide is reduced. Now look more closely!

The reaction

$$zinc(s) + copper\ oxide(s) \rightarrow zinc\ oxide(s) + copper(s)$$

can be divided into two 'half-reactions':

$$zinc \rightarrow zinc\ oxide$$

$$copper\ oxide \rightarrow copper$$

Zinc cannot become zinc oxide without forming a zinc *ion*, and to do this it must lose two electrons. The half-reaction is

$$zinc\ atom \rightarrow zinc\ (2+)\ ion + 2\ electrons$$

$$Zn(s) \rightarrow Zn^{2+}(s) + 2e$$

Also, copper oxide cannot become copper without forming a copper *atom*, and to do this the copper ion must gain two electrons. The half-reaction is

$$copper\ (2+)\ ion + 2\ electrons \rightarrow copper\ atom$$

$$Cu^{2+} + 2e \rightarrow Cu(s)$$

The two electrons gained by the copper ion are transferred from the zinc atom, which turns into an ion. This is sometimes called an 'electron-transfer' reaction. The two simultaneous half-reactions can be added together, giving

$$Zn(s) + Cu^{2+}(s) \rightarrow Zn^{2+}(s) + Cu(s)$$

The oxide ion retains the structure O^{2-} throughout, and simply changes partners – from the copper to the zinc.

Q1 Work through this argument again for yourself, using the reaction between magnesium and lead (II) oxide, which takes place in just the same way.

When magnesium burns in air, forming magnesium oxide, the process is similar:

$$magnesium\ atom \rightarrow magnesium(2+)\ ion + 2\ electrons$$

$$oxygen\ atom + 2\ electrons \rightarrow oxide(2-)\ ion$$

Electrons are removed from the magnesium atom to make the oxide ion.

Q2 Using chemical symbols, write half-equations for this process. Then combine them to show the full oxidation–reduction reaction.

Q3 Do the same for the reactions between (a) sodium and oxygen to form sodium monoxide, Na_2O; and (b) iron(II) chloride, $FeCl_2$, and chlorine to form iron(III) chloride, $FeCl_3$.

Fig. 4 Explosions and fires are rapid oxidation–reduction reactions.

Oil-rig!

In all oxidation–reduction reactions the electrons *from* the substance *oxidised* are transferred *to* the substance *reduced*. Some people use the word 'OIL-RIG' to help them remember this loss and gain of electrons:

Oxidation **I**s **L**oss – **R**eduction **I**s **G**ain!

Fig. 5 Oxidation–reduction in action: this film for a disc camera undergoes several oxidation–reduction processes before you get your final picture.

Oxidation number

The term **oxidation number**, or sometimes 'oxidation state', refers to the number of electrons which have been lost or gained by an atom in forming an ion. Metal ions with a charge of +1, +2 etc. have an oxidation number of 1, 2 etc. Ions formed by the addition of electrons to the atoms of non-metals, with charges of –1, –2 etc. have oxidation numbers of –1, –2 etc. An atom which has lost one electron has undergone 'one unit of oxidation'. This is why it is given an oxidation number of +1. The atom of an element on its own is given the oxidation number 0.

The oxidation number is usually written in Roman numerals, and included in the name of the substance where necessary. For instance, there are two oxides of copper, known as copper(I) oxide and copper(II) oxide. These are quite different compounds. One is red-brown and contains the copper(I) ion, Cu^+. The other is black and contains the copper(II) ion, Cu^{2+}.

Q4 Suggest oxidation numbers for (a) the copper ion in copper sulphate crystals; (b) copper atoms in a copper bracelet; (c) chloride ions in copper chloride; (d) argon atoms in a light bulb; (e) sodium ions in sodium chloride.

Fig. 6 Our own living system is a mass of oxidation–reduction processes. To work in a hostile environment you must carry the substances needed to support these processes on your back.

Introducing electrochemistry

An electric current seems mysterious and invisible, although you can see and feel its effects. An electric current flows when electrons move. Chemical reactions, also, occur through the movement of electrons from place to place. So there is a link between the two.

How does electricity pass through substances?

Many solid substances, like metals and graphite, conduct electricity. Other solids do not. Some liquids and solutions also conduct. Even gases will allow electrons to pass under certain conditions.

☐ A substance which carries an electric current is called a *conductor*.

The atoms in conductors do not move when an electric current passes. Their outer electrons can move within the framework provided by the rest of the atoms. A potential difference between two points will cause some electrons to move, so a current flows.

A substance which contains ions will also conduct electricity if it is molten or dissolved. Melting or dissolving an ionic substance 'unlocks' the ions from the lattice which makes up the solid. A current can flow if the ions are free to move (Figs. 5 and 6).

☐ A substance which will carry an electric current only when it is molten or dissolved is called an **electrolyte**.

Chemical reactions take place as the current passes, and the process is known as **electrolysis** (see Fig. 3). The **power supply** [A] is connected to the **electrodes** [B], maintaining a potential difference in the circuit. This causes electrons in the connecting wires to move. The electrodes become charged:

☐ One electrode becomes negative because electrons (which are negatively charged) are moving towards it. This is the **cathode**.
☐ The other becomes positively charged because electrons are drawn away from it. This electrode is called the **anode**.
☐ *Positively charged ions* move to the *negatively charged electrode*, where they meet the supply of electrons and join them to form atoms.
☐ *Negatively charged ions* move to the *positively charged electrode*, where they give up their 'surplus' electrons and also become atoms. The electrons released at the positive electrode are moved round the connecting wires by the battery, so providing a further supply at the negative electrode.

Michael Faraday and the idea of ions

Michael Faraday, whose picture is shown in 1.2 Fig. 2, was the person who realised what is going on when molten substances and solutions allow electricity to pass. He was intrigued to find that water would conduct electricity, but that ice was an insulator. This led him to investigate a large number of substances which could be melted. He found that, except for the metals, the substances which conducted electricity when molten would not do so when solid. During the 1830s he introduced the word **ion** to mean an electrically charged atom. This idea is explained in 1.11.

Faraday did all his scientific work at the Royal Institution in London. His apparatus and diaries are still there. Part of his laboratory has been reconstructed, and is open to the public.

Fig. 1 Conduction: the metal terminals of these dry batteries are connected to graphite rods. Mobile electrons in graphite and metals will allow electric currents to flow.

Fig. 2 No current flows through these glass insulators because they contain no free ions or electrons.

Fig. 3 This blue copper sulphate solution contains ions, so a current can flow through it lighting the bulb.

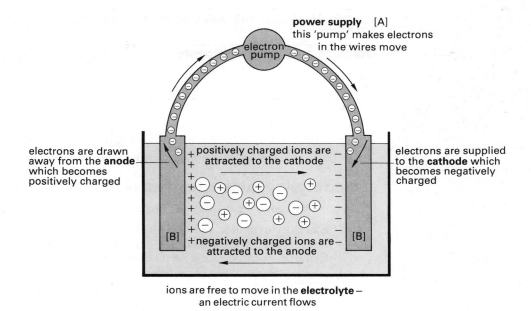

power supply   [A]
this 'pump' makes electrons
in the wires move

electron pump

electrons are drawn away from the **anode** which becomes positively charged

+ positively charged ions are attracted to the cathode _

electrons are supplied to the **cathode** which becomes negatively charged

[B]

+negatively charged ions are attracted to the anode—

[B]

ions are free to move in the **electrolyte** — an electric current flows

Fig. 4 *The flow of current through an electrolyte. Figs. 1 and 2 in 4.8 show what happens at the electrodes in more detail.*

Solid substances which will not conduct electricity

Ionic substances do not conduct electricity when they are in the solid state. This is because the ions are packed together in a rigid lattice, and cannot move. When the ions cannot move they unable to release or collect electrons at an electrode, so there is no continuous route for electrons to move round the circuit.

Solids which contain small covalent molecules, or continuous 'giant molecule' structures, are also quite unable to conduct electricity. Some of these substances, like poly(ethene), are used as insulators.

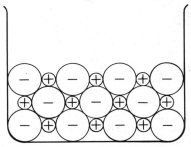

Fig. 5 *The ions in this solid are packed tightly together. Since they cannot move, the solid does not conduct electricity.*

Q1 Draw two diagrams to show simple arrangements for testing (a) a solid sample and (b) a liquid sample, to see whether or not they will conduct electricity.

Q2 Here is a list of substances which could be tested with the arrangements you have drawn. Put them into two columns: conductors of electricity and non-conductors. Against each substance write down the letter which gives a reason for your choice, taken from the following list:
    A: because it contains ions which are free to move
    B: because it contains ions which are not free to move
    C: because it does not contain ions
    D: because it contains delocalised electrons which are free to move.

Substances: copper sulphate crystals, graphite pencil 'lead', sodium chloride solution, polystyrene tile, iron nail, ethanol, wax, sugar solution, molten aluminium oxide.

Q3 Molten glass is said to conduct electricity. Using a labelled drawing, show how you would put this idea to the test. If it proved to be correct, what conclusions would you draw?

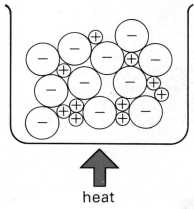

heat

Fig. 6 *Once the ions have been set free by melting (or dissolving) an ionic substance, a current can flow.*

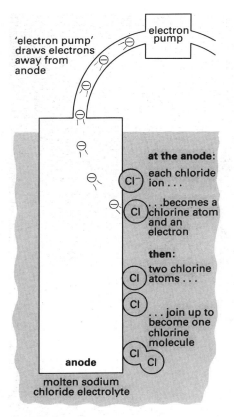

Chemical changes at the electrodes during electrolysis

Electrolysis is not just a magic process. It is a set of chemical reactions. Chemical changes take place at the electrodes as soon as the current begins to flow. The ions from the electrolyte always take part in these chemical reactions. Sometimes the electrodes themselves are also changed.

Electrolysing molten sodium chloride

This process is used for making the metal sodium from salt.

> Electrolyte: molten sodium chloride
> Ions present: sodium ions, Na^+, and chloride ions, Cl^-
> Electrodes: carbon, or a metal unaffected by molten salt

☐ At the **anode** (+):
Choride ions are attracted, and give up their electrons. Chlorine atoms are formed:

$$Cl^- \rightarrow Cl + e$$

Chlorine atoms become covalently bonded together in pairs, forming chlorine molecules:

$$2Cl \rightarrow Cl_2$$

☐ At the **cathode** (−):
Sodium ions are attracted, find a supply of electrons, and are converted into sodium atoms:

$$Na^+ + e \rightarrow Na$$

In summary, chlorine is released at the anode, and sodium collects at the cathode. Sodium metal is manufactured in this way (Fig. 3).

Q1 Write a single chemical equation which sums up what has happened in this process.

Q2 Magnesium is manufactured by electrolysis of a mixture which contains molten magnesium chloride. Write a careful account of what happens at each electrode in this process.

Q3 Suggest three other metals which could be made by electrolysis of a molten salt. Check your ideas with *Datapage R3*.

Making sodium Figure 3 shows the cells in which sodium is made by electrolysis. The cells are made of steel and have a ceramic lining. Each one contains a group of graphite anodes and a steel cathode. Sodium is obtained by electrolysing a molten mixture of sodium and calcium chlorides. The purpose of the calcium chloride is to lower the melting point of the mixture, and so to reduce energy costs. These cells are operated at about 600°C. Sodium is used in making petrol additives, in extracting the metal titanium, and in some nuclear power stations. There is more about the uses of sodium in 5.1.

Fig. 1 This is what happens at the anode when molten sodium chloride is electrolysed.

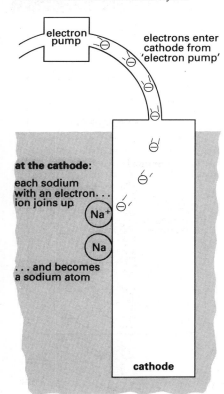

Fig. 2 This is what happens at the cathode when molten sodium chloride is electrolysed.

Fig. 3 Sodium metal is made by electrolysing molten sodium chloride in these vessels.

Electrolysing molten lead bromide

Lead bromide is often used in schools to show electrolysis, because the products at both electrodes are very easy to see (Fig. 4).

> Electrolyte: molten lead bromide
> Ions present: lead ions, Pb^{2+}, and bromide ions, Br^-
> Electrodes: carbon, or a metal unaffected by molten salt

☐ At the **anode** (+):
Bromide ions are attracted, and give up their electrons. Bromine molecules are formed, and brown fumes of bromine can be seen:

$$2Br^- \rightarrow Br_2 + 2e$$

☐ At the **cathode** (−):
Lead ions are attracted, find a supply of electrons, and are converted into lead atoms. Molten lead collects around the cathode:

$$Pb^{2+} + 2e \rightarrow Pb$$

In summary, lead bromide is split into its elements:

$$PbBr_2(l) \rightarrow Pb(l) + Br_2(g)$$

Q4 Make a large copy of Fig. 4, suitable for use as a wallchart, and label it in your own words to explain fully what is happening.

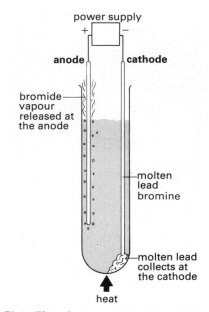

Fig. 4 Electrolysing molten lead bromide in the laboratory.

117

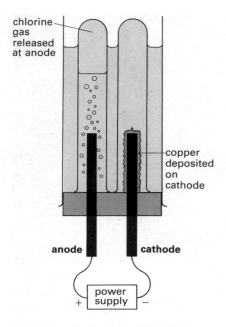

Fig. 1 Electrolysing copper chloride solution: chlorine collects at the anode and a coating of copper forms on the cathode.

Fig. 2 These metal plates have been electroplated in a plating bath. The metal used to electroplate them is hanging on the hooks.

Putting electrolysis to work – I

Electrolysis is used commercially in various ways, for instance:

☐ in the 'metal-finishing' trades for electroplating (see below) and anodising (see 5.3);

☐ for extracting reactive metals, such as sodium (see 4.8);

☐ in metal refining, e.g. for obtaining pure copper (see 4.10);

☐ in making chlorine and sodium hydroxide (see below and 7.10).

Electrolysing copper chloride solution

To decide how to use electrolysis you need to understand what happens at the electrodes. Copper chloride solution is an easy example:

> Electrolyte: copper chloride solution
> Ions present: copper ions, $Cu^{2+}(aq)$, chloride ions, $Cl^-(aq)$, and also the ions from water (see 4.10)
> Electrodes: carbon or platinum

☐ At the **anode** (+):
Chloride ions are attracted. They release their electrons, and chlorine is evolved.

$$2Cl^-(aq) \rightarrow Cl_2(g) + 2e$$

☐ At the **cathode** (−):
Copper ions are attracted, find a supply of electrons, and are converted into copper atoms:

$$Cu^{2+}(aq) + 2e \rightarrow Cu(s)$$

The overall process is:

$$CuCl_2(aq) \rightarrow Cu(s) + Cl_2(g)$$

Any object used as the cathode will become coated with a layer of copper. This is the principle of electroplating. To copper plate an object you must arrange for it to be the cathode in a solution containing copper ions. Copper sulphate solution is often used.

> **Q1** Copper chloride is not a suitable electrolyte for copper plating. Can you suggest why?

Making chlorine and sodium hydroxide by electrolysis

Chlorine is produced at the anode when sodium chloride solution (brine) is electrolysed. Sodium hydroxide is formed in the electrolyte, and hydrogen is released at the cathode. This is how chlorine, sodium hydroxide and 'hypochlorite bleach' are made. More details of the process can be found in 7.10.

> **Q2** What ions are present in a solution of sodium chloride? What would happen to these during electrolysis?

Fig. 3 These iron pram wheels have been electroplated to protect them and give a bright, attractive finish.

Electroplating

When electrolysis is used to put a layer, or 'plating', of one metal on the surface of another this is known as **electroplating**. Often the purpose of electroplating is to give a protective coating to the metal beneath, and at the same time to make a more attractive finish. **Chromium-plating** is one of the commonest types of electroplating. It is found on bath taps, car bumpers, electric kettles, towel rails, and many other household articles. Chromium does not corrode, it can be polished to give a bright attractive appearance, and it is a hard metal which resists scratches and wear.

Fig. 4 These silver-plated objects look like silver but cost less!

More precious items may be **silver-plated**. Electroplating on to a cheaper metal is used to save the full cost of a solid silver item. Silver-plated articles may be marked 'EPNS', which stands for 'electroplated nickel silver'. 'Nickel silver' is an alloy which contains copper, zinc and nickel – but no silver! It is often used as the base metal for silver-plated articles.

Electroplating is carried out in an electrolytic cell, usually known as a 'plating bath', which contains a suitable electrolyte. A solution of a chromium salt or a silver salt would be used for chromium-plating and silver-plating respectively. The article to be plated is made the cathode in the cell, so that metal ions move to it when the current is switched on. The reactions at the cathodes in the above processes are:

chromium plating: $Cr^{3+}(aq) + 3e \quad \rightarrow \quad Cr(s)$

silver plating: $Ag^+(aq) + e \quad \rightarrow \quad Ag(s)$

> **Q3** Write a set of instructions for someone who has been asked to chromium-plate the buckle for a belt. Include a labelled diagram.

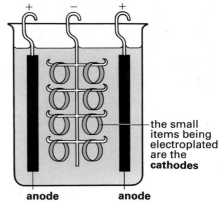

the small items being electroplated are the **cathodes**

anode　　　anode

Fig. 5 Small articles to be electroplated are usually placed in a plating bath like this.

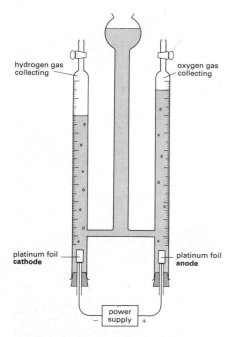

Fig. 1 *Hofmann's apparatus for electrolysing acidified water.*

Fig. 2 These slabs of impure copper will be used as anodes in the refining process shown in Fig. 3.

Putting electrolysis to work – II

Electrolysing 'water'

Pure water is a poor conductor of electricity. It contains $H^+(aq)$ and $OH^-(aq)$ ions, but very few are present. For electrolysing 'water' a special laboratory apparatus is sometimes used (Fig. 1). Some dilute sulphuric acid is added to increase the current flow.

> Electrolyte: dilute sulphuric acid (= 'acidified water')
> Ions present: hydrogen ions, $H^+(aq)$, hydroxyl ions, $OH^-(aq)$,
> sulphate ions,
> $SO_4^{2-}(aq)$
> Electrodes: platinum

☐ At the **anode** (+):
Sulphate ions and hydroxyl ions are attracted. Hydroxyl ions release their electrons more readily than sulphate ions, and oxygen is evolved.

$$4OH^-(aq) \rightarrow 2H_2O(l) + O_2(g) + 4e$$

☐ At the **cathode** (−):
Hydrogen ions are attracted, find a supply of electrons, and are converted into hydrogen molecules:

$$2H^+(aq) + 2e \rightarrow H_2(g)$$

Hydrogen collects in the cathode side of the apparatus, and oxygen in the anode side. When platinum electrodes are used the volumes of gas collected are always in the ratio 2 parts hydrogen to 1 part oxygen:

$$2H_2O(l) \rightarrow 2H_2(g) + O_2(g)$$

> **Q1** It is possible to make hydrogen commercially by electrolysing water. This is not the cheapest method, but it is used when specially pure hydrogen is needed. Design a simple 'plant' which would do this, and make a sketch of it.

Electrolysing copper sulphate solution between carbon or platinum electrodes

This electrolysis, often a laboratory demonstration, works as follows:

> Ions present: copper ions, $Cu^{2+}(aq)$, hydrogen ions, $H^+(aq)$,
> sulphate ions, $SO_4^{2-}(aq)$, and hydroxyl ions, $OH^-(aq)$

☐ At the **anode** (+):
Sulphate ions and hydroxyl ions are attracted. Hydroxyl ions release their electrons more readily than sulphate ions.

$$4OH^-(aq) \rightarrow 2H_2O(l) + O_2(g) + 4e$$

☐ At the **cathode** (−):
Copper ions are attracted, and are converted into copper atoms:

$$Cu^{2+}(aq) + 2e \rightarrow Cu(s)$$

Fig. 3 Copper-refining cells contain large numbers of anodes and cathodes connected together, so that large amounts of copper can be processed at the same time. These 'starting sheets' are cathodes, about to be lowered into place.

Copper refining by electrolysis

Copper must be very pure if it is to be used in electrical wiring. It is refined by electrolysis, using huge cells (Fig. 3). Slabs of impure copper are made the anodes, and thin sheets of already purified copper are used as cathodes. These cathodes are known as 'starting sheets'. The electrolyte is a solution containing copper ions.

☐ At the **anode** (+):
Copper atoms in the electrode release electrons and become ions.

$$Cu(s) \rightarrow Cu^{2+}(aq) + 2e$$

☐ At the **cathode** (−):
Copper ions from the electrolyte gain electrons to become atoms.

$$Cu^{2+}(aq) + 2e \rightarrow Cu(s)$$

The overall effect is to remove copper from the impure anodes and deposit it on the cathodes. The conditions are arranged so that impurities from the anodes are not carried to the cathodes, but settle as a sludge at the bottom of the cell. This material, called 'anode slimes', contains precious metals, such as gold, silver and platinum.

Copper slabs like the one in Fig. 2 are used as anodes in the refining process shown in Fig. 3. These anodes are already 99.5% copper, but the electrolysis builds up the pure copper 'starting sheets' into cathodes which are 99.99% pure. Copper as pure as this is suitable for making electric wire.

> **Q2** Solutions of copper chloride and copper sulphate are blue. This colour gradually disappears when the solutions are electrolysed, unless copper electrodes are used. Explain fully why this happens.

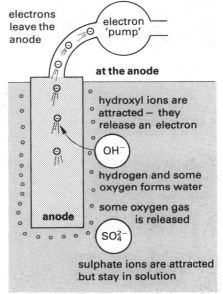

Fig. 4 Electrolysing copper sulphate solution – the anode.

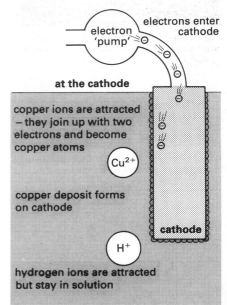

Fig. 5 Electrolysing copper sulphate solution – the cathode.

Energy changes during chemical reactions

Fig. 1 *The outer sections of these 'Hotcans' contain granules of calcium oxide and a plastic sachet of water. Puncturing the sachet releases the water and causes an exothermic reaction which heats the food in the can.*

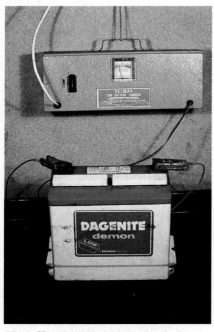

Fig. 2 *Charging a car battery: chemical reactions in the battery can store and release electrical energy.*

As you read this page you are converting some of the energy stored in your food into heat and movement. Some foods provide more energy than others, and this information often appears on food packaging. You would choose high-energy foods if you were doing hard physical work, and low-energy foods if you were slimming. The energy content of a food is measured in kilojoules per 100 grams (kJ/100 g).

Energy and foods

High-energy foods	kJ/100 g	Low-energy foods	kJ/100 g
most fats	>3000	most raw vegetables	<100
sweet biscuits	2000	most fresh fruit	<200
hard cheeses	1500	boiled rice	500
most pasta	1500	eggs	650
roast meat	>1000	most bread	<1000

(**Important note:** These are *approximate* figures only. Different ways of cooking and different amounts of sugar make a big difference.)

> **Q1** Daily requirements for teenage girls are about 10 000 kJ per day, and for teenage boys about 12 000 kJ per day. Work out roughly how many kJ you consumed (a) during your last cooked meal (b) in the food you have eaten between meals today.

Chemical reactions and heat energy

Quite often there is a noticeable change in temperature when a chemical reaction takes place. Many reactions get warm, and some – like burning and explosions – give out a great deal of heat. In a few cases, however, the temperature of the reacting mixture falls. To understand this you need to remember that chemical bonds are broken and new bonds are made during a chemical reaction. (More details are given in 1.9.)

- ☐ Energy is *required* (taken *in*) for *breaking* chemical bonds.
- ☐ Energy is *released* (given *out*) in *forming* chemical bonds.

The temperature change you notice as the reaction takes place depends on the balance of these two processes.

- ☐ An **exothermic** reaction is one in which heat energy is *given out*.
  (You notice a *temperature rise* because more energy comes from forming new bonds than is used up in breaking the old ones.)
- ☐ An **endothermic** reaction is one in which heat energy is *taken in*.
  (You notice a *temperature drop* because more energy is needed to break the old bonds than comes from forming new ones.)

The energy change taking place during a chemical reaction is measured in **joules**. This is the same unit as the one used for giving the energy value of a food. One joule is a very small amount of energy, so energy changes are usually measured in **kilojoules**. One kilojoule (1 kJ) is 1000 joules. The amount of energy needed to boil enough water for just one cup of tea is about 100 kJ. To cook a slice of toast you would use another 200 kJ. The chemical reaction used to heat the 'Hotcans' shown in Fig. 1 gives out 1.1 kJ for every gram of calcium oxide used.

Fig. 3 *High-energy foods provide the energy for hard physical work like this.*

Measuring the heat change during a chemical reaction

A chemical reaction occurs when the substances which react together (the reactants) are converted to the products. The heat change during the reaction is the difference between the amount of heat energy in the products (let's call it H_p) and the amount of heat energy originally in the reactants (H_r).

$$H_p - H_r = \Delta H \qquad \text{(This heat change is called 'delta H'.)}$$

☐ For an *exothermic* reaction H_p is less than H_r, and ΔH is *negative*.
☐ For an *endothermic* reaction H_p is greater than H_r, and ΔH is *positive*.

Chemical reactions and other forms of energy

The energy released when new chemical bonds are formed often appears as heat, but not always. After all, while chemical bonds are being formed and broken, electrons are moving from place to place. This produces an electric current (Fig. 2). In this **electrochemical cell** the energy change appears in the form of electricity.

Heat is often the form of energy taken in when chemical bonds are broken, but again, not always. This question includes some examples:

> **Q2** Write down the forms of energy (other than heat) which are released or must be supplied when the following processes take place: (a) magnesium ribbon is burned; (b) an article is silver-plated; (c) a mixture of petrol vapour and air is ignited in a car cylinder; (d) a photograph is taken; (e) a gun is fired; (f) the chemicals in a torch battery react together; (g) hydrogen atoms fuse together to make helium in the sun; (h) a car battery is charged.

Fig. 4 *Light energy from the sun and from flashguns like these is needed for the chemical reactions which occur when you take a photograph.*

Questions

** **1.** Draw an outline diagram showing how the Periodic Table is arranged. Label (a) Group I, (b) the first Period, (c) the region of the Table where you would find the non-metals.

** **2.** Draw an outline diagram of the Periodic Table, showing where you would find the following elements: the Alkali Metals; the Halogens; the Transition Metals; the Noble Gases.

* **3.** Describe *three* ways in which you could distinguish a metal from a non-metal.

** **4.** Many of the oxides of non-metals can be dissolved in water to make a solution. What colour changes might you expect to see if you added universal indicator to one of these solutions? Explain your answers.

** **5.** Make a list showing *five* metals in their Reactivity Series order. For each metal, give one piece of evidence which justifies its place in your list.

** **6.** Describe and explain what you would see when the following metals are placed in cold water: sodium; calcium; magnesium; zinc.

** **7.** Zinc is above copper in the Reactivity Series. Describe and explain one way for demonstrating that this is true.

** **8.** Explain, with examples to show what you mean, the terms *oxidation* and *oxidising agent*.

*** **9.** The compound with the formula $FeCl_2$ is known as iron(II) chloride.
(a) Explain why it is given this name.
(b) This compound can be converted to $FeCl_3$ by reaction with chlorine gas. Write ionic half equations for this process and name the new substance formed.

** **10.** Draw a diagram which shows the meanings of the following terms used in electrolysis: electrode; anode; cathode; electrolyte.

** **11.** Explain what is meant by an electrical *insulator*. What substances could be used for making this type of insulator?

** **12.** What new substances are formed when the following substances are melted, and then electrolysed: sodium chloride; lead bromide? Describe what you would expect to see in each case.

*** **13.** Write ionic equations for the processes taking place at the electrodes when molten sodium chloride and molten lead bromide are electrolysed.

** **14.** Explain how electrolysis is used (a) to make chlorine, (b) in electroplating, (c) in refining copper.

* **15.** Many water taps are *chromium-plated*. What does this mean, and how is chromium-plating carried out?

** **16.** What gases are released when acidified water is electrolysed? Describe what you would see during this process.

* **17.** (a) What is a *high-energy food*?
(b) Give one example of a high-energy food, and say when you would choose it.

** **18.** Explain the meaning of the terms *exothermic* and *endothermic*, and give examples to illustrate your answer.

** **19.** Look at the Periodic Table 4.2 (Fig. 3) and suggest *two* elements, other than silicon, which might be 'borderline cases' between metals and non-metals. Give reasons to support your suggestions.

** **20.** The metal, M, forms a chloride with the formula MCl_2.
(a) In which Group of the Periodic Table would you find the metal M?
(b) What would be the formula of the oxide of M?
(c) M reacts with water, forming a hydroxide. Write an equation for this reaction, and name the gas which is given off.
(d) What would you expect to see when Universal Indicator paper is dipped into the solution left at the end of reaction (c)?

*** **21.** The element, X, is in Group V of the Periodic Table.
   (a) It forms two different chlorides and two different oxides. Suggest likely formulae for these compounds.
   (b) Both oxides react with water to form acid solutions. What does this tell you about element X.

* **22.** The element caesium, symbol Cs, is in Group I of the Periodic Table.
   (a) Say whether caesium is a metal or a non-metal, and explain your answer.
   (b) The symbol for chlorine is Cl. Its valency is 1. Write the formula for caesium chloride.
   (c) Would you expect the reaction between caesium and chlorine to be vigorous or rather slow? Explain your answer.

* **23.** The element indium, symbol In, is in Group III of the Periodic Table. It is a good conductor of heat and electricity.
   (a) What would you expect a piece of indium to look like? Explain your answer.
   (b) Describe an experiment you could do to check whether indium is a metal or a non-metal.

** **24.** The element germanium, symbol Ge, forms an oxide GeO_2. It is a hard but brittle solid, and an electrical 'semi-conductor'. Explain, giving your reasons,
   (a) where in the Periodic Table you would expect to find this element; and
   (b) whether you would describe germanium as a metal or a non-metal.

* **25.** You have been given a previously unknown element to study. It is a metal, and it reacts rapidly with water.
   (a) Where would you place this metal in the Reactivity Series?
   (b) What would you expect to see if a freshly cut piece of this metal was left in the atmosphere?
   (c) How would you store this metal to keep it safely for a few months?
   (d) Why do you think this metal was unknown to people living 200 years ago?

** **26.** The element nickel, Ni, is a Transition Metal. When nickel is placed in a solution of copper sulphate it becomes coated with copper. If zinc is placed in nickel sulphate solution it becomes coated with nickel.
   (a) What would you expect to see when a piece of zinc is placed in copper sulphate solution?
   (b) List the three metals copper, zinc and nickel in their Reactivity Series order, with the most reactive first.
   (c) Describe and explain what you would expect to see when a mixture of powdered nickel and copper oxide is heated.
   (d) Nickel oxide and copper oxide can be reduced by heating them with carbon. Write word equations for these processes.

** **27.** Explain which substance has been oxidised and which reduced in the following reactions:
   (a) lead oxide + carbon → lead + carbon dioxide
   (b) hydrogen + copper oxide → copper + steam
   (c) sodium + oxygen → sodium oxide
   (d) hydrogen chloride + zinc → zinc chloride + hydrogen

*** **28.** Write formulae equations and, where possible, ionic equations for the reactions (a) to (d) in Q27.

*** **29.** Suggest oxidation numbers for (a) the calcium ion in Plaster of Paris (calcium sulphate); (b) the iron atom in a cast iron drain cover; (c) the oxide ion in magnesium oxide; (d) the neon atoms in a fluorescent tube.

*** **30.** The full name for the compound $FeCl_3$ is iron(III) chloride. Give full names, including the oxidation number, to the following compounds: CuO; Cu_2O; $FeCl_2$; Fe_2O_3; PbO_2; $HgCl_2$.

*** **31.** Explain fully why (a) an ionic substance conducts electricity when it is molten, but not when it is solid; (b) an ionic substance will conduct electricity when dissolved in a suitable solvent.

*** **32.** 'Galvanised iron' is used for making dustbins, wheelbarrows and corrugated roofing sheets. It is iron which has been coated with zinc. Draw a diagram to show how this material could be made by electroplating.

** **33.** Draw a labelled diagram which shows what happens when an electric current is passed through molten potassium chloride, an ionic substance.

** **34.** Peanuts are high-energy foods. They contain 50% fat. If you burn a peanut you can measure its energy content.
(a) Draw a suitable arrangement for doing this.
(b) List the measurements you would make.
(c) Suggest why the result would probably be less than the correct value, which is about 2600 kJ per 100g.

C. Can you use this information?

** **35.** *Datapage F* gives a list of elements in order of their reactivity. How, if at all, would you expect the metal barium to react with (a) sodium oxide; (b) zinc oxide; (c) copper oxide; (d) sodium sulphate solution (think carefully about this one!).

** **36.** Use *Datapage F* to suggest *four* different experiments which would fix the position of the metal magnesium between its neighbours in the Reactivity Series.

** **37.** When a muslin bag containing mercury is hung in a solution of silver nitrate, spiky crystals gradually appear on the outside of the bag. Use *Datapage F* to suggest what may be happening here, and write an equation.

** **38.** *Datapage R3* gives some information about elements which may be extracted commercially by electrolysis.
(a) Why are the temperatures needed to make aluminium and sodium so high?
(b) Suggest why materials like graphite, titanium and lead are chosen for the anodes in these processes.
(c) Electrolysis is not the principal method for making zinc or copper. Suggest when this process might be used.

** **39.** Manufacturers of silicon compounds refer to this element as 'silicon *metal*', although chemists would argue that this is not correct. Look again at 4.2 and suggest some reasons in favour of calling silicon a metal.

* **40.** Draw a simple Periodic Table, using the information in 4.1. Include the elements sodium, calcium, chlorine, helium, carbon, aluminium, nitrogen, oxygen, sulphur and neon.

D. Taking it further

*** **41.** It has recently been reported that the noble gas radon will react with the compound bromine trifluoride, and produce ions with the formula Rn^{2+}. What conclusions would you draw from this discovery?

*** **42.** Arsenic is listed in *Datapage C* as a 'semi-metal'. What information there suggests this description, and what other facts would you need to confirm this conclusion.

*** **43.** Some information about a chemical test for nitrates is given in 7.5. Read about it, and explain why this is described as a reduction reaction.

Quick questions

1. Read about element 104 (in 4.1) and suggest a suitable name for element 105.

2. Which elements would you expect to be (a) the most reactive metal; (b) the most reactive non-metal in the Periodic Table?

3. There is a reaction when magnesium metal and sand (silicon oxide) are heated together, but not if the metal chosen instead is iron. What does this tell you about the reactivity of silicon?

4. What two substances must be present for iron to rust?

5. Lithium is an alkali metal. How do you think it could be made from lithium chloride?

Group

Period	I	II
1		
2	Li 3	Be 4
3	Na 11	Mg 12
4	K 19	Ca 20
5	Rb 37	Sr 38
6	Cs 55	Ba 56
7	Fr 87	Ra 88

↑

the alkali metals

Fig. 1 The Alkali Metals are in Group I of the Periodic Table.

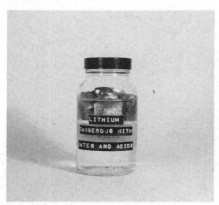

Fig. 2 The alkali metals must be kept free of both air and moisture during storage. Small quantities are usually stored in bottles containing enough mineral oil to cover the metal completely.

5.1

The alkali metals:
lithium, sodium, potassium

All the metals in Group I of the Periodic Table (Fig. 1) react with water to form alkalis. For this reason they are called the **alkali metals**.

What are the alkali metals like?

☐ All the alkali metals are quite soft. All except lithium can be easily cut with a knife.

☐ They have low melting points (for example sodium melts at 98°C), and they are less dense than most other metals.

☐ When freshly cut they are a silver colour, but the surfaces quickly tarnish in air.

☐ They conduct heat and electricity well.

☐ All the alkali metals give vivid flame colours (see *Datapage N*).

Chemically, the alkali metals are very reactive.

☐ All the alkali metals tarnish in **air** because they react rapidly with oxygen, forming a surface layer of the metal oxide. For instance:

sodium + oxygen → sodium oxide

$$4Na(s) + O_2(g) → 2Na_2O(s)$$

☐ The alkali metals react vigorously with **water**, forming an alkaline solution of the hydroxide. Hydrogen is given off. For instance,

potassium + water (or ice) → potassium hydroxide + hydrogen

$$2K(s) + 2H_2O(g, l \text{ or } s) → 2KOH(aq) + H_2(g)$$

☐ The reactions between **acids** and the alkali metals are too violent to be carried out without special equipment. Hydrogen is evolved very vigorously and the usual salts are formed.

The alkali metal atoms have one electron in the outer shell. They form cations with a single positive charge (for example the sodium ion, Na^+). This means that, in forming compounds, all alkali metals show a valency of 1.

How reactive are the alkali metals?

Lithium is the least reactive of the alkali metals. It reacts briskly with water, giving a steady stream of bubbles. In air it tarnishes quite slowly. Potassium is so reactive that it tarnishes in air within seconds of a freshly cut surface being exposed. Sodium is more reactive than lithium, but less reactive than potassium. The reactivity of the alkali metals increases in the order Li<Na<K.

Q1 Suggest a method for finding out what happens if lithium is allowed to react with ice. What would you expect to see?

128

Fig. 3 Small amounts of sodium are used in the powerful yellow lamps used for street lighting.

How are the alkali metals used?

Lithium is only known to most people from the 'lithium batteries' used in watches and cameras. Lithium metal is used in a few special alloys, but the main use of lithium is in compounds for lubricating greases, enamels and glass.

Small, but important amounts of **sodium** are used in the powerful yellow lamps employed for street lighting. The main uses for sodium metal are in the manufacture of 'anti-knock' compounds for petrol, and in the production of titanium. In some nuclear power stations, liquid sodium is circulated through the reactor to transfer the heat energy to the boilers.

Sodium compounds are of great importance, and sodium chloride is the source of nearly all of these. Sodium hydroxide, often known as 'caustic soda', is used in some domestic floor and oven cleaners, because it helps to remove grease. It must be used and stored very carefully. Its large-scale uses include the purification of bauxite for aluminium manufacture, and the making of soap, rayon, paper and bleaches (7.10).

> **Q2** Use the index and *Datapage E2* to make short notes on other sodium compounds.

Fig. 4 Making salt (sodium chloride) the old way. Salt crystals were obtained by evaporating brine in open pans like these, photographed in Stafford in the 1890s.

Potassium is not a commercially important metal, but its compounds are widely used in agriculture. Potassium chloride (known to the trade as 'chloride of potash') is added to many fertilisers as a source of potassium. Potash is mined off the north-east coast of England.

Calcium and its compounds

Fig. 1 A steady stream of hydrogen bubbles is produced when calcium metal is put into water. The indicator has changed colour around it. Why?

Fig. 2 This quarry in Portland, Dorset, produces limestone – a form of calcium carbonate.

Fig. 3 Lime is made by heating limestone to a high temperature in rotating kilns like this.

☐ Calcium is a fairly hard, brittle metal. It corrodes in moist air, forming a white crust of calcium oxide and calcium hydroxide:

$$2Ca(s) + O_2(g) \rightarrow 2CaO(s)$$

followed by

$$CaO(s) + H_2O(g) \rightarrow Ca(OH)_2(s)$$

☐ Calcium also reacts rapidly with water, giving off hydrogen:

$$Ca(s) + 2H_2O(l) \rightarrow Ca(OH)_2(s) + H_2(g)$$

The solution quickly becomes cloudy because calcium hydroxide is not very soluble in water.

☐ Calcium compounds give a brick red 'flame test' (see *Datapage N*).

Lime water

A solution of calcium hydroxide in water is known as 'lime water'. This is usually made by keeping a bottle of purified water with a layer of calcium hydroxide at the bottom. This saturated solution is used in the well-known test for carbon dioxide. Details of the lime water test are given in 3.5.

What is the difference between lime and limestone?

Limestone and chalk are forms of calcium carbonate, $CaCO_3$. So, too, is marble – formed when these rocks are under great pressure. When strongly heated, calcium carbonate breaks down:

$$CaCO_3(s) \xrightarrow{\text{heat}} CaO(s) + CO_2(g)$$

Calcium oxide, CaO, is popularly known as 'quicklime'. When treated with water it turns into calcium hydroxide, 'slaked lime':

$$CaO(s) + H_2O(l) \rightarrow Ca(OH)_2(s + aq)$$

Quicklime takes its name from an old English word meaning 'living', because a lump of it appears to swell up and writhe about when water is added. This happens because the reaction gives out enough heat to turn some of the water to steam, and this forces the quicklime to split apart. Ordinary garden lime is slaked lime. The word 'slake' is another word from the past. It means 'satisfy a thirst'.

Q1 Use a reference book to find out what the expression 'being in the limelight' has to do with quicklime. Then try heating a small piece of lime in a Bunsen flame as strongly as possible.

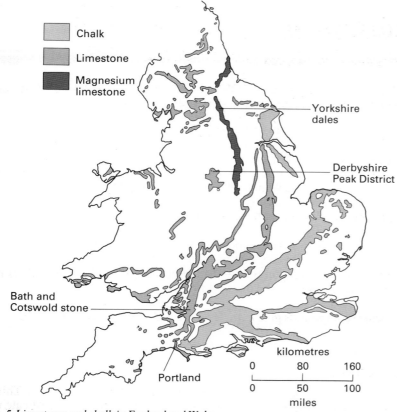

Chalk
Limestone
Magnesium limestone

Yorkshire dales

Derbyshire Peak District

Bath and Cotswold stone

Portland

kilometres
0   80   160
0   50   100
miles

Fig. 5 *Limestones and chalk in England and Wales.*

Fig. 4 *Many of these buildings in the centre of Cardiff are faced with Portland limestone.*

How are lime and limestone used?

Limestone has been widely used as a building stone. The main British limestones are found in the places shown in Fig. 5. St Paul's Cathedral was built of Portland stone, and the centre of Cardiff (Fig. 4) has many buildings faced with this fine-quality limestone. Other famous limestones used for buildings, often in parts of the country where they are quarried, include Bath stone, Cotswold stone and the carboniferous limestones of the Derbyshire Peak District and the Yorkshire Dales.

Large amounts of limestone are quarried in Britain – about 80 million tonnes in a typical year. Figure 2 shows a large limestone quarry in Dorset. Some limestone is used as a building stone, but a great deal is converted to quicklime for use in three main ways:

☐ iron and steel manufacture
☐ making cement
☐ making glass

Liming the soil

Garden lime, which is used to correct the pH of acid soils, is calcium hydroxide. It is made from the quicklime obtained by heating limestone in a kiln (Fig. 6). Slaked lime and limestone are both used as agricultural lime. Powdered limestone is most often used, because it is cheaper than any form of lime which has been heated.

> **Q2** An article in your local newspaper reveals plans to extend a nearby limestone quarry. Write a letter to the paper, *either* supporting the plan by explaining the main uses of limestone, *or* opposing the plan on whatever reasonable grounds you wish.

Fig. 6 *In many country areas of Britain you can still see the remains of old lime kilns. Farmers made their own lime from local supplies of chalk or limestone. This recent picture, taken in Crete, shows how the work was done.*

131

Aluminium

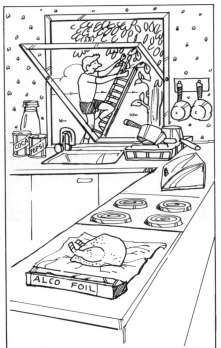

Fig. 1 How many aluminium articles can you spot?

Fig. 2 These compact discs are just about to be coated with aluminium.

Fig. 3 Aluminium is both light and a conductor. Thousands of miles of aluminium cable carry high voltage electricity around the UK.

Aluminium is the most abundant metal in the earth's crust (see *Datapage 11*). Most of it, unfortunately, is locked up in clays and rocks from which it is very difficult to extract. The only important aluminium ore is **bauxite**, an impure form of aluminium oxide, Al_2O_3.

Bauxite is mined in Australia, and also in Guinea, Jamaica, Brazil and Yugoslavia. These countries are not major producers of aluminium *metal*, however. Forty per cent of the world's aluminium is produced in the USA and Canada – countries which have very little bauxite. In Europe the major aluminium producers are West Germany and Norway, using entirely imported ore. Britain has large aluminium smelters at Holyhead in Anglesey, and at Lynemouth in Northumberland.

Britain is one of many aluminium-producing countries which has to import all of its bauxite. Extracting aluminium uses so much electricity that it is often cheaper to bring the ore to the electrical supply than to generate electricity close to where the ore is mined.

How is aluminium used?

☐ Much aluminium is used in the form of alloys, containing one or more other metals. It is found in the home as cooking foil, drinks cans, saucepans, stepladders, and many replacement window frames.

☐ The aircraft industry makes great use of aluminium alloys, which combine lightness with strength. Aluminium is used in overhead power cables because it is light and conducts electricity well.

☐ A thin aluminium deposit forms a reflective layer for mirrors and car headlights. Milk bottle tops contain about 0.1 g of aluminium.

Q1 Collect suitable pictures and make a chart: 'Using aluminium'.

What is the chemical nature of aluminium?

Aluminium is a much more reactive metal than you might think. It reacts readily with oxygen to form a tough oxide coating, which protects it from many of the reactions which would be expected. Once that coating is removed, aluminium becomes a very reactive metal.

Although aluminium does not appear to be affected by air or water, it does react with both acids and alkalis. Acids will slowly dissolve aluminium, producing aluminium salts and hydrogen. Strong alkalis will also react. Sodium hydroxide, for example, dissolves aluminium to form sodium aluminate and hydrogen. Fruit juices are often acidic, so jam is not normally made in aluminium containers. Alkaline cleaning materials should not be used for aluminium saucepans.

What is anodised aluminium?

The surface coating of oxide on aluminium can be made thicker by an electrolytic process called **anodising**. The aluminium is made the anode in an electrolyte bath containing dilute sulphuric acid. As the current is passed, oxygen is evolved at the anode. This combines with the aluminium, forming more aluminium oxide on its surface, so giving greater *protection*. Dyes can be mixed with the electrolyte so that the new layer is also colourful and *decorative*. The anodising process is used to make coloured aluminium kitchenware, like kettle and saucepan lids.

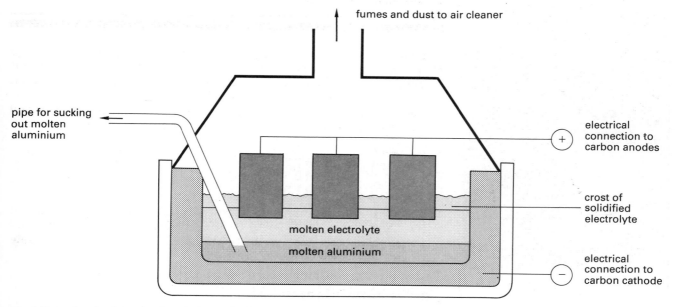

Fig. 4 *Extracting aluminium by electrolysing molten bauxite.*

How is aluminium extracted from its ore?

Aluminium is a reactive metal, so it must be obtained from its ore by electrolysis. The bauxite ore is first treated to produce pure aluminium oxide. This is dissolved in molten cryolite (another aluminium compound, with the formula Na_3AlF_6) and electrolysed between carbon electrodes. A carbon lining to the electrolyte bath acts as the cathode, and the molten aluminium is often removed by sucking it out from the bottom of the container (Fig. 4). The overall process is:

$$2Al_2O_3(l) \rightarrow 4Al(l) + 3O_2(g)$$

and the electrode processes may be represented:

$$\text{Cathode}\ (-) \quad 4Al^{3+} + 12e \rightarrow 4Al(l)$$
$$\text{Anode}\ (+) \quad\quad 6O^{2-} \rightarrow 3O_2(g) + 12e$$

The operating temperature is nearly 1000°C, so the carbon anodes burn away in the oxygen, forming carbon dioxide.

Q2 Summarise the process for extracting aluminium as a flow-chart.

An aluminium-air battery

Researchers in Canada have recently developed a battery that runs merely on water, air and sheets of aluminium! Electricity comes from a chemical reaction which gradually turns these materials into aluminium hydroxide. Every so often you have to top up the electrolyte (an alkaline solution of salt), and add another sheet of aluminium. In theory, that is all. The success of the battery will depend on trials planned for the next few years, and on the eventual cost of aluminium when compared with other materials used in batteries.

Fig. 5 *In an aluminium smelter there are large numbers of cells, like the one shown in Fig. 4, connected together.*

133

Making iron

Iron and its alloys, which are called 'steels', are metals of enormous importance. Even during the industrial recession of the 1980s, the EEC countries produced more than 100 million tonnes of steel per year. The UK contributed about 15 million tonnes of this, mainly from large steelworks in Scotland and South Wales. To make 1 tonne of iron, about 4.5 tonnes of raw materials are needed:

- ☐ iron ore (about 1.7 t)
- ☐ limestone (about 0.25 t)
- ☐ coke (about 0.5 t)
- ☐ hot air (about 2.0 t)

Q1 From these figures, estimate the amounts of iron ore and coke used in the UK in a typical year.

Two of these raw materials, coke and iron ore, are shown in Figs. 1 and 2. The coke is made by heating coal in airtight ovens, so that all the gas and tar is driven out, leaving spongy lumps of unburned carbon. Iron ore and limestone are quarried from the ground, and crushed to a fine powder before use. Nearly all the iron ore used in Britain is now imported, but the limestone is usually available from nearly quarries.

Iron ore

Most iron ore used in the UK is imported from countries such as Australia, Brazil, Canada and Sweden, and about a quarter of a million tonnes of ore is mined each year in the UK.

The preferred ore is the form of iron oxide known as haematite, Fe_2O_3, which contains 70% iron. In practice, a number of ores from different sources are blended together to produce a material of uniform composition.

How is iron made?

Iron is made in a **blast furnace** (Fig. 3). The process works like this. Suitable amounts of iron ore and coke are mixed together and pre-heated, forming a biscuity material called 'sinter'. This is mixed with limestone and put into a blast furnace. Hot air is blown in and the following reactions take place.

(1) The limestone decomposes at the temperature of the furnace:

$$CaCO_3(s) \rightarrow CaO(s) + CO_2(g)$$

(2) Some of the coke burns in the hot air, forming carbon dioxide:

$$C(s) + O_2(g) \rightarrow CO_2(g)$$

(3) Carbon dioxide reacts with hot coke, forming carbon monoxide:

$$CO_2(g) + C(s) \rightarrow 2CO(g)$$

(4) Carbon monoxide reduces the iron ore to iron:

$$3CO(g) + Fe_2O_3(s) \rightarrow 2Fe(l) + 3CO_2(g)$$

Liquid iron flows to the bottom of the furnace, and can then be run off.

Fig. 1 Raw materials for iron-making: iron ore is dug out of the ground.

Fig. 2 Raw materials for iron-making: a stock pile of coke.

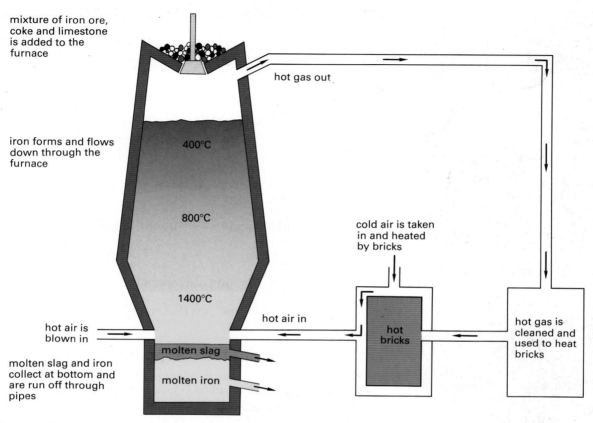

mixture of iron ore, coke and limestone is added to the furnace

hot gas out

iron forms and flows down through the furnace

400°C

800°C

cold air is taken in and heated by bricks

1400°C

hot air in

hot air is blown in

hot gas is cleaned and used to heat bricks

molten slag

hot bricks

molten slag and iron collect at bottom and are run off through pipes

molten iron

Fig. 3 *Iron is made in a blast furnace by passing hot air through a mixture of iron ore, coke and limestone.*

(5) The limestone has a further function. It reacts with acidic impurities in the iron ore, such as sand. A material known as 'slag' is formed:

$$\text{calcium oxide} + \text{silicon oxide} \rightarrow \text{calcium silicate}$$

$$\underset{\text{(heated limestone)}}{CaO(s)} + \underset{\text{(sand)}}{SiO_2(s)} \rightarrow \underset{\text{(slag)}}{CaSiO_3(l)}$$

Slag is also liquid at the temperature of the furnace. It floats on top of the molten iron, and runs off first when the furnace is 'tapped'. Blast furnace slag is sold for road-making.

> **Q2** Copy the diagram of the blast furnace, and label it with word or formula equations to show what goes on inside.
>
> **Q3** The coke used in a blast furnace acts as the *reducing agent*. (For more information see 4.5 and 4.6). Explain fully what this statement means.

How is iron used?

The iron which comes from a blast furnace is not normally used directly. Although some is made into iron castings, most is turned into the different forms of **steel**. (Details are given in 5.6). Large quantities of steel are used to make cars, bridges, buildings and oil platforms.

Fig. 4 *Tapping molten iron from a blast furnace.*

Fig. 1 This iron pillar in Delhi, India, is believed to be around 1500 years old.

Iron and its compounds

Iron was one of the earliest metals used by people. It is a relatively cheap, strong metal and huge amounts of it are now made every year. Its main disadvantage is that it rusts!

What is the chemical nature of iron?

Iron is element number 26, and it is one of the transition metals. (There is more about transition metals in 5.7.) Like most other metals it is shiny and hard, and it conducts heat and electricity well.

Iron is a fairly reactive metal. It reacts with acids, forming a salt and hydrogen. For instance:

iron + hydrochloric acid $\rightarrow$ iron(II) chloride + hydrogen

$$Fe(s) + 2HCl(aq) \rightarrow FeCl_2(aq) + H_2(g)$$

Like other transition metals, iron can form more than one kind of ion. The iron(II) ion [$Fe^{2+}(aq)$], once called the 'ferrous' ion, is pale green in solution. The iron(III), or 'ferric', ion [$Fe^{3+}(aq)$] is brown.

What is known about the compounds of iron?

One of the best known of all the iron compounds is 'haemoglobin', which is responsible for the red colour of blood. A healthy diet must include foods rich in iron compounds, such as red meat, liver or prunes. Nursing mothers and other people who need extra iron are given 'iron tablets' containing iron sulphate.

A simple laboratory **test for iron** uses sodium hydroxide solution. When this is added to a solution containing iron ions, the possible reactions are:

$$Fe^{2+}(aq) + 2OH^-(aq) \rightarrow Fe(OH)_2(s) \text{ [iron(II) hydroxide: grey-green]}$$

or

$$Fe^{3+}(aq) + 3OH^-(aq) \rightarrow Fe(OH)_3(s) \text{ [iron(III) hydroxide: rusty brown]}$$

Fig. 2 A healthy diet must include iron compounds. Nursing mothers need extra iron, which they get from 'iron tablets'.

Q1 There are two ways of distinguishing between iron(II) compounds and iron(III) compounds in solution. Write instructions to a friend who has this task, explaining exactly what to do.

Q2 How, and under what conditions, would you expect iron to react with (a) dilute sulphuric acid, (b) copper sulphate solution, (c) sulphur? Explain each answer as fully as you can.

Here is a summary of some important chemical reactions of iron:

Reaction with	Conditions	What is seen	Name of product
air	moisture present present	rusting	'hydrated iron oxide
water	as steam at high temperature	iron reacts	iron(III) oxide and hydrogen
oxygen	high temperature	iron burns	iron(III) oxide
sulphur	heat mixture	glows	iron sulphide
chlorine	heat metal	glows	iron(III) chloride

Fig. 3 *This tin of roast veal dates from 1824. The label reads, "This cannister was taken by Capt. Parry to the Arctic Regions in the year 1825 and brought back by him to England on his return. It accompanied him on his second voyage to that region and a second time brought back to England when it was presented by him to Mr. Nutland of the Admiralty and on the 23rd of October 1850 presented by Mr. Nutland to Mr. Stramers. The can was opened in the 1930's, when the meat was said to have been in 'perfect' condition. At the same time it was established that the can was made from tinplate (iron plated with tin) made in S. Wales using Cornish tin."*

Why does iron rust?

Simple experiments show that both air and water are needed for rust to form on a piece of iron. Rusting is a complicated process which takes place in several stages.

Iron is oxidised by moist air:

$$2Fe(s) + O_2(g) + 2H_2O(l) \rightarrow 2Fe(OH)_2(s)$$

The resulting iron hydroxide is further affected in a similar way:

$$4Fe(OH)_2(s) + air + water \rightarrow 2Fe_2O_3.xH_2O(s)$$

The amount of water in the rust, shown here as '$x\,H_2O$', is variable.

How can rusting be prevented?

If the surface of iron or steel is to be protected from rusting it must be coated with something which keeps out both air and water. The type of coating used depends on

☐ how severe the rust problem is likely to be
☐ what the protected surface must look like
☐ how much you are prepared to spend
☐ how long you want the protection to last.

Around a typical house and garden you would find iron and steel articles protected from rusting in various ways. Beyond the *painted* iron railings you might see a *galvanised* dustbin containing some *tin-plated* food cans. Parked outside is a car with a *bitumen-coated* underbody, *chromium-plated* bumpers and some well-*greased* moving parts. The wire mesh fence is *plastic-coated*. In the kitchen there are some *stove-enamelled* items, like the cooker and the fridge, and a *stainless steel* sink unit.

Fig. 4 *Zinc alloy bars like this are used to prevent oil rigs and pipelines from rusting. They are called 'sacrificial anodes'. Can you find out how they work?*

Iron and steel

Fig. 1 The world's first cast iron bridge still stands at Ironbridge, Shropshire. It was built in 1779.

The technology of iron-making was developed in China and in India many centuries before the first blast furnaces were built in Europe. Charcoal was the form of carbon first used for reducing the iron ore. Coke was first used by Abraham Darby in 1709. Large-scale production developed in the UK during the 19th century, thanks to the use of steam-engines to deliver a powerful 'blast' of pre-heated air. The next step was the introduction of a large-scale method for making steel, by Sir Henry Bessemer in 1859. A steelworks today has several blast furnaces and operates continuously, day and night.

Cast iron is blast-furnace iron with a small number of additives, chosen to suit the way in which the cast iron will be used. To make a casting the molten iron is poured into a box containing sand moulded into the shape of the article required. Many gratings, drain covers, and cylinder blocks for car engines are made from cast iron. Cast iron is a strong but brittle material, and contains about 4% of carbon.

Wrought iron is made from blast-furnace iron by removing as much carbon as possible. It is easy to shape and bend, so it is often used for iron railings, chains and gates. The traditional process for making wrought iron has now all but disappeared, since it required arduous manual work of great skill. Much of the material now sold as 'wrought iron' is actually soft steel strip.

> **Q1** The iron bridge at Ironbridge, Shropshire (1779) contains nearly 400 tonnes of cast iron. The Eiffel Tower (1889) is built from over 7000 tonnes of wrought iron. Why do you think these materials were chosen, and why would we choose differently today?
>
> **Q2** After reading the rest of this section, collect pictures to make a chart with the title 'Making and using steel'.

Fig. 2 These engine blocks for cars are made from cast iron.

What is the difference between iron and steel?

Iron is an element, but the different types of steel are alloys which contain a high proportion of iron. (There is more about alloys in 5.10.) The best known steels are **mild steel** and **stainless steel**. Mild steel is an alloy of iron and a small amount of carbon which is used to make things like steel girders and motor car bodies. Stainless steel is an alloy of iron, chromium and nickel, usually in the proportion 74:18:8. Here is some more information about the different types of steel.

Fig. 3 Wrought iron was used to make these gates at Hampton Court Palace because it can easily be bent into decorative shapes.

Some types of steel

Type	Typical composition	Likely uses
(i) Carbon steels		
low carbon	< 0.3% carbon	rivets, car bodies
medium carbon	0.3–0.8% carbon	springs, railway lines
high carbon	0.8–1.5% carbon	knives, razor blades
(ii) Alloy steels		
chromium steel	up to 5% Cr	ball bearings
cobalt steel	up to 10% Co	magnets
molybdenum steel	up to 4% Mo	gun barrels
stainless steel	often 18% Cr, 8% Ni	sinks, cutlery
tungsten steel	up to 18% W	tools, armour plate
vanadium steel	up to 2% V	spanners, tools

Fig. 4 This hot rolling mill makes girders from mild steel – a strong alloy of iron and carbon.

How are steels made?

There are two stages in the production of steel from iron:

☐ removal of impurities from the iron
☐ addition of alloying elements.

Much steel is now made using the **basic oxygen method** (Figs. 5 and 6). The impurities are 'burned out' of the molten iron by a blast of oxygen, which is directed into the metal through a water-cooled pipe. After a suitable interval, samples are taken for analysis and then the alloying elements are added. A converter of this type can make a 400 tonne batch of steel in less than an hour.

Some of the special alloy steels are made in an **electric arc furnace**. The raw material for this type of furnace is mainly scrap iron, which does not contain the impurities from the blast furnace. Oxygen is therefore not used. An electric arc furnace can deal with anything from cans to car bodies, and plays an important part in the re-cycling of materials which would otherwise be wasted.

Shaping steel

Newly made steel leaves the furnace as a liquid, at a temperature above 1500°C. In some steelworks it is poured into moulds, where it solidifies as rectangular blocks, called **ingots**. The alternative is to keep the steel molten until it is ready for casting into shape.

Ingots of steel are shaped by passing them backwards and forwards between pairs of heavy rollers. When this process starts the steel ingots are still red hot, and this is why the machinery shown in Fig. 4 is called a '**hot rolling**' mill. Molten steel is shaped by squeezing it through a mould so that it comes out almost like toothpaste from a tube. This process is called **continuous casting**, and it is much less expensive than traditional rolling methods. Thanks to recent developments it is now possible to produce large girders directly from molten steel in this way.

Fig. 5 Basic oxygen steelmaking: pouring molten iron into a converter.

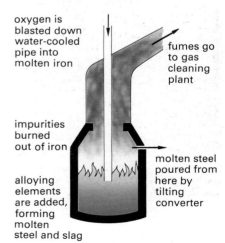

oxygen is blasted down water-cooled pipe into molten iron

fumes go to gas cleaning plant

impurities burned out of iron

molten steel poured from here by tilting converter

alloying elements are added, forming molten steel and slag

Fig. 6 Basic oxygen steelmaking: inside the converter.

The transition metals

The metals at the centre of the Periodic Table are known as the **transition metals**. (There is more about transition metals on *Datapage C*.) Elements 21 to 30, scandium to zinc, are known as the first transition series, and they have a number of properties in common.

Group	I	II			
Period					
1					
2	Li 3	Be 4			
3	Na 11	Mg 12	transition metals		
4	K 19	Ca 20	Sc 21	Ti 22	V 23

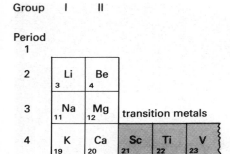

Fig. 1 The start of the first transition series in the Periodic Table.

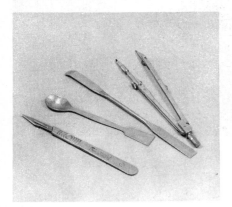

Fig. 2 These compasses, the scalpel handle and the spatulas are all made of nickel, an unreactive transition metal which does not corrode easily.

Fig. 3 Transition metals in use: an AlNiCo magnet. (Which metals do you think it contains?).

What is special about the transition metals?

For reasons which are beyond the scope of this book, the transition metals have many similarities. They all

☐ are hard, dense metals
☐ have high melting points (above 1000 °C)
☐ are fairly low in the Reactivity Series
☐ form more than one kind of ion.

Many of them

☐ form coloured compounds
☐ behave as catalysts.

Here is some information about four transition metals:

Some properties of selected transition metals

Property	Chromium	Manganese	Iron	Copper
symbol	Cr	Mn	Fe	Cu
atomic number	24	25	26	29
rel. atomic mass	52	55	56	63.5
M.P. (°C)	1850	1244	1535	1087
density (g/cm^3)	7.2	7.2	7.9	8.9
common valencies	3,6,7	2,4,7	2,3	1,2
coloured ions	Cr^{3+}(aq) green	MnO_4^{-}(aq) purple	Fe^{2+}(aq) pale green	Cu^{2+}(aq) pale blue
	$Cr_2O_7^{2-}$(aq) orange	Mn^{2+}(aq) pink	Fe^{3+}(aq) brown	

Q1 Cobalt and nickel are metals from the first transition series. Using the *Datapages* and the *Index*, list the information needed for adding *one* of them to this table.

Q2 Chromium is an important transition metal, with both household and industrial uses. Most of the ore comes from just two countries: South Africa and the USSR. Write a short newspaper article pointing out what problems would arise if the metal became unavailable.

Titanium – element number 22

Element number 22 (in Fig. 1) is a transition metal. As you will see on *Datapage 11* it is one of the 'top ten' elements in the Earth's crust. Although they are expensive to manufacture, titanium alloys are widely used in the aircraft industry. They are strong and resistant to corrosion. Titanium dioxide is the white pigment often used for making paint.

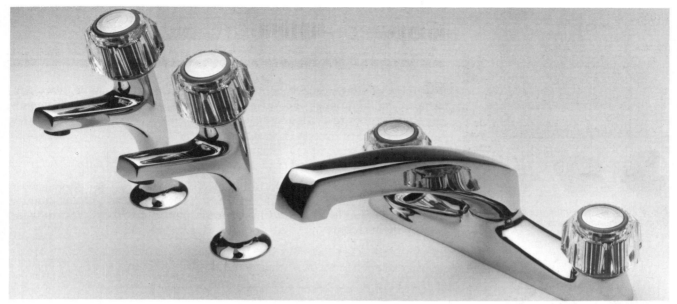

Fig. 4 Chromium plated bathroom fittings. The unreactive chromium coating helps prevent rusting.

Why are industrial catalysts so important?

A catalyst is a substance which alters the rate of a chemical reaction. Most industrial catalysts have been developed to speed up processes for making important chemicals. Very few of the products which we take for granted could be made at all without the use of catalysts.

Some industrial processes using catalysts

Product	Name of process	Catalyst
ammonia	Haber	iron oxide
carbon dioxide	steam reforming	nickel oxide
margarine	hydrogenation	nickel
nitric acid	Ostwald	platinum/rhodium
nylon	–	cobalt naphthenate
SBR rubber	–	calcium and nickel phosphate
sulphuric acid	contact	vanadium(v) oxide

[All these catalysts are transition metals or their compounds.]

How do catalysts work?

There is no single answer to this question, since different catalysts work in different ways. One important way is illustrated by the Haber process, which is shown in Fig. 4.

Q3 Manganese forms an oxide (MnO_2) which is a catalyst for the decomposition of hydrogen peroxide. What experiments would you do to check that this oxide was indeed a catalyst?

Did you know?

The original headquarters of the chemical firm ICI is Imperial Chemical House in London. Its doors are made entirely of one transition metal. Which?

Nickel.

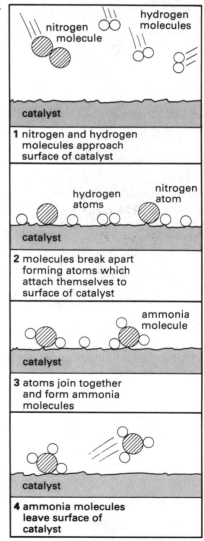

1 nitrogen and hydrogen molecules approach surface of catalyst

2 molecules break apart forming atoms which attach themselves to surface of catalyst

3 atoms join together and form ammonia molecules

4 ammonia molecules leave surface of catalyst

Fig. 5 The catalyst used in making ammonia is thought to work in this way.

Copper – the pink metal

Just think of all the objects containing copper which you handle every day. About 7 million tonnes of copper are produced each year, mostly from new ore, but some by re-cycling scrap copper.

How is copper used?

The main uses for copper are in the electrical industry – for copper wire, and for electrical fittings made out of brass (which is an alloy containing copper). Copper is also used in domestic piping, for roofs, and in some saucepans and coins.

Q1 Look around at home, and make a list of all the items you can find which are made from copper, or a copper alloy such as brass or bronze. Give one possible reason for the choice of copper in each case.

Some alloys of copper

The three alloys of copper which are most widely used are:

☐ the **brasses** – containing copper and zinc
☐ the **bronzes** – containing copper and tin
☐ the **cupro-nickel** alloys – containing copper and nickel.

The best known brass contains 70% copper and 30% zinc. It was originally known as 'cartridge brass', and used for cartridge cases. Today it is used for a large variety of products, ranging from light fittings to door knobs and car radiators. Many different brasses have been developed, all with different properties. Since zinc is a cheaper metal than copper, it is worth choosing a brass which has the highest zinc content possible for the application required.

There are many bronzes, too. The simplest contain over 90% copper, alloyed with tin. Church bells have traditionally been cast from 'bell metal', a bronze containing 80% copper and 20% tin. This is expensive and fairly brittle, however. For engineering purposes, a number of other bronzes have been developed, which combine corrosion resistance with strength. Phosphor-bronze (containing a little phosphorus) and aluminium bronze (containing up to 7% aluminium) are widely used.

Cupro-nickel alloys are used in many coins. Details are given in 5.10. 'Nickel silver', used for cutlery and articles to be silver-plated, is a cupro-nickel alloy containing zinc (but no silver!).

Where is copper ore found?

In the 1980s the countries with the most productive copper mines were Chile, the USA, Zambia, Zaire, Peru and the USSR. Copper ore is mined underground and from large open-cast pits like the one shown in Fig. 3. The scale of operation is very large: two million tonnes of material are mined each week from this enormous hole in the ground!

Q2 Make an estimate of the annual production of refined copper from this mine, assuming that the ore contains 0.5% of copper, and that 60% of the material taken out of the pit is waste rock.

Fig. 1 These copper containers and the altar they stand on were made in Egypt over 4000 years ago!

Fig. 2 Bronze, an important alloy of copper, has been used for making this statue of the Hindu god Siva.

Fig. 3 Copper mining on the grand scale: 2 million tonnes of material are removed from this mine every week.

How is copper metal produced?

Despite the enormous mines, copper is not a plentiful metal. It is now commonly extracted from ore deposits which contain as little as 0.5% of the metal. These deposits may contain a whole variety of copper minerals. Two of the more important ones are chalcopyrite, $CuFeS_2$, and malachite, $CuCO_3$.

The ore from a copper mine must first be crushed to a fine powder. This is carried out in large rotating drums (Fig. 4, step 1), which contain hardened steel balls to break up the rock. Crushing is necessary because less than 1% of the ore is copper, and you can only get at it by breaking the rock up into small particles.

The powder is then treated by froth flotation (step 2) to separate the particles which contain copper. Froth flotation works like this: the powdered rock is mixed with water and a detergent. Special additives in the mixture cause the bits of powder which contain copper to float up with the froth to the surface. The froth is collected and dried, giving a powder which is rich in copper for the extraction stage.

Extracting the metal is a complex process, in which the ore is first roasted in air (step 3) and then reduced (step 4). The molten copper is cast into slabs. These slabs are used as cathodes in a refining process which relies on electrolysis (step 5).

Q3 Use information from *Datapages R* and *S* to suggest why the prices of copper, silver and iron are so different.

Did you know?

At the Tower of London there is a Turkish cannon, dated 1464, which weighs 17 tonnes. Which copper alloy is it made from?

Bronze, of varying composition, but on average about 11% tin with 89% copper.

1 rock containg copper ore is **crushed**

2 ore is separated from rock by **froth flotation** - ore particles float on a special liquid

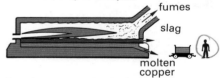

3 molten copper is obtained by **roasting** ore with carbon

4 molten copper is purified in a **reduction furnace**

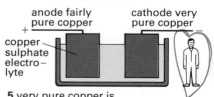

5 very pure copper is made by **electrolysis**

Fig. 4 Making copper from copper ore.

143

Copper and its compounds

Fig. 1 Copper is an unreactive metal: the dome of this London mosque has a copper covering.

Fig. 2 The new £2 coin is made from an alloy which contains 70% copper.

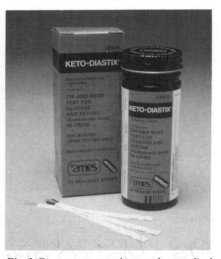

Fig. 3 Copper compounds at work: a medical kit for testing urine samples. The copper compound in this kit changes colour when it reacts with 'reducing sugars'. If these are present, the patient may have diabetes.

Copper is a fairly unreactive metal, but it tarnishes in air, forming an oxide layer on the surface. It is below hydrogen in the Reactivity Series, so it does not react with water or with dilute hydrochloric or sulphuric acids. (There is more about the Reactivity Series in 4.3.)

It does react with nitric acid, however, giving a salt (copper nitrate) and brown fumes of dinitrogen tetroxide, N_2O_4. This gas is formed when the nitrogen monoxide, NO, from the reaction combines with oxygen in the air. The reaction is complicated, but for a 1:1 mixture of concentrated nitric acid and water, it is often written:

copper + nitric acid $\rightarrow$ copper nitrate + nitrogen monoxide + water

$$3Cu(s) + 8HNO_3 (aq) \rightarrow 3Cu(NO_3)_2(aq) + 2NO(g) + 4H_2O(l)$$

Copper *reduces* the nitric acid, which behaves as an *oxidising agent* in this reaction.

Some important copper compounds

> **Q1** Copper is a transition metal. (There is more about these in 5.7.) What predictions can you make about its properties and its compounds?

Copper oxide, CuO, is a black substance which forms on the surface of copper when it is heated in air. The full name for this compound is copper(II) oxide ('Oxidation numbers' in 4.6 tells you why). It is produced when most copper salts are strongly heated. For instance:

copper nitrate $\rightarrow$ copper oxide + nitrogen dioxide + oxygen

copper carbonate $\rightarrow$ copper oxide + carbon dioxide

copper hydroxide $\rightarrow$ copper oxide + water

copper sulphate $\rightarrow$ copper oxide + sulphur trioxide

> **Q2** Write balanced equations for each of these reactions.

When copper oxide is heated with carbon, or in a stream of hydrogen, it is reduced to copper:

$$2CuO(s) + C(s) \rightarrow CO_2(g) + 2Cu(s)$$

$$CuO(s) + H_2(g) \rightarrow H_2O(g) + Cu(s)$$

> **Q3** Explain how you would carry out each of these reactions, and describe what you would expect to see happening.

Copper(I) oxide, Cu_2O, is the red substance which you often see forming on the surface of a piece of copper while it is being heated. It is also seen when using Benedict's or Fehlings' tests for reducing sugars. The valency (oxidation number) of copper in this oxide is +1.

Fig. 4 Trucks as big as this are used to bring copper ore from the mine shown in 5.8 Fig. 3. They can carry 160 tonnes at a time.

Copper sulphate is well known in its hydrated form, $CuSO_4.5H_2O(s)$, which has pale blue crystals. When heated, it breaks down in stages:

(1) Four water molecules are lost (at about $100\,°C$)

$$CuSO_4.5H_2O(s) \quad \rightarrow \quad CuSO_4.H_2O(s) + 4H_2O(g)$$

(2) The fifth water molecule is lost (at about $250\,°C$), leaving anhydrous copper sulphate, $CuSO_4(s)$, which is white.

(3) Finally, copper sulphate breaks down to copper oxide:

$$CuSO_4(s) \quad \rightarrow \quad CuO(s) + SO_3(g)$$

Q4 When cold water is added to anhydrous copper sulphate there are two obvious changes: it turns blue, and it becomes hot. Explain why these things happen.

How do you recognise copper compounds?

☐ Most copper salts in solution are blue, because of the blue colour of the $Cu^{2+}(aq)$ ion.

☐ Copper salts give a green flame test (*Datapage N*) which is a brighter, sharper green than the 'apple green' of barium.

☐ Adding sodium hydroxide solution to a solution of a copper salt produces a pale blue precipitate of copper hydroxide, $Cu(OH)_2$:

$$2NaOH(aq) + Cu^{2+}(aq) \quad \rightarrow \quad Cu(OH)_2(s) + 2Na^+(aq)$$

☐ Adding ammonia solution gives first the same pale blue precipitate of copper hydroxide, and then – as more ammonia is added – a clear solution with a deep inky blue colour.

Fig. 5 Copper compounds at work: copper compounds in this spray are being used to prevent these vines from becoming diseased.

145

Making money – and some other alloys

Fig. 1 Joining metals with the lead–tin alloy called solder is a simple process.

The name **alloy** is given to metallic substances which are mixtures of two or more elements. Many alloys contain two or three metals, and a few contain non-metals as well. A very large number of the substances we think of as metals are, in fact, alloys. The properties of alloys are always different from those of the separate elements they contain.

Why make alloys?

☐ to improve hardness:
for example adding carbon to iron makes a hard **steel**,
adding tin to copper makes **bronze**, which is harder than copper.

☐ to improve resistance to chemical attack:
for example **stainless steel** is made from iron, nickel and chromium.

☐ to improve the working properties of materials:
for example adding zinc to copper gives **brass**, an alloy which can readily be pressed or stamped into shapes.

☐ to give strong magnetic properties:
for example **Alnico** magnets contain aluminium, nickel and cobalt.

☐ to lower the melting point of the metal:
for example **solder**, used for joining metals together, usually contains tin and lead. **Wood's metal**, a mixture of bismuth with tin, lead and cadmium, melts at about 70°C. It is used in automatic sprinkler systems – and is sometimes found in joke shops in the shape of teaspoons which melt in your tea!

☐ to replace more expensive metals:
for example the coinage alloy **cupro-nickel** contains only copper and nickel, but looks like silver.

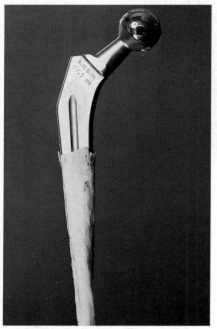

Fig. 2 Hip joints like this one are made from an alloy of chromium, cobalt and molybdenum. The shaft is made of titanium.

Alloys at work – building Concorde

Concorde is designed to carry up to 128 passengers at twice the speed of sound. This makes enormous demands on the materials used to construct the aircraft. They must be as light as possible and able to withstand very great stresses. Moreover, the temperature of the surface of the aircraft varies from –20°C to +120°C during a flight. This causes considerable expansion and contraction of its 'skin'. The nose and the edges of the wings become especially hot.

Q1 Suggest three reasons for the temperature changes which occur during Concorde's flight.

The alloy used for the airframe and skin of Concorde is a specially strengthened aluminium alloy known as RR58. It is about 95% aluminium, with copper, magnesium and small amounts of iron, silicon and nickel added. Titanium alloys, which can withstand higher temperatures than RR58, are used where necessary, but these are very expensive.

Fig. 3 Concorde's airframe and 'skin' are made of a light but strong alloy of aluminium known as RR58.

Alloys at work – making coins

> **Q2** Imagine that you had the task of choosing the alloy for a new coin. Make a list of the properties you would want it to have.

Coins for many countries are made at the Royal Mint, which is in Llantrisant, South Wales. British coins are made from several different alloys, chosen for a combination of reasons (Fig. 4). Coins must be strong, and wear-resistant. They will not last long in use if they are easily bent, or if the design is rubbed off. Coins must not easily become corroded. The chosen alloy must not be too expensive, and finally it must be capable of taking an intricate design in the stamping process.

Alloys at work – replacement joints for the human body

The disease called 'arthritis' leads to painful wear in the joints. Worst affected are the large, hard-working joints, such as the hip and shoulder. Many patients have now been fitted with metal-and-plastic replacements, giving dramatic improvements in their condition. The human body is a surprisingly demanding environment for replacement materials. A suitable substance:

☐ must not alter its shape under steady load, or on sudden shock

☐ must be resistant to scratches and indentation

☐ must not suffer 'metal fatigue' (failure after repeated stresses)

☐ must not harbour infection

☐ must be resistant to corrosion from body fluids.

> **Q3** Select one metal, important for the alloys in which it is used. (*Datapage K* give you some to choose from.) Then collect materials for an illustrated folder on the alloys of your chosen metal.

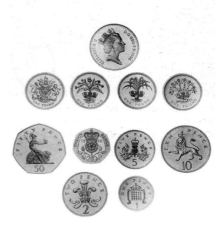

Fig. 4 British coins are all alloys. The table below shows which metals these alloys contain.

Alloys used for UK coins

Coins	% Copper	% Nickel	% Tin	% Zinc
Bronze:				
1p and 2p	97	–	0.5	2.5
Cupro-nickel:				
5p, 10p and 50p	75	25	–	–
20p	84	16	–	–
Nickel-brass:				
£1	70	5.5	–	24.5

The 20p coin contains more copper than the other 'silver' coins. Have you ever noticed that its colour is slightly different?

Questions

A. What can you remember?

** **1.** Describe and explain what you see when a small piece of sodium is put into water.

** **2.** What is 'lime water'? Describe how you could make some lime water, starting from the metal calcium.

** **3.** Limestone is calcium carbonate. Describe and explain the reactions which take place (a) when limestone is heated strongly, and (b) when water is added to the cooled product which remains.

** **4.** Aluminium is obtained from purified bauxite by electrolysis. Draw a labelled diagram to show how this process is carried out.

** **5.** Make a list of some ways in which aluminium is used. Against each use write down a reason for choosing aluminium for this particular purpose.

** **6.** Aluminium does not appear to be a very reactive metal. Its position in the Reactivity Series (*Datapage F*) suggests that it should be. How do you account for this?

** **7.** Draw a diagram of a blast furnace for making iron. Label it by writing equations for the processes which are going on inside.

* **8.** List the raw materials used in a blast furnace for making iron. Alongside each raw material write down how it is obtained.

** **9.** Explain *three* ways in which the chemical behaviour iron is like that of other metals which you know.

** **10.** The following household items made from iron are treated to prevent rust: washing machine casing; bicycle wheel; garden wire; corrugated iron roof; biscuit tin.
Describe a suitable rust-prevention method for each item, and say why it has been chosen.

** **11.** Explain, with a labelled diagram, the 'Basic Oxygen' method for making steel.

** **12.** What are the 'Transition Metals', and where in the Periodic Table are they found?

** **13.** What is a *catalyst*? Give one laboratory example, and one industrial example to illustrate your answer.

** **14.** List *four* important uses of copper, and explain in each case why it is used in this way.

** **15.** Describe what you would expect to see when some copper(II) oxide powder is mixed with powdered carbon, and heated in a test tube. How would you test the gas which is give off?

** **16.** An electroplating works is believed to have spilled some copper sulphate solution into a nearby stream. Suggest a method for testing the water to see if it is contaminated with copper compounds.

* **17.** Explain, giving *two* examples, what is meant by an 'alloy'.

** **18.** Aluminium alloys are widely used in buildings and in the home. Give four examples of these uses, and explain why the alloy has been chosen in each case.

B. What have you understood?

** **19.** Explain why the elements of Group I are called the Alkali Metals.

*** **20.** Sodium chloride cannot be made safely by adding sodium to hydrochloric acid. Suggest a better way of making solid sodium chloride from sodium metal.

21. 'Garden lime, which is used to correct the pH of acid soils, is calcium hydroxide.' (See 5.2) What does this sentence tell you about the properties of calcium hydroxide?

22. Much aluminium is produced in Europe and N. America, countries which are far from where the ore is mined. Explain the reasons for this.

23. Draw a diagram which explains how aluminium is *anodised*. Give two reasons for treating aluminium in this way.

24. Explain the difference between iron and steel.

25. What is 'cast iron'? Explain why it is a suitable material for making drain covers, but not suitable for making horse shoes.

26. Brass is an alloy of copper and zinc. What would you expect to see if you added (a) dilute hydrochloric acid, and (b) dilute nitric acid to some small pieces of brass.

C. Can you use this information?

27. The reaction between sodium metal and hydrochloric acid would be very violent. Taking into account the chemistry involved, draw an apparatus which might allow this reaction to be carried out without danger to the operator.

28. Iron bars have sometimes been used to hold together the stonework on buildings. When the iron rusts, a number of new substances are formed (see 5.5), and the stonework may be forced apart. Why do you think this happens?

29. Calcium is used in a 'competition reaction' (see 4.4) to extract uranium from one of its oxides.
(a) What does this tell you about the position of uranium in the Reactivity Series?
(b) Uranium has a valency of 4 in this oxide. Write an equation for the reaction of uranium oxide with calcium.
(c) Find the melting points of calcium and uranium (*Datapage C*), and draw an apparatus which might be suitable for this process.

30. Seven of the top ten elements in the earth's crust (see *Datapage I1*) are metals.
(a) Which is the most abundant metal of all?
(b) What fraction of the earth's crust is iron?
(c) Draw a bar chart showing the amounts of the metals Al, Fe, Ca, Na, K, Mg and Ti present in the earth's crust.

31. Use information from 5.1 to make a summary table showing the uses of lithium, sodium and potassium.

32. Find out from *Datapage S3* which is the most expensive metal of all. How many times more expensive is it than solid silver?

33. Using information from *Datapage S*, draw a bar chart which shows the current prices of silver, tin, copper and lead.

34. Look at the changes in metal prices which have taken place during this century (*Datapage S5*). They are all index-linked to the present day, so it is possible to make some comparisons. Using graphs, or by some other method, comment upon these figures.

35. There has been a spectacular growth in the production of aluminium during this century (see *Datapage R4*). Suggest possible reasons for this, and comment on the corresponding figures for the other metals listed on the same *Datapage*.

36. Use information from *Datapage R1* to make two lists of metals:
(a) those which come from ores containing more than 20% of metal,
(b) those which come from ores containing less than 1% of metal.

37. Table 2 on *Datapage R* gives some information about the different materials which are put into a blast furnace, and those which come out of it. Present this information in the form of two pie charts.

D. Taking it further

** **38.** Write a short newspaper article about gold, using information from *Datapage R, S, T.*

** **39.** The earliest iron furnaces were quite small, about a metre high, and made from clay set into the ground. They used charcoal to reduce iron ore. The metal did not melt, and was taken out of the furnace after it had cooled down. What advantages does the modern blast furnace have over this process?

** **40.** A manufacturer is choosing a new metal for making car bodies. What important arguments could be put for and against the following suggestions: (a) aluminium; (b) stainless steel; (c) brass?

** **41.** Copper and lead sheeting are often used for the roofs of public buildings. What would be the advantages and disadvantages of using aluminium in the same way?

Quick questions

1. Give the names and chemical symbols of three alkali metals.

2. In forming compounds the alkali metals show a valency of 1. Why is this?

3. Give the name and formula of one important ore of each of the following metals: aluminium, copper, iron.

4. Name two parts of Britain where you would expect to find limestone quarries.

5. Give the names of two copper alloys.

Fuels

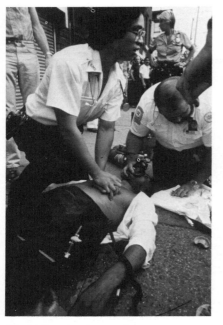

Fig. 1 The injured man is being given oxygen, a gaseous fuel.

Fig. 2 This tanker is loading LPG (Liquefied Petroleum Gas).

Fig. 3 Solid fuels of all kinds: firelighters soaked in paraffin, coal and charcoal.

The word 'fuel' is used to cover every kind of energy source, from dried animal dung to the rods in a nuclear reactor. Anything that can be burned to produce heat for warmth or cooking is a fuel. Anything that will run a car, a train or an aeroplane is also a fuel. Food, of course, is often thought of as 'body fuel'.

The table below and the photographs on this page give some examples of different fuels. They can be solids, liquids or gases.

Some fuels

Solids	Liquids	Gases
charcoal	petrol (gasoline)	methane (natural gas)
coal	diesel fuel (DERV)	butane (camping gas)
wood	ethanol ('meths')	hydrogen (rocket fuel)

Q1 Sort these fuels into two lists: 'naturally occurring fuels' and 'manufactured fuels'. Add any other fuels you can think of.

Combustion

Fuels are all burned to produce heat, even if that heat energy is later converted into another form, such as electricity. Another name for the burning process is **combustion**. The combustion of a fossil fuel (coal, oil and natural gas) can be represented:

$$\text{fossil fuel} + \text{oxygen} \rightarrow \text{carbon dioxide} + \text{water}$$

Incomplete combustion

Sometimes the supply of oxygen from the air is not sufficient for the full combustion process. For example, when the air-hole of a bunsen burner is closed, there is not enough air mixed with the gas to burn it all to carbon dioxide and water. There is **incomplete combustion**, giving a cooler flame, which contains unburned carbon. This makes it yellow and sooty:

$$\text{natural gas} + \text{air/oxygen} \rightarrow \text{carbon} + \text{carbon dioxide} + \text{water}$$

A car engine 'ticking over' is another example of incomplete combustion. One of the combustion products is carbon monoxide (see 3.10). This forms because the amount of oxygen supplied from the air is not enough to burn the fuel completely:

$$\text{petrol} + \frac{\text{air/}}{\text{oxygen}} \rightarrow \text{carbon} + \text{carbon monoxide} + \text{carbon dioxide} + \text{water}$$

Carbon monoxide is very poisonous, so it is always dangerous to run a car engine in a confined space, such as a garage or workshop.

Q2 Write down four other examples of combustion processes. In each case say whether you think the combustion is complete or incomplete, and give a reason for your answer.

Fig. 4 This coalmine in Staffordshire supplies an adjacent power station. The heat energy produced by burning the coal – a fossil fuel – is converted into electricity.

Fossil fuels

The 'fossil fuels' are coal, oil and natural gas. They have been formed in the earth from once-living material. Coal comes from fossil plant material, while oil and natural gas are derived from organisms which lived in the sea. There is more about this in 6.2 and 6.4.

It takes many millions of years for fossil fuels to be formed in the earth. Today they are being used up very rapidly, and the known reserves of oil and gas may well be used up during our lifetimes. Coal is rather more plentiful. This raises various problems. First, there are some practical questions, for example:

☐ How long can we expect to go on using oil and natural gas as we do at present?
☐ How much more expensive will the fuels become as they have to be brought from ever more inaccessible places?
☐ How will we make plastics and fertilisers when we no longer have oil and natural gas as starting materials?
☐ What alternative sources of energy will be sufficient to meet our future needs?
☐ Have we the skill to develop the new sources and to use them safely?

Then there are some 'moral' questions, for example:

☐ Should we be saving our oil and gas for more important uses, rather than simply burning them up?
☐ Have we a responsibility to our descendants to see that the earth's resources are not squandered?
☐ Should we be searching for renewable energy sources, rather than depleting the energy stores we have?

The information in this chapter will help you to think some more about these questions.

Fig. 5 Oil is a fossil fuel. This oil production platform is in the North Sea. The flares on the right are due to the burning of fossil fuel gases.

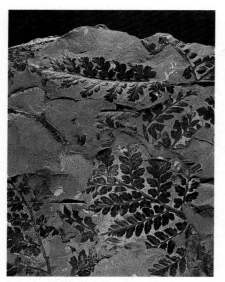

Fig. 1 *Coal is formed from dead plant material over millions of years. Here you can see plant fossils in a piece of coal.*

Fig. 2 *The first and last stages in the formation of coal: peat and anthracite.*

Fig. 3 *This stamp, issued in 1881, was dyed with the first 'coal tar dye' – mauveine.*

Coal

Coal is our most abundant fossil fuel. In Britain it is found among Carboniferous rocks, which began forming more than 300 million years ago. Coal comes from dead plant material which once grew in swampland. Earth movements and changes in climate cause new layers of sand and mud to cover the decaying vegetation. The gradually forming coal becomes more and more compressed beneath other material as time passes. Eventually, little but carbon is left.

Q1 What kinds of plant can you see in the coal sample shown in Fig 1? In what kinds of conditions do these plants grow today?

Different types of coal

Peat is the first step in the coal-forming process. Time passes and the peat becomes more compressed under further layers of sand and mud. This gradually turns into 'brown coal' or 'lignite', then into the harder forms of coal, and finally – under the right conditions – into anthracite. You can see the first and last of the four stages in Fig. 2. The table below shows how the proportion of carbon increases. Anthracite is the purest fuel – it is nearly 100% carbon and contains no water.

Some types of coal

Type of coal	Appearance	% Carbon	% Moisture	Heat value
		(approximate figures)		
peat	soft, brown, fibrous	20	70	low
lignite	crumbly, dark	55	35	fair
bituminous	hard, black, dusty	80	little	good
anthracite	shiny, black very hard	95	none	high

Q2 The figures in the above table do not add up to 100% for any of the individual forms of coal. There is no mistake, so what explanation can you give for this?

Using coal

Most of the world's coal is used for heating purposes. About 80% is used in this way, either on fires directly, or in power stations to drive generators. The other 20% of coal is used in metal-smelting, mainly to make coke for blast furnaces (see 5.4).

Peat is sometimes cut from boggy ground, left to dry, and then used in household fires. It is not used commercially as a fuel in the industrialised countries. **Lignite**, the brown coal, is an important fuel in countries where it can be mined easily. In West Germany, for example, the amount of brown coal produced each year is about the same as the amount of ordinary coal mined each year in Britain. It comes from open-cast mines (6.3, Fig. 4) and is used in power stations.

Ordinary **household coal** is of the 'bituminous' type. Bituminous coals are widely used in power stations and in the manufacture of coke. **Anthracite**, the purest form of coal, is used for solid fuel central heating, and for generating electricity.

Fig. 4 Coal was formed from plants growing in conditions like this: a swamp of giant ferns more than 300 million years ago.

Making better use of coal

Although coal is a good fuel, it also contains valuable chemicals. Simply to burn it all, however efficiently, would be very wasteful.

Coal is an important source of chemicals and other types of fuel. In countries where coal is plentiful and cheap to mine (for example South Africa), it is worth converting it into oil or gas. Coal can be treated with solvents under high pressure to remove some of its chemicals directly. It is even possible to turn coal into gas underground, without having to mine it. These and other projects mean that coal must be thought of as an important raw material, as well as a fuel.

Better methods of burning coal and coal products are constantly under development. A particularly promising method, which improves heat efficiency and reduces air pollution, is a system called 'fluidised-bed combustion'. This is shown in Fig. 5. Burning coal produces acidic gases such as sulphur dioxide. Lime is an alkali which reacts with sulphur dioxide. If lime is added to the fluidised bed it will greatly reduce the amount of sulphur dioxide pollution which reaches the atmosphere as the coal is burned.

Q3 Mauveine, used to colour the stamp shown in Fig. 3, was a 'coal tar dye'. Using a reference book, find out more about these dyes and the work of W.H. Perkin.

Q4 Coal-fired power stations contribute to the problem of 'acid rain' (see 6.13). Find out more about this, and explain how the problem is being tackled.

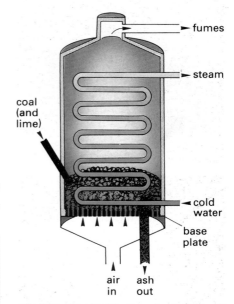

Fig. 5 The 'fluidised bed' combustion of coal increases heat production and reduces air pollution.

Mining and using coal

Fig. 1 A modern coal mine.

Most British coal is found at a depth of a few hundred metres, and is obtained by **underground mining** (Fig. 2). Other coal deposits which are fairly near the surface are worked by **open-cast mining** (Fig. 4). It is not usual to find different kinds of coal in the same mine, because different types of coal take different lengths of time to form.

> **Q1** Use *Datapage Q2* to make a map to show the main coal-producing areas of the world, and which types of coal they produce.
>
> **Q2** Coal in one place is likely to be all of the same age. Explain why this is.

Almost all of Britain's coal is produced north of a line drawn from Bristol to Hull. The only large mines to the south are those in East Kent. Between the 1940s and the 1980s coal production more than doubled, and the number of miners employed was greatly reduced. New mines are being opened up and old ones closed, and the industry is at a time of rapid change. In a typical mine there are many miles of underground roadways. Several coal faces are worked at different depths. The coal is brought to the surface six tonnes at a time. It is then washed, yes, *washed* – to remove unwanted rock and debris, for even coal must be clean before it is ready for sale.

Fig. 2 Mining coal underground. Today, much of the work is done by machines.

Coal, health and the environment

Coal is an excellent fuel, which is widely used. Mining and using coal has always been linked with certain risks, however, both to the miners and to people living in districts where coal is mined and used.

Around two dozen men are killed each year in British coal mines, and many more contract pneumoconiosis, the dreaded 'dust disease' of the lungs. These are horrifying figures, and work is constantly going on to reduce the dangers which cause them. Conditions in the mines today are unrecognisably better than they were even a generation ago, and improvements are continuing. Nevertheless, one part of the 'price' of coal is that, until remotely controlled machines can do all the work, lives and health will be put at risk in digging it out.

When coal is mined it is not possible to bring only the coal to the surface. Waste material has to be brought out of the mine, too. Some of this is in quite large pieces which can be tipped and landscaped fairly easily. A more difficult problem is the slurry of fine mud which is formed when coal is washed. If this is not properly drained the tip becomes unstable. A dreadful tragedy occurred in 1966 at Aberfan in South Wales, when part of a sliding tip engulfed a primary school. More than 100 children were killed. Even greater care is now taken to make sure that coal tips cannot slide.

Fig. 3 These coke ovens turn coal into coke for use at a steel works.

Open-cast coal mining involves digging out huge trenches, and this disturbs the landscape a good deal (Fig. 4). Careful planning allows the ground to be restored as mining continues. It is possible to replant the land and restore its appearance quite quickly. By law, any agricultural land which is mined must be restored to agricultural use.

> **Q3** The burning of household coal produces a number of undesirable effects. Use a library to find out about the Clean Air Acts and why they were introduced.

Fig. 4 Mining coal by the 'opencast' method. The machine digs huge trenches to scoop out the coal, but the landscape can be restored once the coal is dug out.

Coke

Coke is a fuel made from coal. It is made on a large scale for industrial use, particularly at steel works. Some is also sold for domestic heating. It is manufactured in **coke ovens** – special closed furnaces in which coal is strongly heated (Fig. 3). A great deal of **coal gas**, also a valuable fuel, is produced at the same time. All the tarry material in the coal is driven out, and a hard spongy substance, **coke**, is left. No air is allowed to reach the coal, as it would burn away. Mechanical rams are used to empty the furnaces, and as soon as the hot coke emerges it is drenched with water to stop it from catching fire.

Until North Sea gas was found, Britain relied on coal gas for the public supply. Coal gas is just one of the by-products of coke-making. The others are **coal tar** (a mixture of valuable organic chemicals) and **ammonia** (which is used to make fertilisers).

Fig. 5 These are smokeless fuel 'briquettes' for use on household fires.

Smokeless fuels

Although it is not very easy to light, coke burns with a hot clean flame. It is one of the so-called 'smokeless' fuels (Fig. 5). Because of the need to reduce air pollution from domestic fires, British Coal has developed a number of manufactured fuels which produce very little smoke. Products such as 'Homefire', 'Multiheat', 'Phurnacite' and 'Roomheat' are made by heating crushed coal to drive off the tarry material. While still hot it is mixed with a binder to form a material which can be shaped into small blocks or 'briquettes'.

Turning coal into 'smokeless' fuel has great benefits for the users and their neighbours. People who live near plants where smokeless fuel is made will tell you another side to the story! Figure 6 gives you an idea why.

Fig. 6 A smokeless fuel works. Would you like to live nearby?

Oil

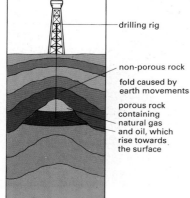

- ancient sea

layers of mud, and the remains of small living creatures build up on top of one another over millions of years

- drilling rig

- non-porous rock

fold caused by earth movements

porous rock containing natural gas and oil, which rise towards the surface

Fig. 1 *Oil gathers beneath the earth's surface in this way.*

Fig. 2 *An early oil well, drilled at Oil Creek in Pennsylvania, in about 1870.*

Crude oil, or 'petroleum', is a raw material of enormous importance. It supplies a chemical industry which is so large that dozens of its products are to be found in every home. It is also a major source of fuels.

How was oil formed?

Like coal, crude oil is a 'fossil' material formed from things that were once living. It is believed that petroleum and natural gas have been formed by the action of bacteria on a mixture of plant matter and the bodies of marine animals. These accumulate on the sea bed and become covered by many further layers of sediment. Once formed, the oil and gas tend to rise towards the surface, but usually they are trapped in a fold beneath layers of non-porous rock. Figure 1 illustrates this.

It is important to realise that the oil is not present as an underground lake. It is dispersed as tiny droplets, trapped under pressure in a porous rock, like sandstone. The same is true of natural gas, which is often found immediately above the oil.

How is oil discovered and extracted?

Oil and natural gas usually occur together, and the methods of searching for them are essentially the same. Once an oil and gas field has been found, exploration wells are drilled, to establish the size and quality of the deposit. Later on production wells are built, so that the oil and gas may be brought to the surface. There is more about this in 6.5.

Where is oil found?

Figure 4 shows the major oil-producing areas of the world. This pattern has changed considerably since the first commercial drilling for oil was undertaken in the USA in 1859 (Fig. 2). Many of the land-based oilfields have been in production for many years now, and most new discoveries take place beneath the sea bed. The first North Sea oil was brought ashore to Britain in 1975, and production is expected to continue into the next century. It is not easy to tell how long a particular oilfield will last. New discoveries and new extraction techniques often make an oilfield last longer than was originally expected. Nevertheless, oil is in quite short supply, and it is certain that important changes in the pattern of use will take place in our lifetime.

Q1 Use *Datapage P4* to make a table showing the 10 major oil-producing countries of the world.

Oil is widely distributed, and there are more than 70 oil-producing countries in the world. The three major ones are the USSR, the USA and Saudi Arabia (in this order), which between them produce more than half of the world's oil. Britain, which in 1981 became self-sufficient in oil, produces about 4% of the world total.

Did you know?

What was the first use made of the crude oil discovered in the USA during the early nineteenth century?

As 'American Medicinal Oil', a liniment.

Fig. 3 *There are four main oil-producing areas of the world: the USA, the Middle East, the countries around the Caribbean Sea (Venezuela, Colombia, Mexico and Trinidad), and the USSR. Many other areas are also important, as you can see from this map.*

Oil from beneath the sea bed

Much of today's oil is brought from beneath the sea bed. Special drilling methods have been developed for this. In shallow water, less than 100 metres deep, it is possible to use **jack-up** rigs, which can be floated out to where they are needed, and then jacked up on their own legs (Fig. 4). In deeper and rougher waters it is necessary to use **semi-submersible** rigs mounted on huge floats or pontoons (Fig. 5). Specially built drilling ships can also be used. These have heavy anchors and computer-controlled motors driving propellers which will move the ship in any required direction. This makes it possible to hold the ship's position accurately over the hole being drilled.

Fig. 4 *A jack-up rig, used in the search for oil below the sea bed in shallow water.*

How is crude oil used?

Crude oil is used in two main ways:

☐ as a source of fuels
☐ as a chemical starting material.

Fuels made from oil include petrol, diesel, kerosine (for aircraft), and fuel oil (for ships and for heating systems). Lubricating oils and bitumen products are also very important. Oil is used as a starting material for making solvents, plastics, dyestuffs, paints, medicines and other chemicals.

There is more about this in 6.6.

Fig. 5 *A semi-submersible rig for use in the North Sea.*

159

The search for oil

Although there are a few places in the world where natural hydrocarbons like oil and gas seep to the surface, this is rare. Normally, there is no sign at the surface of what lies below.

Looking for oil

The first task is for the geologist. Sedimentary rocks which are capable of holding oil and gas make up a large proportion of the earth's crust, both on land and beneath the sea bed. Nevertheless, large quantities of oil have only been found in a fairly small number of places. Figure 1 shows the kind of geological region which is worth exploring for oil.

Aerial and satellite surveys can provide detailed pictures of surface features which give clues about the underlying rock. Promising areas can then be surveyed more closely. Trailing an instrument called a 'magnetometer' behind an aeroplane (Fig. 2) reveals local variations in the earth's magnetic field. These indicate changes in the structure of the rock beneath. More clues can be obtained by measuring the small variations in the pull of gravity at the earth's surface. Taken together, these measurements show whether it is worth carrying out further measurements at ground level. **Seismic** surveying is the most important of these (Fig. 4).

Seismic survey

An important survey method, used both at sea and on land, is known as a 'seismic survey'. Shock waves in the earth are produced by setting off small explosions, or simply by thumping the earth with a heavy weight! At sea, compressed air guns are used.

Depending upon what is below, the shock waves are reflected back along different routes. By listening at different places on the surface with sensitive instruments called **geophones**, the length of time taken for the reflected waves to return is measured. The information received by the geophones is processed to show how the rocks are lying beneath the surface.

Exploration drilling

Promising areas are then drilled. Sometimes the drilling is carried out simply to gain more geological information. The rotary drill cuts into the earth while a liquid slurry, called 'drilling mud' is pumped down the drill pipe. It emerges at the bottom of the hole and is forced back to the surface through the space between the drill pipe and the sides of the hole (Fig. 3). As it returns it carries up the chippings which allow a 'map' of the underlying rocks to be built up. The chippings are also examined under a microscope for traces of oil. Once oil has been found, many more holes must be drilled to establish the size and quality of the deposit.

As the drill passes through the earth it meets both hard and soft rocks, in addition to water, gas and oil, which may be under pressure. Sometimes there are gaps or 'fissures' underground, so that the drilling mud escapes and seeps away. All these changes are closely watched by the drillers. Special care must be taken to avoid 'blowouts' – an uncontrolled rush of oil and gas to the surface. Blowouts can be very dangerous, as well as wasteful. Oil rigs are fitted with 'blowout preventers', a series of strong valves and seals, which can control the flow of oil.

Fig. 1 A promising area for oil. This fold in the rock, or 'anticline', is in Iran.

Fig. 2 Looking for oil with instruments carried in an aircraft. The lines show how the aircraft checks one area at a time.

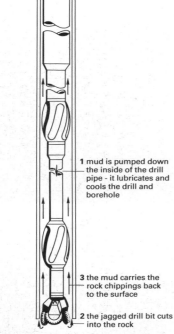

1 mud is pumped down the inside of the drill pipe - it lubricates and cools the drill and borehole

3 the mud carries the rock chippings back to the surface

2 the jagged drill bit cuts into the rock

Fig. 3 Rock chippings carried by the drilling mud carry important clues back to the surface during exploratory drilling for oil.

Fig. 4 *A seismic survey being carried out in Oman. Small quantities of dynamite will be placed in these boreholes.*

Production wells

A production well is a much larger and more permanent structure than an exploration rig. The platforms built for use in the North Sea are among the largest moveable structures ever built. The main frameworks are built in a dockyard before being floated out to sea. Then they are turned on end, and anchored firmly to the sea bed. The machinery and workshops, living quarters for the crew, and helicopter landing pad are then added.

Most of the pipes leading to a production platform do not go straight down into the earth. They are splayed out, almost like the ribs of an upturned umbrella. In this way, one platform can draw oil from quite a wide area.

North Sea oil and gas are so well known that it would be easy to forget that oil has also been found on the British mainland – in the East Midlands and near the South Coast (Figs. 5 and 6). Some of this oil lies beneath areas of natural beauty, with unique wildlife, so care will be needed in developing these oilfields.

Fig. 5 *A drilling rig in use at Beckingham oilfield in Nottinghamshire.*

Extracting the last drop of oil

If left to the effects of natural pressure, a well-drilled oil reservoir may give up as much as half of all the oil it contains. There are various ways of increasing this yield. One is to displace the oil by pumping down water under high pressure. More effective, but more expensive methods include the use of hydrocarbons or other chemicals. It is sometimes possible to increase the flow from an oil well by injecting steam under pressure, to heat the oil, and make it less viscous. Attempts have even been made to cause the same effect by setting fire to some of the oil in the nearby rock! These methods of driving out almost the last drop of oil are known as 'enhanced oil recovery'. As oil runs short it will be vital to make the most of each deposit.

Q1 Make your own wallchart with the heading "The Search for oil".

Fig. 6 *These pumps are drawing oil from the Wytch Farm oilfield in Dorset. Because of their rocking movement they are known in the trade as 'nodding donkeys'.*

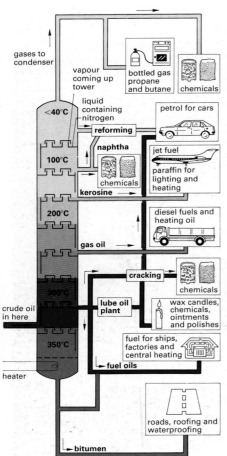

gases to condenser

vapour coming up tower

bottled gas propane and butane

chemicals

<40°C

liquid containing nitrogen

reforming

petrol for cars

naphtha

100°C

chemicals

jet fuel

paraffin for lighting and heating

kerosine

200°C

diesel fuels and heating oil

gas oil

cracking

chemicals

300°C

lube oil plant

wax candles, chemicals, ointments and polishes

crude oil in here

350°C

fuel for ships, factories and central heating

heater

fuel oils

roads, roofing and waterproofing

bitumen

Fig. 1 Fractional distillation ('fractionation') of crude oil.

Oil refining

The different crude oils, from different parts of the world, are not the same. North Sea oil, for example, is black-brown and of medium density. Some Middle Eastern oils are lighter and more brown in colour, while crude oil from Venezuela is very dark and sticky. The task of the oil business is to make the best possible use of every drop of crude oil extracted from the earth. This job is done at an **oil refinery**, using two kinds of process: **separation** and **conversion**.

Separation by fractional distillation

Crude oil is a mixture, so the separation process is needed first. The different substances found in crude oil have different boiling points. Because of this they can be separated by the process of **fractional distillation**. This involves heating the oil in a column like the one in Fig. 1. The temperatures show you that the column is heated from the bottom. This means that substances with the lowest boiling points rise right to the top of the column before their vapours condense. Heavy oils have high boiling points and condense near the bottom of the column. Each 'fraction' is a new mixture containing substances with similar properties.

Figure 1 also shows how the main fractions are used. A whole series of distillations is carried out in an oil refinery, and even then the substances in the oil are not completely separated. Crude oil fractions are mixtures of hydrocarbons. For more details see 6.7 and *Datapage P1*.

> **Q1** Use *Datapage P1* and a reference book to make notes on the uses of these fractions: fuel gases; kerosene; fuel oil; bitumen.

Conversion

Conversion processes are needed because some fractions are not as useful as others. The 'lighter' fractions contain small molecules. They make good fuels and valuable chemical raw materials. The 'heavier' ones contain large molecules. They are tarry and have fewer uses. Although some of the heavier fractions are suitable for road-making, the distillation process yields more than is needed for this purpose. To avoid wastage they are converted to 'lighter' materials which are more useful.

Many conversion processes have been developed. The most important of these is **cracking**. This is just what the name suggests – breaking up the larger molecules to produce smaller ones. One way of doing this is to heat the oil fraction very strongly. This process is called **thermal cracking**, and was the original method used. However, it is more efficient to run the process at a lower temperature, using a catalyst (**catalytic cracking**). A catalytic cracker is shown in Fig. 3.

Cracking not only breaks the larger hydrocarbon molecules into smaller ones. It also rearranges the structures of these molecules. Cracking usually increases the proportion of **alkenes** (see 6.9) in the final mixture.

> **Q2** Explain carefully why 'cracking' processes are so important in the oil industry.

Fig. 2 *A large oil refinery at Grangemouth in Scotland.*

Changes in supply and demand

The fortunes of the oil industry and world-wide economic changes are very closely linked. In recent years (mid-70s to mid-80s) the demand for fuel oil has not grown as expected. European oil refineries are not being fully used, and some of the Middle Eastern oil-producing countries have started to refine their own oil. New methods for extracting valuable products are being developed. At the same time the oil companies are aiming to develop 'flexible' refineries which can adapt their range of products to match changes in the pattern of demand.

Pollution problems and oil

Oil is a fossil fuel containing sulphur and nitrogen, so when oil products are burned, the air may be polluted with sulphur dioxide and nitrogen oxides (see 6.13). Another pollution risk is spilling the crude oil itself. Major spills have occurred from accidents with oil rigs and large tankers. Sometimes, oil is even dumped at sea deliberately when tankers are cleaned out. Oil spills are a serious threat to human safety and to wildlife.

Q3 Spilled oil is sometimes burned. Sometimes it is collected behind a temporary floating barrier (or 'boom'). On other occasions it is best dispersed with detergent. Unfortunately, all these methods cause further problems of their own. Find out more about this, and suggest what the problems may be.

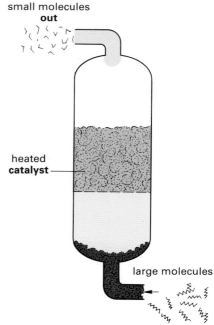

small molecules **out**

heated **catalyst**

large molecules

Fig. 3 *Catalytic cracking.*

163

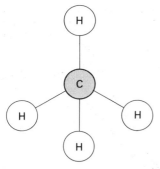

Fig. 1 Methane, CH_4, the most important hydrocarbon in natural gas.

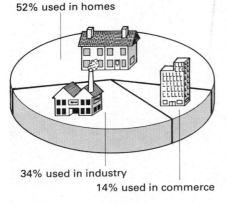

52% used in homes

34% used in industry

14% used in commerce

Fig. 2 Who uses gas?

Natural gas and other hydrocarbons

Compounds which contain hydrogen and carbon *only* are known as **hydrocarbons**. Because carbon atom has four electrons in its outer electron shell, it is capable of forming four covalent bonds to other atoms. The simplest hydrocarbon has the formula CH_4. Its structure is shown in Fig. 1. This compound is **methane**, and it is the main hydrocarbon in natural gas.

What exactly is natural gas?

Natural gas, like crude oil, is a mixture of hydrocarbons. As with oil, different gas fields produce natural gas of different types. The main variation from one gas field to another is in the sulphur content of the natural gas. Some natural gas contains so much hydrogen sulphide that it is an important source of sulphur (see 3.12). The natural gas around Britain is low in sulphur, however. Here are some typical figures for North Sea gas:

What's in North Sea gas?

Field	% methane	% ethane	% propane	% carbon dioxide	% nitrogen
Indefatigable	92	3.4	0.8	0.5	2.7
Leman	95	2.8	0.5	0.04	1.3

Figure 3 shows the main gas fields around Britain. Most are in the North Sea, but in 1985 the first gas was brought ashore from the Morecambe Bay gas field, which is about 40 km off Blackpool.

How is natural gas used?

Gas is supplied to millions of homes and businesses throughout Britain. About half of it is used by 'domestic' consumers for heating and cooking. About one sixth is used by commercial customers, such as hotels, restaurants, shops and offices. The rest is used by industry, in two ways – for heating and as a chemical raw material.

> **Q1** The main industrial uses of natural gas are as follows:
>
> | | |
> |---|---|
> | chemicals | 43% |
> | engineering | 16% |
> | metals | 10% |
> | pottery, cement, bricks and glass | 7% |
> | other uses | 24% |
>
> Make a pie chart to show these figures, and illustrate it with suitable pictures from magazines. How would you expect the demand for gas to change during the next 10 years?

Hydrocarbons

If the carbon atom could do no more than form four covalent bonds to hydrogen atoms, then methane would be the only hydrocarbon. Actually, it can form single, double and even triple covalent bonds to other carbon atoms. This extends the possibilities enormously.

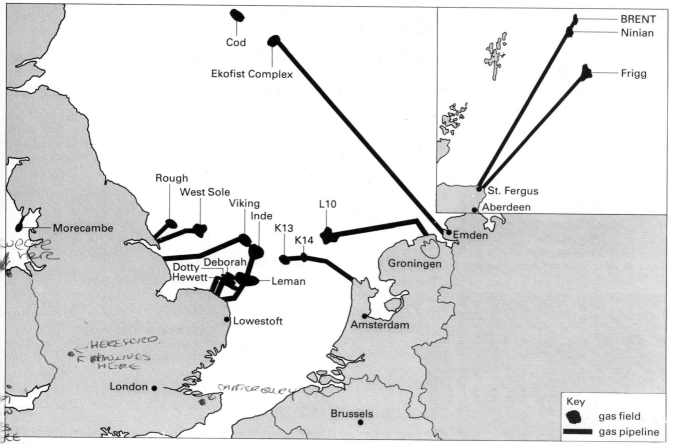

Fig. 3 *The gas fields around Britain. Most are in the North Sea, which provides over 90% of the gas consumed in Britain.*

Alkanes

Hydrocarbons in which all the carbon-to-carbon links are single covalent bonds are known as **alkanes**.

Some alkanes

Number of carbon atoms	Name of hydrocarbon	Formula of hydrocarbon	B.P. (°C)
1	methane	CH_4	−164
2	ethane	C_2H_6	−89
3	propane	C_3H_8	−42
4	butane	C_4H_{10}	−1
5	pentane	C_5H_{12}	+36

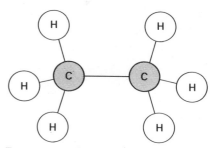

Fig. 4 *Ethane, C_2H_6.*

The alkanes are a 'family' of compounds with similar structures, similar properties and the same ending to their names. Their formulae all fit the general type $C_nH_{(2n+2)}$ where n is the number of atoms of carbon. A family of compounds like this is known as a **homologous series**.

Q2 Plot a graph which shows the boiling points of the alkanes in relation to the number of carbon atoms in the molecule. Allow room to include boiling points of up to +300 °C, and alkanes with up to 20 carbon atoms. Use your graph to predict the boiling points of alkanes with 6, 9, 12 and 16 carbon atoms. Compare your estimates with the figures given in *Datapage G*.

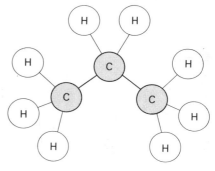

Fig. 5 *Propane, C_3H_8.*

165

The chemistry of alkanes

Crude oil and natural gas contain many alkanes, together with other hydrocarbons. The gas in the domestic supply is largely **methane**. Most of its natural impurities have been taken out. A tiny quantity of a strongly smelling substance has been added, so that gas leaks are noticed quickly. **Butane**, sometimes mixed with **propane**, is used in camping gases and also for gas lighter fuels and portable blow lamps. **Liquefied petroleum gas (LPG)** is a widely used fuel which contains mainly propane and butane.

Q1 Summarise the information in this paragraph by drawing a table with the following headings: name of alkane; formula; uses.

Fig. 1 *An alkane burning – domestic natural gas is mainly methane.*

The chemical behaviour of alkanes

The most important chemical reaction for many alkanes is what happens when they burn. Many alkanes are used as fuels. In a good supply of air they burn to carbon dioxide and water. For example, for propane:

$$C_3H_8(g) + 5O_2(g) \rightarrow 3CO_2(g) + 4H_2O(g)$$

$$\text{propane} + \text{oxygen} \rightarrow \text{carbon dioxide} + \text{water}$$

In other ways, alkanes are surprisingly unreactive.

Reaction with chlorine

Fig. 2 *Camping gas contains a mixture of alkanes.*

One reaction worth noting is that simple alkanes will react rapidly with chlorine. Methane and chlorine react when ultraviolet light splits chlorine molecules into atoms:

$$\overset{\text{ultraviolet}}{\underset{\text{(from sunlight)}}{}}$$
$$Cl_2(g) \rightarrow 2Cl(g)$$

A chlorine atom then reacts with a methane molecule and releases a hydrogen atom:

$$Cl(g) + CH_4(g) \rightarrow CH_3Cl(g) + H(g)$$

This hydrogen atom is highly reactive:

$$H(g) + Cl_2(g) \rightarrow HCl(g) + Cl(g)$$

As a result, another chlorine atom is produced. This, in turn, reacts with another methane molecule. The process continues until all the methane or all the chlorine has been used up. This is known as a **chain reaction**. It is such a rapid process that once it starts there is an explosion. Reaction which take place include:

$$CH_3Cl(g) + Cl_2(g) \rightarrow CH_2Cl_2(g) + HCl(g)$$

$$CH_3Cl_2(g) + Cl_2(g) \rightarrow CH_2Cl_3(g) + HCl(g)$$

$$CHCl_3(g) + Cl_2(g) \rightarrow CCl_4 + HCl(g)$$

Fig. 3 *Candles also contain a mixture of alkanes.*

The organic products of the reaction between methane and chlorine have the formulae CH_3Cl, CH_2Cl_2, $CHCl_3$ and CCl_4. They are the result of a series of **substitution reactions**, so called because the chlorine atoms have been *substituted* for the hydrogen atoms originally present in the methane molecule.

Fig. 4 *A control room at British Gas where supply and demand are monitored and controlled.*

Isomerism

Molecules with the *same formula*, but with *different structures* are known as **isomers**. One way to learn about this is by building a model.

> **Q2** Take 4 carbon atoms and 10 hydrogen atoms from a simple molecular model kit. You will need 13 'bonds'. Assemble all the atoms to make a complete molecule. Each carbon atom should be joined to one or two other carbon atoms. All remaining bonds should be carbon–hydrogen links. Now draw the model you have made.
>
> **Q3** Is there another way of assembling the same pieces to make a different molecule? Keep your first molecule, and try again with a new set of parts – or look at what someone else has made.

Figures 5 and 6 show the two possible answers to questions 2 and 3. At one time, both molecules were called butane, because both have the same formula. But their atoms are linked together in different ways. This causes them to have different *structures*, and therefore different *properties*.

> **Q4** Look at the two molecules with the formula C_4H_{10}. Both exist as gases at room temperature, but imagine millions and millions of them crowded together, as they would be in a liquid.
> (a) Which molecule would form the denser liquid?
> (b) Which would form the liquid with the higher boiling point?
> Information to check your answer can be found on *Datapage G*.

There are just two isomers with the formula C_4H_{10}, but the number of possibilities increases enormously in larger molecules. The word **isomerism** is given to the existence of two or more compounds with the same formula, but different three-dimensional structures.

Figs. 5 & 6 *Isomerism: two different molecules with the same formula, C_4H_{10}, but different structures.*

167

Alkenes

Key to bonds

—— single covalent bonds

⌒ double covalent bond

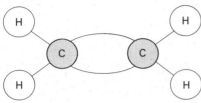

represented as:

Fig. 1 An ethene molecule, the simplest alkane.

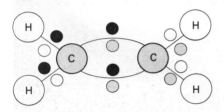

Key to electrons

○ from hydrogen atoms

● from left-hand carbon atom

◐ from right-hand carbon atom

Each pair of electrons makes one covalent bond.

*Fig. 2 An ethene molecule. A double covalent bond consists of **two** shared pairs of electrons.*

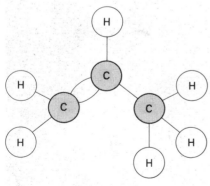

Fig. 3 A propene molecule.

Another homologous series of hydrocarbons is known as the **alkenes**. The special feature of an alkene is that it contains at least one pair of carbon atoms linked by a *double* covalent bond. A double bond is formed when two atoms are linked by *two* shared pairs of electrons (Fig. 1). The single bond between carbon atoms in alkanes has been represented as … C–C … The double bond between one pair of carbon atoms in alkenes is shown as … C=C …

Some alkenes

Number of carbon atoms	Name	Formula	B.P. (°C)
2	ethene	C_2H_4	−104
3	propene	C_3H_6	−47
5	pentene	C_5H_{10}	+30*
6	hexene	C_6H_{12}	+63*

* These figures refer to pent-1-ene and hex-1-ene respectively.

Q1 From this information, and from the information about alkanes in 6.8, make the following predictions about the alkene with four carbon atoms:
    (a) its name and formula;
    (b) whether or not it would show isomerism (use models);
    (c) its approximate boiling point.

How is ethene used?

Ethene is a very important industrial chemical. Much of it is used in the manufacture of ethanol and certain plastics.

Ethanol is formed in the reaction between ethene and steam, at high temperature. A catalyst is used.

$$\text{ethene} + \text{steam} \xrightarrow{\text{catalyst}} \text{ethanol}$$
$$C_2H_4(g) + H_2O(g) \xrightarrow{\text{catalyst}} C_2H_5OH(g)$$

Plastics

Ethene is the starting point for three very widely used plastics: Poly(ethene), PVC and poly(styrene). Poly(ethene), often known as 'polythene', is made by polymerisation of ethene at high pressure. This is when lots of small molecules, in this case ethene, are joined together to make one giant molecule, in this case poly(ethene). ('Poly' means many.) You can read more about polymers in 7.13. Polythene is used in packaging. PVC is used for the insulation on electrical cables, and for brightly coloured rainwear. Poly(styrene) has many uses too. The cups from drinks machines are nearly always poly(styrene). The ones which split if you crush them in your hand are high-density poly(styrene). The foam-plastic ones are made from 'expanded polystyrene'.

Q2 Green bananas are often kept in 'ripening rooms' containing ethene for a few days before they are sold. Green tomatoes, too, will change colour when kept in ethene. Suggest some possible reasons for this practice.

Fig. 4 Ethene is used to ripen bananas. Here they are being taken from the ripening room.

The chemical behaviour of alkenes

Alkenes have a greater variety of chemical reactions than alkanes. This is because their double bonds contain electrons which can be released to take part in **addition reactions**. Under suitable conditions, addition reactions can take place with gases such as hydrogen or chlorine:

$$> C{=}C < \quad +H_2(g) \quad \rightarrow \quad > CH{-}CH <$$
(alkene)

$$> C{=}C < \quad +Cl_2(g) \quad \rightarrow \quad > CCl{-}CCl <$$
(alkene)

Fig. 5 Made from ethene: polythene wrapping on snack foods.

These reactions are used to convert alkenes to other useful materials. An addition reaction between hydrogen and the alkenes in suitable vegetable oils is used to make margarine (see 7.12). Addition reactions between chlorine and alkenes are used in making solvents and the starting materials for plastics. Making polythene from ethene is also an addition reaction (see 7.14).

Recognising alkenes –
the bromine test for unsaturation

The addition reaction between bromine and alkenes is used as a chemical test for the presence of a double bond. When bromine water is shaken with an alkene the yellow-brown colour of the bromine disappears. This happens because bromine reacts with alkenes to form substances which are not coloured.

Hydrocarbons which contain no double bonds are known as **saturated hydrocarbons**. Those which have double or even triple bonds between some pairs of carbon atoms are called **unsaturated**. Unsaturated hydrocarbons usually react with bromine water.

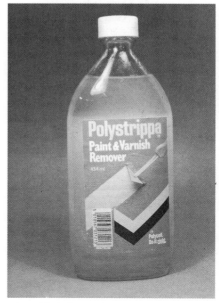

Fig. 6 Made from ethene: a solvent for removing paint.

169

Minerals and ores

Fig. 1 A mineral but not an ore: malachite.

Fig. 2 A mineral and an ore. This kidney iron ore gets its name from its shape.

Very few raw materials occur on the earth ready for use. Most require some processing first of all. Even coal needs to be washed, to remove unwanted dirt and rock which is mixed with it.

The solid raw materials in the earth are often referred to as **mineral resources**. They range from substances as precious as diamonds to materials as ordinary as sand and gravel. Usually they have to be quarried or mined in some way, and nearly always they have to be separated from the unwanted material which surrounds them. A list of some important minerals is given on *Datapage R1*.

What is a mineral?

The word 'mineral' is used in more than one way. A mineralogist thinks of a mineral as a pure crystalline inorganic substance, found in the earth's crust. Collectors of minerals are interested in very attractive samples like the malachite in Fig. 1. A wider meaning of the word 'mineral' is used by geologists, geochemists and mining engineers – it includes all the substances listed on *Datapage R1*, and many more. Most minerals are chemical compounds, although a few (such as gold and diamonds) are elements.

What is an ore?

The word 'ore' is used to describe a mineral resource which

☐ is found in the earth's crust
☐ is a chemical compound
☐ contains a metal
☐ can be used as a commercial source of that metal.

Figure 2 is a photograph of one form of iron ore or haematite.

Extracting metals from their ores

The method used for extracting a metal from its ore is related to the position of that metal in the Reactivity Series (see 4.3). The higher the metal is in the Series, the more difficult it is to extract from its ore. Only the most unreactive metals occur as the 'native' element, uncombined with any other substance.

Q1 Name three metals which might be found 'native', and give reasons for your choice.

Q2 Find out from an encyclopaedia how *one* of the following metals is extracted from its ore: lithium, vanadium, chromium, magnesium. Write down a simple explanation of the method which is used.

Did you know?

How many of the chemical elements have been found in their native state?

Twenty-two elements. How many of these can you think of?

Fig. 3 *Mining a very ordinary mineral, but a vital one. This limestone is being crushed to a suitable size for making foundations for buildings and roads.*

The amounts of different minerals which were produced in the UK in some recent years are shown below.

Mineral production in the United Kingdom

Mineral	UK production (thousands of tonnes)				
	1971	1979	1981	1983	1985
coal	122500	122400	127000	119000	94000
crude oil	–	77900	89000	125000	127500
sand and gravel	108000	111500	100000	107000	106000
limestone and dolomite	93000	97000	79000	93000	94000
natural gas	–	58000*	58000*	55000*	57000*
igneous rock	36000	36000	31000	37000	37000
miscellaneous clays	34000	28000	23000	27000	23000
sandstone	11500	13500	12000	15000	15000
chalk	17500	14000	12000	12000	12000
gypsum and ahydrite	4100	3500	2900	2900	3200
rock salt	1800	1600	1350	1300	1600
potash	–	440	466	504	562
iron ore	10000	4269	731	384	274
slate	67	500	350	494	190
fluorspar	224	154	185	131	150
barytes	20	45	63	36	70
lead/copper/zinc (as metal)	14	5.3	18.5	13.4	8.6
tin (as metal)	3.8	3.7	3.7	4.0	5.3

* These figures refer to the energy equivalent in tonnes of coal.

Q3 Use the information from this table to comment on the production changes during recent years for (a) crude oil, (b) natural gas, (c) coal, (d) iron ore, (e) rock salt.

Fig. 4 *Mining a very precious mineral: diamonds. This is the Premier mine which produced the Cullinan diamond.*

Fig. 5 *Metal-mining in Britain: Cornish tin at Geevor.*

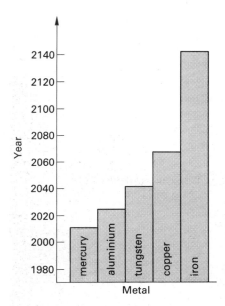

Fig. 1 *One opinion (published in 1975) about how long our mineral resources may last.*

Fig. 2 *Lead is too valuable to throw away when the battery wears out. It is re-cycled.*

Fig. 3 *Recycling glass: a bottle bank.*

6.11

Making best use of our mineral resources

How long will our mineral resources last?

No-one can really tell how long our supplies of mineral resources will last. Many people believe that some minerals may run out in the next 50 years, but it is extremely difficult to make accurate predictions.

On the positive side, it is known that the world has enough aluminium and iron ores to last many centuries. There is no immediate shortage of coal, and there may be new sources of oil. Some minerals will run out soon, however, leaving us with some difficult choices:

☐ finding new sources of supply (much deeper in the earth, perhaps)
☐ doing without familiar minerals, and solving problems in new ways
☐ re-using minerals which have already been extracted.

World circumstances change very rapidly. In the mid-1980s, for instance, the demand for oil and uranium was well below what the producers could supply, yet 10 years earlier there had been shortages.

Figure 1 gives one opinion of how long some of our mineral resources will last.

New minerals or old?

When you have finished with an aluminium drinks can, you probably throw it away. Although aluminium is not cheap, the cost of collecting and re-using old cans is greater than making completely new ones. If you decided to get rid of a piece of silver jewellery, however, you would probably sell it to someone who would use the metal for something else. The silver would be **re-cycled**.

Lead re-cycling

One metal which is re-cycled more than any other is lead. When a car battery no longer works, the lead in it can be re-used (Fig. 2). In fact, nearly half the lead used each year throughout the world has been used before for something else. This happens because the cost of re-cycling the lead can be about the same as mining and smelting new lead. The more lead there is in use, the more becomes available for re-cycling, so the price falls. The price of new lead also varies, according to successes or problems in mining and production.

Glass re-cycling

One of the best known examples of re-cycling is the 'bottle bank' for re-using glass (Fig. 3). The firms who use bottle banks need to keep the costs right down. They provide:

☐ separate compartments for glass of different colours (so that they do not have to pay for the glass to be sorted)
☐ skips which can easily be loaded on to lorries (to cut down collection costs).

Q1 Copper is a fairly expensive metal (see *Datapage S4*). Suggest how a 'copper bank' might be run to keep re-cycling costs down to a minimum. Include sketches if you wish.

Fig. 4 This land, once a quarry, has been restored for public use.

Some environmental problems involved in using minerals

Extracting large amounts of mineral resources leaves very large holes in the ground. If these holes are in an underground mine, they can lead to subsidence (Fig. 5). If they are at ground level, as in quarries or open-cast mines, they can be unsightly and wasteful of land (Fig. 6).

The importance of avoiding these problems is well recognised, and there are ways of dealing with them. However, there are always difficult decisions to be made. The value of the mining activity must always be balanced against the costs of its consequences. For example, a main railway used to run above the Selby coalfield in Yorkshire. Before mining could start, a choice had to be made. Either a zone of coal a mile wide had to be left untouched, to prevent possible subsidence, or the railway had to be re-routed. A 14-mile track diversion was built in 1983, at a cost of £60 million.

Quarries and open-cast workings are reclaimed by a process of 'landfill' – either by tipping domestic rubbish, or by working in such a way that unwanted material removed from one part of the hole is transferred to finished sections of it elsewhere. Mining companies are required to restore the land to a very high standard. An example can be seen in Fig. 4.

Two more mining problems are noise and dust. The two tend to go together, since they are caused by the blasting and crushing processes which are often needed. Sometimes they are also caused by the heavy lorries used to transport the product. It can be unpleasant to live near a working quarry, but methods are available for limiting the inconvenience, and these are closely watched by local groups.

Fig. 5 Careless mining can lead to problems like this: subsidence!

Fig. 6 This familiar sight in Cornwall is the result of mining for China clay.

Water

Fig. 1 This reservoir holds enough water to provide the whole of England and Wales with the water it needs for just one day.

water vapour condenses to form clouds

water droplets in clouds become large enough to fall as rain

water evaporates

rivers and streams flow back to the sea

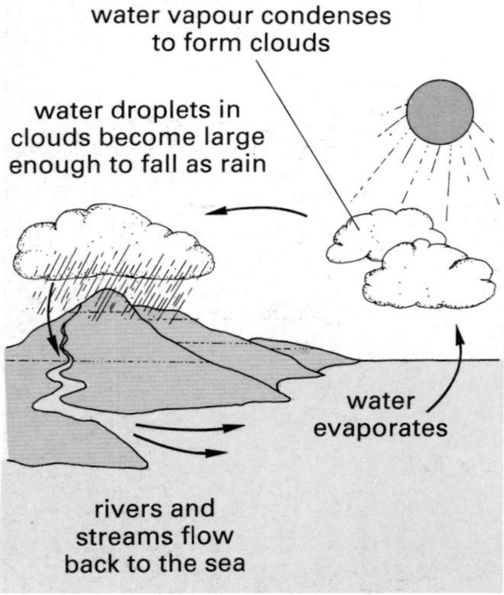

Fig. 2 The natural water cycle.

% of population receiving fluoridated water supply (1977)

- □ 0
- □ <10
- □ 11–30
- ■ 31–45
- ■ 46–90
- ■ >90

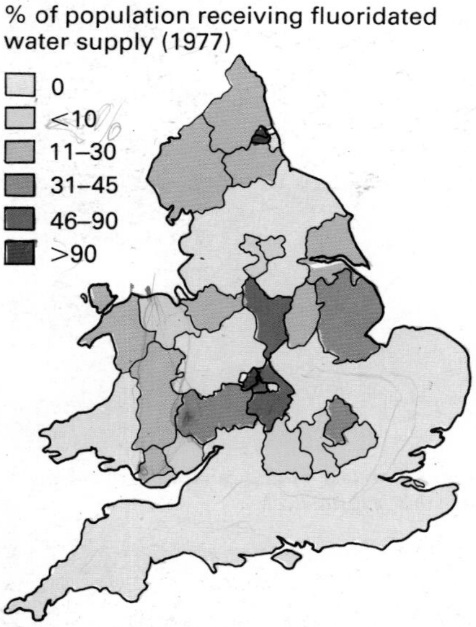

Fig. 3 Sodium fluoride is added to the public water supply in these areas to help prevent tooth decay.

The amount of water used every day in England and Wales alone would almost completely empty the reservoir shown in Fig. 1. This is 3000 million gallons (14000 million litres), or 60 gallons (272 litres) per day for every single person. Nearly two-thirds of this is used in the home. The rest is used to make things. For instance, nearly 1.5 million litres of water are needed to make 1 tonne of aluminium, and

making 1 tonne of steel uses	200000 litres
filling one car with petrol	4000 litres
making 1 large newspaper	180 litres
producing 1 litre of milk	6 litres

The water cycle

The re-circulation of water, which takes place all over the globe, is known as the **water cycle** (Fig. 2).

(1) The water which falls as rain runs into streams and rivers, and eventually reaches the sea.
(2) Evaporation from lakes and the sea causes water vapour to build up in the atmosphere.
(3) This vapour condenses on cooling, to form clouds. Rain begins to fall when the condensed water droplets reach a certain size.

What's in the water from the tap?

Water for the public supply contains few micro-organisms and very little solid material. However, there are substances dissolved in it. Rainwater dissolves oxygen and carbon dioxide from the atmosphere, especially as it runs slowly through the air which is trapped between soil particles. The water also dissolves salts from the soil and rocks over which it flows.

Other substances are sometimes added to the water supply on purpose. One of these is **sodium fluoride**. The idea of putting sodium fluoride into the water supply came from the discovery that adding this substance – in the right quantities – helps to prevent tooth decay. Some people believe that it is wrong to add chemicals to drinking water, and point out that sodium fluoride is poisonous. Too much of it does cause mottled teeth, and swallowing solid sodium fluoride could be fatal! Nevertheless, a number of Water Authorities have decided to add sodium fluoride in carefully controlled amounts (Fig. 3). Children who live in areas with sodium fluoride in the water supply have healthier teeth than those who don't.

Q1 Is there sodium fluoride in your tap water? Give the arguments 'for' and 'against' adding fluoride. What is your own opinion?

Purifying the water supply

Before water can be used for drinking or food preparation it must be purified.

(1) The water is filtered through coarse gratings to remove floating rubbish, and then through sand and gravel beds.
(2) The most dangerous impurities are micro-organisms, which cause disease if allowed to multiply in drinking water. For this reason, water is usually treated with chlorine. This kills most of the organisms, reducing their concentration to a safe level.

some of the bacteria present in water are removed by microbes grown esp. for that purpose in the sand

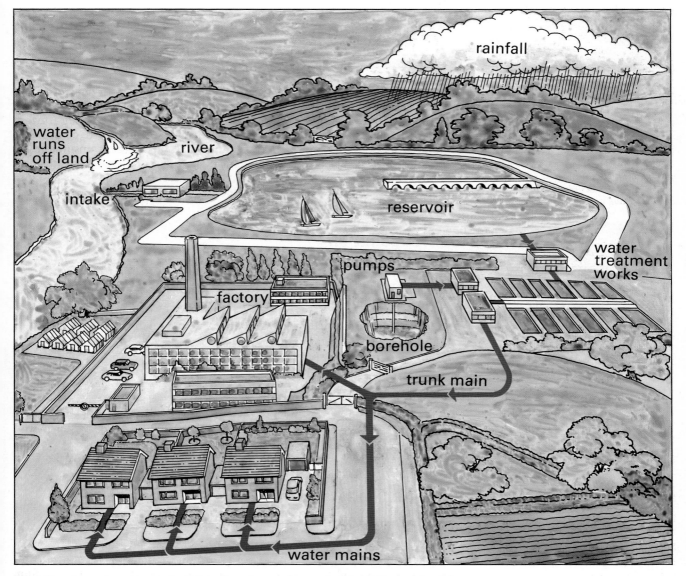

Fig. 4 How does water get to your tap? Water from rivers and reservoirs is treated to remove solid material and kill dangerous micro-organisms, before being piped to homes and factories.

Sea water

The 'salt' in sea water is a mixture of substances which have dissolved in the water during its passage to the sea. The amount of dissolved material is surprisingly constant in the open oceans – about 35 g in 1 kg of sea water. Enclosed seas contain much more because of evaporation. The Dead Sea, for instance, contains around 275 g of salts in every kilogram of water.

'Sea salt' is mostly sodium chloride, but other ions are also present. Here is what you would find in a solid sample of 'sea salt'.

Sea salt

Cations		Anions	
Na^+	84%	Cl^-	87%
Mg^{2+}	10%	SO_4^{2-}	12%
Ca^{2+}	3%	HCO_3^-	0.6%
K^+	3%	Br^-	0.3%

Fig. 5 The concentration of salt in the Dead Sea is about 8 times greater than in the open oceans.

175

Water pollution

Fig. 1 We take water for granted, but this Welsh reservoir ran dry during a recent summer drought.

Fig. 2 Some rivers are still seriously polluted.

The public water supply is constantly being re-used. It is rather a shock to realise that water discharged as waste into one part of a river may re-appear (after suitable treatment!) through the taps of people living further downstream. This means that great care must be taken to control the quality of water. In some parts of Europe the tap water is unsuitable for infants to drink because it contains a high concentration of nitrate ions. These come from fertilisers which have been washed off the fields and into the rivers. Constant checks are needed to make sure that dangerous levels of pollutants do not build up.

River pollution

In Britain there are some very clean rivers, but there are others which are a disgrace. Between 2000 and 3000 kilometres of the larger rivers in Britain are too heavily polluted for fish to survive in them. This pollution can take many forms, but the two most important ones are

☐ poisonous substances which kill plant and animal life
☐ organic matter containing micro-organisms which use up dissolved oxygen from the water while 'feeding'.

Why is dissolved oxygen important?

Dissolved oxygen is vital for the survival of fish and many other organisms which live in water. Water which contains large quantities of organic matter can, in the presence of micro-organisms, become starved of its dissolved oxygen. The process may be represented:

oxygen + organic matter + micro-organisms

↓

carbon dioxide + water + organic debris + more micro-organisms

Where the micro-organisms are multiplying in this way the oxygen dissolved in water is used up, and there is not enough left for other water creatures to survive. When this is going on, the water is said to have a high **Biological Oxygen Demand** (BOD). The BOD of a water sample is found by measuring its oxygen content, keeping it for a fixed period of time at a fixed temperature, and then measuring the amount of oxygen left. The amount of oxygen used up in this time, measured in milligrams of oxygen per litre of water, is known as the Biological Oxygen Demand. Nitrates in the water can make the problem worse. You can find out why in 7.5.

Q1 Visit a local river or stream and make a list of the different types of pollutant you can see in it. What other types of pollutant may be present, but invisible to the naked eye?

Q2 Suppose you had the task of checking for pollution in a nearby river. Describe some simple tests of 'water quality' which you could use.

Did you know?

About how many times is water in Britain re-used between falling as rain, entering the public supply, and eventually returning to the sea?

It varies of course, but the average is about 3 times.

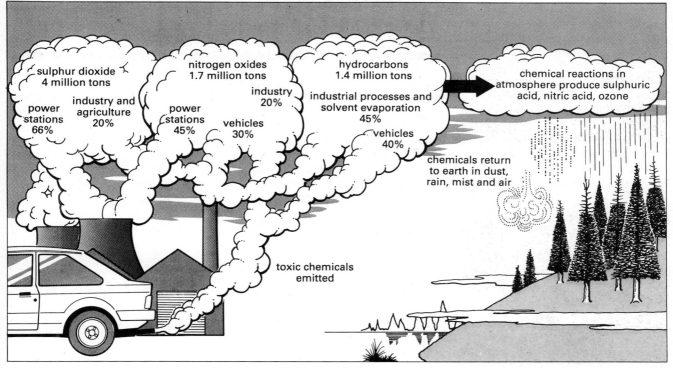

Fig. 3 *Some possible causes of acid rain.*

Acid rain

Rainwater is always slightly acidic because it contains dissolved carbon dioxide. Its natural pH value is around 5.5. In recent years there has been great concern that rainfall with a much lower pH may be responsible for damage to trees and freshwater life.

Three substances are believed to be responsible for acid rain:

☐ sulphuric acid – which comes from the sulphur dioxide released by the burning of fossil fuels

☐ nitric acid – which comes from the nitrogen oxides in motor vehicle exhaust

☐ ozone – which is formed in the reaction between nitrogen oxides and the oxygen in the air.

Fig. 4 *Photographs like this persuaded people that acid rain should be taken seriously.*

Figure 3 shows how the problem seems to have arisen. Motor vehicle exhausts and power stations burning fossil fuels appear to be the main culprits, but there is a lot more research to be done.

The problem of acid rain is very complicated. A change in the pH of a lake or river causes other changes too. Acid water may dissolve poisonous metal ions from clay. This in turn may cause problems with nearby trees and other vegetation. Changes in plant life lead to changes in the animal life, and so on.

Q3 The helicopter in Fig. 5 is adding lime to an 'acid' lake. Explain what effect the lime might have.

Q4 Using lime is only a temporary cure for the problem. What other suggestions can you make?

Fig. 5 *Liming an acidified lake may help to correct the problem for a while.*

Hard water

Fig. 1 This scum is the most obvious effect of hardness in water.

Fig. 2 Hard water leaves deposits like this in a kettle.

Fig. 3 Pipes carrying hot water may get blocked like this if the water is hard.

If you stay in another part of the country, you may notice that the water there seems different from the water which comes out of your taps at home. One difference may be in the 'feel' of the water, and the amount of soap you need for washing. Water which requires a lot of soap to produce a lather is known as **hard water**.

The word 'hard' is used here to mean harsh or rough, since hard water drying on your hands leaves them with a chalky feel. 'Soft' water requires little soap, and feels much smoother as you wash. Hardness is a chemical effect, due to substances which have dissolved in the water on its way to the reservoir. Water tends to be hardest in chalk or limestone districts. *Datapage J2* shows how the hardness varies in different parts of the country.

> **Q1** Use *Datapage J2* to make a table showing the water hardness in the following places:
> Birmingham, Cardiff, Glasgow, Liverpool, Leeds, London, Nottingham, Southampton, your own home area.

The dissolved materials in hard water have certain advantages, but also cause problems when the water is used.

Advantages of water hardness

☐ Dissolved salts in drinking water may be a useful supplement to the diet. Calcium salts, in particular, help with healthy bones and teeth. Heart disease seems to occur less frequently in hard water areas, though the hard water may not be the only reason for this.

☐ Hard water does not dissolve undesirable substances as readily as soft water. This is why some drinks, such as 'bitter' beer, are best made with hard water.

Disadvantages of water hardness

☐ Hard water is less suitable for any washing purpose than soft water. It wastes a great deal of soap, and it also leaves a deposit of scum on the articles being washed (Fig. 1).

☐ When hard water is boiled the dissolved salts may be deposited. The heating elements in kettles become 'furred up' (Fig. 2) and hot water pipes may even become blocked (Fig. 3). If boiler pipes become blocked in this way, a serious explosion can occur.

> **Q2** Industries normally require water which has been 'softened' by removing all the dissolved salts. How do you think that using hard water might cause problems in industry?

What causes hardness in water?

The hardness in water is due to ions which react with soap to form a precipitate or scum. The reason that soap forms a scum in hard water is that a precipitation reaction takes place. For example:

sodium soap (aq)   calcium ions (aq)   sodium ions (aq)   calcium soap (s)
(soap)   + (hard water) → (soft water) + (scum)

Fig. 4 *When hard water evaporates slowly it can leave these beautiful stalactites and stalagmites. These are the Dan-yr-Ogof caves in West Glamorgan.*

Simple soaps are salts of the 'soap acids', such as stearic acid, $C_{17}H_{35}COOH$. Sodium stearate, its sodium salt, is a 'sodium soap'. Sodium soaps are soluble in water. Calcium and magnesium soaps are not. They appear as a precipitate or scum when soluble soaps are added to hard water.

Temporary and permanent water hardness

Hardness which can be removed by boiling the water is known as **temporary hardness**. It is due to hydrogencarbonate ions, which break down on heating (or when the water evaporates). For example:

$$\text{calcium hydrogencarbonate (aq)} \xrightarrow{\text{boiling}} \text{carbon dioxide (g)} + \text{water (l)} + \text{calcium carbonate (s)}$$

$$Ca(HCO_3)_2(aq) \xrightarrow{\text{boiling}} CO_2(g) + H_2O(l) + CaCO_3(s)$$

The deposit which furs kettles and blocks pipes is calcium (or magnesium) carbonate. Sometimes this is called 'boiler scale'.

Hardness which cannot be removed by boiling the water is known as **permanent hardness**. Permanent hardness is caused by ions which are not affected by being heated to this temperature. *e.g sulphate ions*

Ions responsible for water hardness
Common cations (permanent hardness)
calcium, Ca^{2+}(aq) magnesium, Mg^{2+}(aq)
Common anion (temporary hardness)
hydrogencarbonate, HCO_3^-(aq)

sulphate ion (permanent)

Coping with hard water

Fig. 1 *This rain, falling on chalky ground, will be hard water when it reaches your tap.*

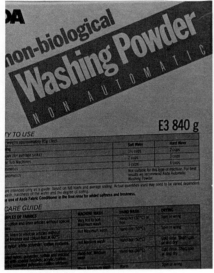

Fig. 2 *The instructions on this washing powder suggest that you use more in hard water areas.*

The substances dissolved in a sample of water tell you its 'history'. Water which has run through a limestone or chalk district contains dissolved calcium salts (Fig. 1). Often it also contains hydrogencarbonate ions.

The hydrogencarbonate ions get into the water like this:

☐ Rainwater dissolves carbon dioxide from the air, and becomes a dilute solution of carbonic acid, H_2CO_3.

☐ This carbonic acid reacts with calcium carbonate (in chalk or limestone), giving calcium hydrogencarbonate:

| carbonic acid (aq) | + | calcium carbonate (s) | → | calcium hydrogencarbonate (aq) |

$$H_2CO_3(aq) + CaCO_3(s) \rightarrow Ca(HCO_3)_2(aq)$$

How can hard water be softened?

Any treatment which removes the ions causing hardness can be used as a water-softening method.

☐ One method would simply be to use lots of soap, until the cations had been removed as scum. Clearly this is of very limited use!

☐ Another method would be to boil or distil the water. Boiling would remove temporary hardness, and distillation would remove all dissolved material.

Distillation uses a lot of heat energy, so it is expensive. It is used when small quantities of purified water are required, as in a laboratory.

☐ A relatively cheap large-scale method of water softening is to add sodium carbonate crystals (washing soda, see 3.6). The carbonate ions react with calcium and magnesium ions in the hard water, to give a precipitate, for example:

| magnesium sulphate (aq) | + | sodium carbonate (s) | → | sodium sulphate (aq) | + | magnesium carbonate (s) |

$$MgSO_4(aq) + Na_2CO_3(s) \rightarrow Na_2SO_4(aq) + MgCO_3(s)$$

Water softened in this way is suitable for washing clothes, and many washing powders contain water-softening chemicals. Some manufacturers make different batches of soap powder for different areas of the country, to allow for variations in water hardness.

Q1 Suggest a method for comparing the hardness of samples of water taken from different parts of the country.

Ion-exchange water softeners

Many industries and quite a few homes use **ion-exchange** water softeners. These contain a material which will exchange all the cations in hard water for sodium ions, as the hard water passes through (see Fig. 4). The material inside an ion-exchanger of this type is a resin, with sodium ions 'loosely attached' to it. As the hard water passes through, the ions in the water change places with the ions on the resin. For example:

sodium resin + calcium ions → calcium resin + sodium ions
(in softened water)

Fig. 3 This household water softener uses ion-exchange.

After many hundreds of gallons of hard water have passed through, all the sodium ions from the resin have been used up, and replaced by other ions from the water. At this stage the resin must be 'regenerated'. The regeneration is simply a matter of exchanging the ions back to what they were, and to do this a concentrated solution of salt is used:

    sodium ions   + calcium resin   →   sodium resin + calcium ions
    (from salt solution)

The calcium ions which are released in this process are washed through with the first few gallons of water after regeneration. This water may be used for purposes where its hardness will not matter.

The ion-exchange process does not remove all the ions from hard water. It simply exchanges them for other ions which have no effect on soap. Water which has been softened by ion-exchange may contain a high concentration of sodium ions, and should not be used for making up baby foods. In hard water areas, drinking water should be taken straight from the mains tap.

De-ionised water

Pure water for laboratory use and for topping up car batteries should contain no dissolved material at all. Sometimes it is made by distillation, which is why it is known as 'distilled water'. The alternative is to use a **de-ioniser**. A de-ioniser works like an ion-exchange water softener, but with two important differences:

☐ it exchanges all positive ions for *hydrogen* ions, $H^+(aq)$;

☐ it contains a second resin which exchanges all negative ions for *hydroxyl* ions, $OH^-(aq)$.

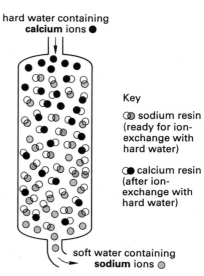

hard water containing
calcium ions ●

Key

⊕ sodium resin
(ready for ion-
exchange with
hard water)

⊕ calcium resin
(after ion-
exchange with
hard water)

soft water containing
sodium ions ⊙

Fig. 4 Ion-exchange works like this.

Questions

A. What can you remember?

* **1.** Explain what is meant by a *fossil fuel*. Give three examples of fossil fuels.

** **2.** There are several different types of coal. Give their names and explain the differences between them.

* **3.** What is *coke*, and how is it made?

** **4.** Britain has oil fields on both land and sea. Where are they to be found?

** **5.** A method called *seismic* surveying is used in the search for oil. Explain what this is, and how it works.

** **6.** Name *four* important fractions obtained in oil refining and explain how they are used.

** **7.** 'Natural gas consists largely of a single hydrocarbon.' Explain what this statement means.

** **8.** Explain what happens when an alkane burns.

** **9.** Ethene is an important alkene. Explain what an alkene is, and why ethene is important.

** **10.** Choose one example of an important *mineral resource*. Explain where it is found, how it is extracted, and how it is used.

** **11.** Explain what treatment must be given to the water collected in a reservoir before it is fit to drink.

** **12.** What is *acid rain*, and why is this a worrying problem?

*** **13.** What is meant by the *biological oxygen demand* of a water sample? How is it measured, and why is it important?

* **14.** Explain what is meant by *hard* water. How does water become hard?

** **15.** What methods can be used to soften hard water?

B. What have you understood?

** **16.** Explain, with examples, what is meant by the terms *combustion* and *incomplete combustion*.

** **17.** 'Oil is used in two main ways.' (see 6.4). Explain what is meant by this statement.

** **18.** What has to be done to turn crude oil into useful substances? Explain how these tasks are carried out at an oil refinery.

* **19.** Explain what is meant by *re-cycling*. Give an example of one material which is re-cycled, and another which is not, explaining the reasons in each case.

** **20.** 'The recirculation of water which takes place all over the globe is known as the *water cycle*.' (See 6.12.) Explain and illustrate this statement.

** **21.** Explain why opencast mining for a mineral deposit is often preferable to sinking a mineshaft. What are the disadvantages of the opencast method?

** **22.** Explain why alkenes will undergo addition reactions, but alkanes will not.

C. Can you use this information?

** 23.** Here is some information about drinking water taken from various places in Britain during the last century.

Date	Location	Type of supply	total solid	nitrogen content	hardness	appearance
1873	Birmingham	shallow well	195	6.4	93	turbid
1877	Machynlleth	mountain stream	2.6	0.09	0.9	clear
1876	Maidenhead	deep well	41	0.9	30	clear
1877	London	River Thames	28	0.24	20	turbid

What conclusions can you draw from these figures?

* **24.** Here is some information about natural gas deposits in different parts of the world.

AREA	% methane	% ethane	% propane	% carbon dioxide	% nitrogen	others
Leman, North Sea	95	2.8	0.5	0.04	1.3	
Lacq, S. France	69	2.8	0.8	9.7	–	15% H_2S
Groningen, Holland	81.2	2.9	0.4	0.9	14.4	
Amarillo, Texas	72.9	19.0	–	0.4	7.7	

Where would you find the natural gas which
(a) has the highest proportion of methane?
(b) could be used as a source of sulphur?
(c) produces the most heat per cubic metre?

** **25.** This information is about some oil refineries in Britain.

Name	Refining capacity (in thousands of tonnes)		
	1964	1974	1984
Esso, Fawley	11,500	19,000	15,600
Shell, Stanlow	10,350	18,000	12,500
BP, Grangemouth	4,500	8,700	8,800
Texaco, Pembroke	4,800	9,000	9,000

Is it possible to draw any conclusions from these figures?
Justify your answer as far as possible.

* **26.** Find the answers to the following questions from *Datapage Q*.
(a) How is most of Britain's coal used?
(b) Which is the world's largest producer of brown coal (lignite)?
(c) Which countries in Europe produces more coal than Britain?

** **27.** Find the answers to the following questions from *Datapage P*.
(a) How is propane used commercially?
(b) What is LPG?
(c) Approximately what percentage of North Sea oil is bitumen?
(d) Arrange the following fuels in order of their boiling points (putting the lowest first): DERV (diesel); heavy fuel oil; aviation spirit; petrol.

D. Taking it further

** **28.** At the end of 6.1 there are three 'moral questions' about the use of fuels. Choose *one* of these, and write an answer in the form of a letter to a science magazine.

** **29.** Wood is regarded in some parts of the world as 'the fuel of the future'. Explain some of the arguments both for and against this view.

** **30.** 'Coal is too valuable to burn' says a newspaper headline. Explain what this statement means.

*** **31.** There is a recent theory that oil is not a fossil fuel at all. It is believed that oil may have been formed deep down inside the earth, early in its history. What evidence would you need to convince you that the conventional theory (given in 6.4) is not correct?

** **32.** A typical N.Sea gas pipeline is about 1 metre in diameter and 400 km long. Its energy content is about 40 MJ m^{-3}.
(a) How many cubic metres of gas does it hold?
(b) How many households would this supply for a year, assuming an average use of 2000 m^3 for each?
(c) What is the energy content of the gas in the pipeline.
NB: The gas is in fact under pressure, but the effect of pressure has been ignored in this question.

Quick questions

1. Name a solid fuel, a liquid fuel and a gaseous fuel.

2. Give the name and one use of (a) an alkane (b) an alkene.

3. What is the difference between *temporary* and *permanent* hardness in water?

4. Name two metal ores found in commercial quantities in Britain.

5. What is a jack-up rig?

How the chemical industry is organised

Fig. 1 *Most people think of something like this when the words 'chemical industry' are mentioned.*

Fig. 3 *Fumes and dust from this works are having a severe effect on the environment.*

Fig. 2 *This chemical plant makes sugar in Kenya.*

Fig. 4 *Sometimes it is necessary to build a complete town around a new industrial development. This is a bauxite mine in Australia.*

All manufacturers – whether of chemical products or anything else – are engaged in a process which may be summed up:

$$raw\ materials\ \rightarrow\ processing\ \rightarrow\ products$$

which means that they are concerned with

$$supplies\ \rightarrow\ manufacture\ \rightarrow\ sales$$

The chemical industry is a business which has grown up to provide a livelihood for those who work in it, and a profit for shareholders who have invested money in chemical companies. At the same time it is there to meet the need for an ever-growing range of materials and products. A well-run business not only matches its output to the needs of its customers. It also anticipates, perhaps even creates, 'needs' which the customer has not yet thought about.

The chemical industry is extremely diverse. There are huge multinational companies making an enormous range of products. There are tiny companies, specialising in just one kind of business. There are the ultra-clean industries of semiconductors and pharmaceutical manufacture. There are also the noisy and dirty processes needed to make the most of raw materials like metal ores, oil and coal.

Processing and manufacture

The major divisions of the chemical industry in the 'developed nations' are:

agricultural chemicals	heavy chemicals
dyestuffs	metals
explosives	paints
fibres	plastics and petrochemicals
fine chemicals and pharmaceuticals	

There is a chemical industry in the developing nations of the 'third world', too. Some of it is imported plant for local production of materials like those listed above. Some is more concerned with basic needs, such as water supply and food production. Some is there to provide raw materials for the industries abroad.

Locating a chemical plant

The decision on where to build a particular chemical plant is an extremely complicated one. These are some of the more important things which have to be thought about:

☐ **Communications** – road, rail, sea and even air access are needed for bringing in raw materials and distributing products.

☐ **Environment** – this must not be affected too much while building the plant or disposing of its waste.

☐ **Power supply** – this must be available, or it must be possible to generate power at the site.

☐ **Utilities** – examples are water and fuel; these must be available at reasonable cost.

☐ **Workers** – these must be recruited, and perhaps moved to the area and housed.

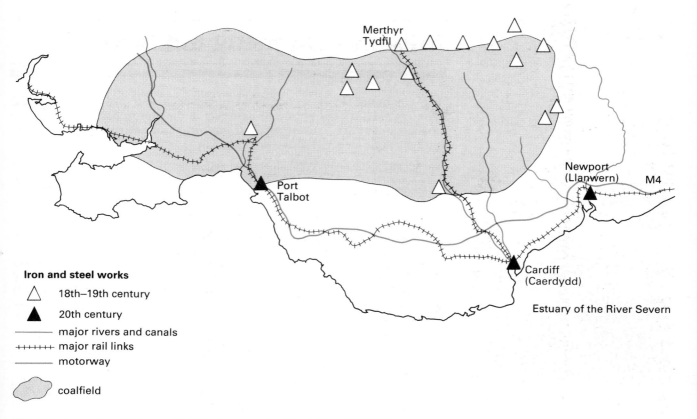

Fig. 5 The iron and steel industry of S. Wales began on the edge of the coalfield, where raw materials were plentiful. The products were transported by canal, and then by rail. The industry moved to the coast when it became necessary to import iron ore. Raw materials and products are now moved by rail and road.

The supply of raw materials

The main raw materials for the chemical industry are oil and natural gas, coal, metal ores, minerals like salt and limestone, and the gases of the air. All of these must be found, extracted and transported to where they are needed. There are important issues here:

☐ Some raw materials are running out. Since new mineral deposits are being found all the time, and new methods for exploiting them are being developed, it is not possible to say precisely how long any particular material will last. Our own supplies of fossil fuels are a good example. Coal will last longer than the others, if we continue extraction at the present rate. The chemical industry is already adapting to likely changes in its supply of raw materials.

☐ Our supply of some minerals, notably tin, mercury, uranium and gold, depends on the fact that miners in some parts of the world work in dangerous conditions for low rates of pay. So long as the world wants these materials, *someone* has to get them out. Social and political changes in different parts of the world may have a considerable effect on the prices and supply of some metal ores.

Who works in the chemical industry?

Figure 6 shows that people with a wide range of skills and qualifications work in the chemical industry. It also gives you some idea of the different kinds of job which have to be done in turning raw materials into products for sale.

Jobs
Administration
Capital projects
Data processing
Finance
Industrial relations
Maintenance
Management
Personnel
Planning
Production
Production scheduling
Purchasing
Quality control
Research
Safety and environment
Sales and marketing
Technical development
Training

People
Accountants
Administrators
Chemical engineers
Chemists
Craft workers
Economists
Engineers
Lawyers
Process operators
Scientists
Secretaries

Fig. 6 A list of the jobs and the people in the chemical industry.

187

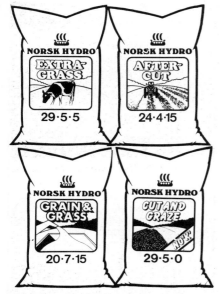

Fig. 1 *The ammonia molecule, NH₃.*

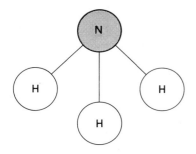

Fig. 2 *Comparing plant growth on an experimental plot. Why is it fairer to compare plants like this than to compare Fig. 5 with Fig. 6?*

Fig. 3 *Some 'nitrogenous fertilizers'. The numbers give information about the amount of nitrogen, phosphorus and potassium which they contain.*

Making and using ammonia

The gas ammonia is a compound of nitrogen and hydrogen, with the formula NH_3. It does not occur naturally in the atmosphere, except in the smallest quantities. Nevertheless, it has an important role in nature. The nitrogen cycle (see 3.4) shows this clearly.

Q1 Look back at 3.4, Fig. 4 (the nitrogen cycle), and explain how ammonia is formed in nature.

Why is ammonia so important?

Nitrogen is one of the elements which plants need if they are to grow. Very few plants can take their nitrogen directly from the air. Most have to rely on the nitrogen compounds which they can absorb from the soil. The only compounds which can be successfully absorbed are ones that dissolve in water. These form solutions which can be drawn in by the roots of the plant. The two kinds of nitrogen compounds which are suitable as fertilisers are:

☐ **Ammonia** and its salts, and **nitrates** (see 7.5).

Q2 Imagine that you had the task of developing a new product for use as a fertiliser. What properties would the substance need to have, to be a suitable material for the farmer to use?

How is ammonia used?

The main use of ammonia is in the fertiliser industry. There are many nitrogen-containing fertilisers, but the most important are:

☐ 'Straight nitrogen' fertilisers, which contain nitrogen only, like ammonia itself and ammonium nitrate
☐ 'Compound fertilisers', which contain the three main plant foods, nitrogen, phosphorus and potassium.

Ammonia is used to make both these kinds of fertiliser. In total, about 1.5 million tonnes of nitrogen are added to the soils of the UK each year.

Q3 These figures show the increase in the use of fertilisers in the UK during the past 60 years:

Year ending:	1929	1939	1949	1959	1969	1979
Thousands of tonnes of plant nutrients used:	190	310	812	1080	1668	2021

Plot a graph of these figures, and predict the weight of plant nutrients likely to be used in 1989 and 1999.

Did you know?

Fritz Haber, who devised the now famous process for making ammonia, spent his last years trying to develop a completely different process. What was it?

Extracting gold from seawater. He was unsuccessful: gold produced in this way was more expensive than gold extracted from the earth.

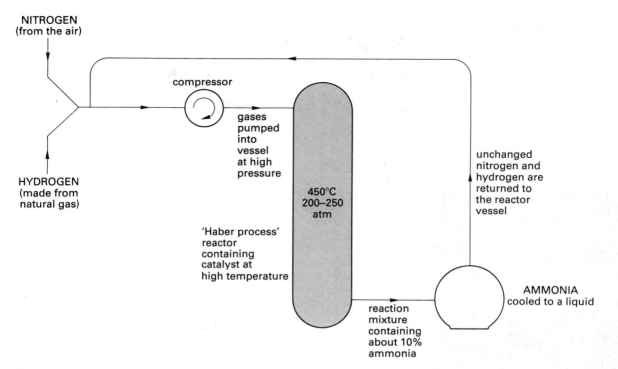

Fig. 4 *The Haber process for making ammonia. Nitrogen from the air is combined directly with hydrogen.*

How is ammonia made?

Almost all the world's ammonia is made by a single process which takes nitrogen from the air, and combines it directly with hydrogen:

$$\text{nitrogen} + \text{hydrogen} \rightarrow \text{ammonia}$$

$$N_2(g) + 3H_2(g) \rightarrow 2NH_3(g)$$

This process was developed by a German chemist, Fritz Haber, during the early years of this century. It became known as the Haber process, and won its inventor the Nobel prize for chemistry in 1918.

Details of the Haber Process are shown in Fig. 4. *Nitrogen* is taken from the air and *hydrogen* is manufactured from natural gas, methane. These are mixed together and pumped into a reactor vessel at *high pressure*. The reactor contains an iron-based *catalyst*, and is at a *high temperature*. Some of the mixed gases combine to form ammonia. This can be liquefied by cooling, and drawn off. More nitrogen and hydrogen are pumped to the reactor, more ammonia is produced, and so on as the gases are continuously circulated.

The production of ammonia is continuous, with more nitrogen and hydrogen being added all the time. The amount of ammonia formed in the reactor varies according to the temperature and pressure at which it is operated. The usual conditions are 450°C, and 200–250 atmospheres pressure. Depending upon the catalyst used, the proportion of ammonia in the reaction mixture is around 10%.

The Haber process has opened the way to large-scale food production, through the manufacture of enormous quantities of fertiliser. In rich countries with good rainfall, agriculture has prospered during this century. Some 'third world' countries have yet to benefit, however.

Fig. 5 *Before the Haber process: the crop was thin and feeble.*

Fig. 6 *After the Haber process: huge wheatfields with a heavy crop of grain.*

189

Ammonia and its salts

Fig. 1 The 'fountain experiment'. Pressure inside the flask drops rapidly as the ammonia begins to dissolve.

Ammonia is a strongly smelling gas which dissolves readily in water. At room temperature, $100\,cm^3$ of water will dissolve almost 100 litres of ammonia gas. The solution which forms has been called 'ammonium hydroxide' because of the reaction:

$$\text{ammonia} + \text{water} \rightarrow \text{ammonium hydroxide}$$

$$NH_3(g) + H_2O(l) \rightarrow \text{`}NH_4OH(aq)\text{'} \rightarrow NH_4^+(aq) + OH^-(aq)$$

It is best to write the formula for ammonia solution as $NH_3(aq)$.

A concentrated solution of ammonia in water is sometimes known as 0.880 ('eight-eighty') ammonia, because its density is $0.880\,g/cm^3$. The 'fountain experiment' (see Fig. 1) shows how rapidly ammonia will dissolve in cold water. To dissolve the ammonia without the fountain effect you can use apparatus like that shown in Fig. 3. Ammonia does not burn in air, but it will burn if mixed with oxygen. It is a reducing agent. For instance, it will reduce heated copper oxide to copper:

$$2NH_3(g) + 3CuO(s) \rightarrow N_2(g) + 3Cu(s) + 3H_2O(g)$$

The alkaline nature of ammonia

Fig. 2 Most of the ammonia has now dissolved but water is still shooting into the flask. The fountain continues until the pressure inside is equal to the pressure outside the flask.

☐ Ammonia is one of the few alkaline gases.
It will form a solution in water which has a pH value greater than 9. It turns universal indicator blue.

☐ Ammonia, like other alkalis, reacts with acids to form salts, e.g.

$$\text{ammonia gas} + \text{hydrogen chloride gas} \rightarrow \text{ammonium chloride}$$

$$NH_3(g) + HCl(g) \rightarrow NH_4Cl(s)$$

☐ This reaction is used as a **test for ammonia:**
A gas thought to be ammonia can be exposed to fumes from a concentrated hydrochloric acid bottle. Wisps of white ammonium chloride 'smoke' will be produced if ammonia is present.

☐ Ammonia acts as a 'hydrogen ion acceptor' in chemical reactions.
In doing so, it forms salts known as ammonium salts. They contain the ammonium ion, NH_4^+. The ammonia molecule has accepted a hydrogen ion (the H^+ ion) from the acid, to form the new ion NH_4^+.

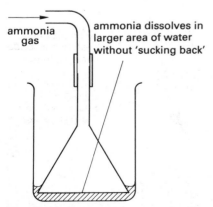

ammonia gas

ammonia dissolves in larger area of water without 'sucking back'

Fig. 3 Ammonia can be dissolved in water without causing a 'fountain' if you use apparatus like this.

Q1 Use the information in this section to make a summary table of all you know about ammonia.

Q2 Look again at the equation at the top of this page, and you will realise that ammonia acts as a 'hydrogen ion acceptor' in its reaction with water. Use this example to explain what is meant by a 'hydrogen ion acceptor'.

Did you know?

What were smelling salts?

Ammonium carbonate, an unstable compound which slowly gives off ammonia, mixed with perfume. Smelling salts were said to give relief to ladies suffering from faintness or headache.

Fig. 4 *This popular fertilizer contains 34.5% nitrogen.*

Some ammonium salts

Ammonium chloride is formed from ammonia and hydrochloric acid (or hydrogen chloride gas). It is a white solid which sublimes when heated. The heating causes ammonium chloride to dissociate:

$$NH_4Cl(s) \rightleftharpoons NH_3(g) + HCl(g)$$

This is the reverse of the reaction in which ammonium chloride is formed. When heated, ammonium chloride splits up again. Ammonium chloride is used in dry batteries.

Ammonium nitrate, NH_4NO_3, is a white solid which is made from ammonia and nitric acid. Its main use is as a 'straight nitrogen' fertiliser. Some is also used in explosives. **Ammonium sulphate** $(NH_4)_2SO_4$, is the salt formed in the reaction between sulphuric acid and ammonia. It is an important fertiliser.

Testing for ammonium salts

Ammonium salts are all soluble in water, and all react with alkalis to give ammonia gas. For example:

$$\begin{array}{c} \text{ammonium} \\ \text{chloride} \\ \text{(ammonium salt)} \end{array} + \begin{array}{c} \text{calcium} \\ \text{hydroxide} \\ \text{(alkali)} \end{array} \rightarrow \begin{array}{c} \text{calcium} \\ \text{chloride} \end{array} + \text{water} + \text{ammonia}$$

$$NH_4Cl(s) + Ca(OH)_2(s) \rightarrow CaCl_2(s) + H_2O(l) + NH_3(g)$$

> **Q3** A white solid, X, sublimes when heated alone. When it is heated with sodium hydroxide solution, a pungent alkaline gas is produced. What does this information tell you about substance X? What further test(s) would be needed to determine the exact identity of substance X?

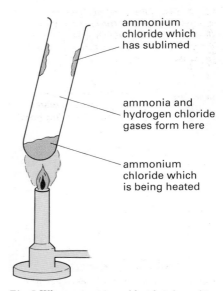

ammonium chloride which has sublimed

ammonia and hydrogen chloride gases form here

ammonium chloride which is being heated

Fig. 5 *When ammonium chloride is heated it sublimes.*

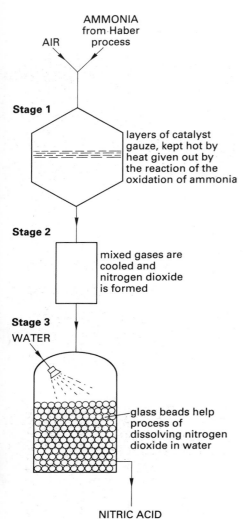

Stage 1

layers of catalyst gauze, kept hot by heat given out by the reaction of the oxidation of ammonia

Stage 2

mixed gases are cooled and nitrogen dioxide is formed

Stage 3
WATER

glass beads help process of dissolving nitrogen dioxide in water

NITRIC ACID

Fig. 1 *The Ostwald process for making nitric acid from ammonia.*

Fig. 2 *The catalyst gauze for the nitric acid process. It is an alloy of platinum and rhodium.*

Nitric acid

Nitric acid is an important industrial chemical, used mainly in the fertiliser industry, but also for making explosives, plastics and fibres.

How is nitric acid made?

Nitric acid is made from ammonia using the Ostwald process. The process is shown in Fig. 1. There are three stages:

(1) Ammonia and air are mixed and passed over a catalyst.
(2) The emerging gases are oxidised with air.
(3) The product from (2) is dissolved in water, forming nitric acid.

The process may be summarised:

$$\text{ammonia} + \text{oxygen} \rightarrow \begin{array}{c}\text{nitrogen}\\\text{monoxide}\end{array} \rightarrow \begin{array}{c}\text{nitrogen}\\\text{dioxide}\end{array} \rightarrow \begin{array}{c}\text{nitric}\\\text{acid}\end{array}$$

$$NH_3(g) + O_2(g) \xrightarrow{(1)} NO(g) \xrightarrow{(2)} NO_2(g) \xrightarrow{(3)} HNO_3(aq)$$

A temperature of about 900 °C is used, and the catalyst consists of several layers of a wire gauze made from the precious metals platinum and rhodium (see Fig. 2).

What is the chemical nature of nitric acid?

Chemically, nitric acid is like the other strong acids, but it has a few extra chemical reactions of its own. Like other acids, it:

☐ neutralises alkalis and bases, forming salts (called nitrates)
☐ reacts with metals
☐ reacts with carbonates and hydrogencarbonates.

In addition, it:

☐ is an oxidising agent
☐ reacts with organic compounds.

> **Q1** Look at 2.7 for information about acids and alkalis. Write word equations and formula equations for the reactions you would expect between dilute nitric acid and (i) potassium hydroxide solution; (ii) magnesium; (iii) copper carbonate.

Unlike the other dilute mineral acids, nitric acid will react with copper (see 5.9). The process is complicated, but it takes place because nitric acid is able to *oxidise* copper atoms in the metal to copper *ions* in solution:

$$\overset{\text{nitric acid}}{Cu(s)} \rightarrow Cu^{2+}(aq) + 2e$$

Did you know?

What does nitric acid do to your skin?

Damages it, certainly! Also stains it yellow because of a chemical reaction with the protein in your skin.

Fig. 3 The mining industry uses huge quantities of explosives.

Nitric acid and the development of explosives

Gunpowder, the first explosive used for warfare and in mines and quarries, is now rarely used except in fireworks. It creates a lot of smoke, and is less powerful than more modern explosives. Nitroglycerine (NG) and trinitro-toluene (TNT) were developed in the middle of the 19th century. Both require nitric acid for their manufacture.

Nitroglycerine and dynamite

Nitroglycerine is an organic substance, properly called 'glyceryl trinitrate'. It is made from glycerine (strictly, 'glycerol'), using a mixture of concentrated nitric and sulphuric acids. Great care is needed in making sure that this reaction does not get out of control (see Fig. 4)! Nitroglycerine on its own was found to be a dangerously unpredictable explosive. Alfred Nobel (Fig. 5), the founder of the Nobel Prizes, made his fortune from the discovery that a much safer explosive could be made by absorbing nitroglycerine in 'kieselguhr'. Kieselguhr is a whitish mineral, which consists largely of the fossil remains of microscopic plants. It is soft, porous and very absorbent. The new safe explosive was called 'dynamite'. It is still widely used in quarrying.

For underground mining, other explosives derived from nitric acid are frequently used. These are based on ammonium nitrate (a powerful oxidising agent), and fuel oil (which is readily oxidised).

Fig. 4 The process for making Nitroglycerine must be watched very carefully. This operator (in the 1890's) was given a one-legged stool, so that his attention would not wander!

Q2 Describe how you could make a solid sample of ammonium nitrate from nitric acid. N.B. Ammonium nitrate crystals decompose when they are heated!

Q3 Here is the equation for what happens when dynamite explodes.

$$4C_3H_5(NO_3)_3(s) \rightarrow 6N_2(g) + 12CO_2(g) + 10H_2O(g) + O_2(g)$$

Why do you think it is such a good explosive?

Fig. 5 Alfred Nobel (1833–1896), inventor of dynamite and sponsor of the Nobel prizes.

193

Fig. 1 Potassium nitrate (saltpetre) was used to make gunpowder in this 18th century mill.

Fig. 2 Nitrates are still used in fireworks.

7.5

Nitrates

The salts of nitric acid are called **nitrates**. Here are some well known or important nitrates:

Name	Formula	Notes
sodium nitrate	$NaNO_3$	'Chile saltpetre', originally used to make nitric acid, now used in food preservation
potassium nitrate	KNO_3	'saltpetre', used in fireworks
silver nitrate	$AgNO_3$	for making photographic chemicals
strontium nitrate	$Sr(NO_3)_2$	for making red flares
ammonium nitrate	NH_4NO_3	for fertilisers and explosives

What is the chemical nature of nitrates?

☐ All nitrates are soluble in water.

☐ All nitrates react with concentrated sulphuric acid, to give nitric acid (see 7.4).

☐ All nitrates break down when heated, giving oxygen. Further decomposition then takes place, according to the position of the metal in the Reactivity Series:

(a) Nitrates of the most reactive metals (K, Na):
These nitrates are least affected by heat. Oxygen is given off.

$$2NaNO_3(s) \rightarrow 2NaNO_2(s) + O_2(g)$$

(b) Nitrates of most metals (for example Ca, Mg, Zn, Pb, Cu):
Further decomposition takes place, leaving the metal oxide as residue. The brown gas, nitrogen dioxide, is given off, together with oxygen.

$$2Cu(NO_3)_2(s) \rightarrow 2CuO(s) + 4NO_2(g) + O_2(g)$$

(c) Nitrates of the least reactive metals (for example Ag):
Complete decomposition to the metal occurs, because the oxide is not stable to heat.

$$2AgNO_3(s) \rightarrow 2Ag(s) + 2NO_2(g) + O_2(g)$$

☐ The reaction used as a **test for nitrates** depends on the fact that *nitrates can be reduced to ammonia*. When a nitrate is warmed with zinc powder and sodium hydroxide solution, ammonia is given off.

Nitrates and the environment

Ammonium nitrate, NH_4NO_3, is a particularly good fertiliser because it contains nearly 35% of nitrogen. All of this nitrogen is available to plants, because it is in a form which dissolves easily in water. Farmers use large quantities of ammonium nitrate fertiliser. In certain conditions, it is possible for some of the nitrate ions to be washed from the land into nearby rivers and streams. Two kinds of problem may result:

☐ Stream water containing too much nitrate will encourage the rapid growth of small plant organisms called 'algae'. When these die they are decomposed by bacteria in a process which requires oxygen. Large quantities of decomposing algae will use up most of the oxygen in the water, and soon other water creatures will die. This process is known as **eutrophication**, and can become very serious (see Fig. 4).

Fig. 3 Farmers must take great care to avoid contaminating streams with fertiliser and animal waste.

Fig. 4 Eutrophication in a lake in Mexico completely clogged with water hyasinth.

☐ Large quantities of water are taken from rivers for drinking purposes. Of course, it is carefully purified first (see 6.12). However, the dissolved nitrate is not removed by the usual purification methods. To adults this may not matter, because the body can tolerate some dissolved substances quite well. For small infants, however, it is a much more serious matter. They may suffer illness or kidney damage from drinking water containing too much dissolved nitrate.

Q1 Plan a wallchart to show how nitrogenous fertilisers used on the land may cause problems in streams, lakes and tap-water.

Q2 How would you get round the problem of making up powdered baby food when the nitrate content of the tap water is high?

Fig. 5 Bottle feeds should never be made up with water which contains a lot of dissolved salts.

Sulphuric acid

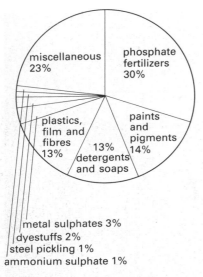

Fig. 1 The uses of sulphuric acid.

Sulphuric acid, H_2SO_4, is one of the chemical industry's most important products. Very little goes on sale directly, because nearly all of it is used for making other materials. Figure 1 shows you the main uses of sulphuric acid. The largest single user of sulphuric acid is the fertiliser industry. This is because sulphuric acid will react with phosphate rock to give phosphoric acid. It is this phosphoric acid which is needed to make phosphate fertiliser.

> **Q1** Most people know sulphuric acid as 'battery acid', but only a small amount is used in this way. Using the information from Fig. 1, collect materials to make a chart illustrating the main uses of sulphuric acid.

How is sulphuric acid made?

Sulphuric acid is made from sulphur dioxide. This gas is made either from sulphur, or from an ore which contains sulphur. There are three stages:

(1) Producing sulphur dioxide by burning a fine spray of liquid sulphur in air:

$$S(l) + O_2(g) \rightarrow SO_2(g)$$

or by roasting zinc sulphide ore in air:

$$2ZnS(s) + 3O_2(g) \rightarrow 2ZnO(s) + 2SO_2(g)$$

(2) Mixing the sulphur dioxide with air and passing it through several layers of catalyst (vanadium(v) oxide) at 450°C. It reacts to form sulphur trioxide:

$$2SO_2(g) + O_2(g) \longleftrightarrow 2SO_3(g)$$

This reversible conversion is known as the **contact process**. It is affected by changes in temperature and pressure.

(3) Absorbing the sulphur trioxide in sulphuric acid to form oleum, a very concentrated form of acid with the formula $H_2S_2O_7$:

$$SO_3(g) + H_2SO_4(l) \rightarrow H_2S_2O_7(l)$$

When oleum is diluted with water it forms sulphuric acid:

$$H_2S_2O_7(l) + H_2O(l) \rightarrow 2H_2SO_4(l)$$

More than 90% of all the acid made in the UK comes directly from sulphur. The rest is a by-product of zinc smelting.

Sulphuric acid production in the UK is around 3 million tonnes per year. There are major works at Avonmouth, on Merseyside, in London, and at Immingham and Teesside in the North East.

> **Q2** Make your own summary of the contact process, using formulae and arrows to build up a flow-chart.

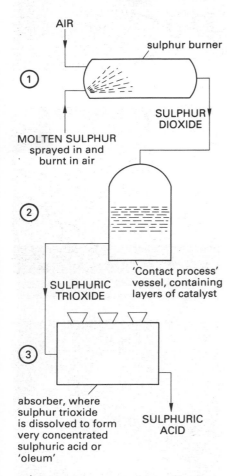

Fig. 2 The Contact process for making sulphuric acid.

Fig. 3 A 'Contact' plant for making sulphuric acid. The large tank on the right contains the catalyst used in the contact process.

What is the chemical nature of sulphuric acid?

Concentrated sulphuric acid is a dense, colourless liquid which boils at a high temperature (>330°C). It is extremely corrosive, and must be handled with great care. It reacts very vigorously with water, so diluting it is hazardous. Sulphuric acid should always be added *to* water, and *not* the other way round. It must be done gradually, with careful stirring, because a lot of heat is given out (Fig. 4).

Fig. 4 Sulphuric acid is diluted by gradually pouring the acid into water. A lot of heat is given out.

> **Q3** Write out precise instructions, step by step, for someone who has to make some dilute sulphuric acid by adding $20 \, cm^3$ of concentrated acid to $200 \, cm^3$ of water.

As a **mineral acid**, dilute sulphuric acid will react with many metals, neutralise bases and alkalis, and produce carbon dioxide when added to carbonates. It is a **dibasic** acid (see 3.6), forming two series of salts – the sulphates and the hydrogensulphates.

Concentrated sulphuric acid is an **oxidising agent**. Like all oxidising agents it is itself reduced when carrying out an oxidation. In particular, it can be reduced by many metals to sulphur dioxide. This allows it to dissolve some metals, like copper, which are below hydrogen in the Reactivity Series.

Concentrated sulphuric acid is also a **dehydrating agent**. That is, it has such a powerful attraction for water that it will even remove the elements of water from certain compounds. With water itself it reacts violently. It will dehydrate:

☐ copper sulphate crystals (blue) → anhydrous copper sulphate (white)
☐ cane sugar (sucrose) → carbon (sugar charcoal)
☐ methanoic acid (formic acid) → carbon monoxide
☐ ethanol (ethyl alcohol) → ethene (ethylene)

Fig. 5 Concentrated sulphuric acid is a dehydrating agent. It reacts with sugar to leave carbon.

Sulphates

The 'normal salts' of sulphuric acid are called **sulphates**. Here are some well known or important sulphates:

Some sulphates

Name	Formula	Notes
ammonium sulphate	$(NH_4)_2SO_4$	fertiliser ('sulphate of ammonia')
barium sulphate	$BaSO_4$	very insoluble in water, used in medicine (barium meals) and in 'drilling mud' for oil rigs
calcium sulphate	$CaSO_4$	different forms are anhydrite, gypsum, and Plaster of Paris
copper sulphate	$CuSO_4.5H_2O$	'blue vitriol', used in electro-plating and as a fungicide
iron(II) sulphate	$FeSO_4.7H_2O$	'green vitriol' or 'Copperas', once used for making sulphuric acid, now put into 'iron tablets'
magnesium sulphate	$MgSO_4.6H_2O$	'Epsom salt', used in medicine
sodium sulphate	$Na_2SO_4.10H_2O$	'Glauber's salt', used in medicine and in glass-making

Green vitriol

Naturally occurring sulphates were once the world's main source of 'oil of vitriol' – sulphuric acid. The word 'vitriolic' still means 'sharp and burning' today. Iron sulphate crystals, 'green vitriol', break down in two stages when heated. First the water of crystallisation is given off. Then it breaks down further. The complete process is:

$$\text{iron sulphate crystals} \xrightarrow{\text{heat}} \text{iron oxide} + \text{sulphur dioxide} + \text{sulphur trioxide} + \text{water}$$

$$2FeSO_4.7H_2O \xrightarrow{\text{heat}} Fe_2O_3 + SO_2 + SO_3 + 14H_2O$$

If the products from this reaction are allowed to collect in the same vessel, the sulphur dioxide and sulphur trioxide dissolve in the water, giving sulphuric acid. The engraving in Fig. 4 shows apparatus which was used in the early 19th century for making sulphuric acid by this method. A coal fire was used to heat the green vitriol in the flasks marked 'C'. Sulphuric acid was collected in the cooler vessels marked 'D'.

Q1 The substance left in the flasks ('C') was a form of iron oxide, known as 'rouge'. Find out what it was used for, and why it was given this name.

What is the chemical nature of sulphates?

☐ The sulphate ion is colourless, so any colour in a sulphate is due to the metal ion.

☐ Many sulphates are soluble in water. One exception is barium sulphate, which is insoluble.

This allows barium salts to be used in the **test for sulphate ions** in solution. The test is in two stages:

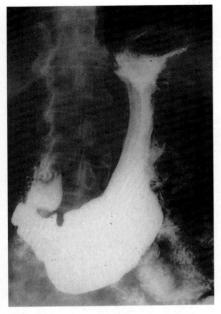

Fig. 1 Barium sulphate does not allow X-rays to pass through. It is also very insoluble in water. People needing an X-ray of their digestive system are first given a porridge containing barium sulphate to eat.

Fig. 2 The plaster used in plasterboard is a form of calcium sulphate.

Fig. 3 The alabaster used for this Egyptian funeral jar is also a form of calcium sulphate.

Fig. 4 *This equipment was used for making sulphuric acid from iron sulphate crystals in the 18th century.*

(1) adding dilute hydrochloric acid to the solution thought likely to contain sulphate ions; and then
(2) adding barium chloride solution.

If sulphate ions are present, a precipitation reaction will take place in which barium sulphate is formed:

$$Ba^{2+}(aq) + SO_4^{2-}(aq) \rightarrow BaSO_4(s)$$

The barium sulphate appears as a dense white precipitate if sulphate ions are present.

> **Q2** You have been provided with some blue crystals, thought to be either copper nitrate or copper sulphate. Describe two ways of deciding which substance it is.

Sulphuric acid also forms 'acid salts', known as **hydrogensulphates**. When sodium hydrogensulphate, $NaHSO_4$, dissolves in water it forms an acid which is strong enough to react with many metals. This happens because the hydrogensulphate ion breaks down, giving a hydrogen ion:

$$HSO_4^-(aq) \rightleftharpoons H^+(aq) + SO_4^{2-}(aq)$$

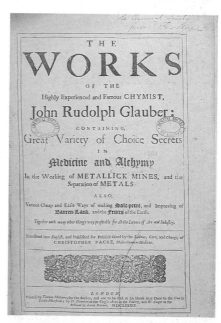

Fig. 5 *Important uses of sodium sulphate were described by J.R. Glauber in this book of 1687. Sodium sulphate crystals are sometimes known as Glauber's salt.*

Chlorine

Mention the word 'chlorine' to most people, and they will probably know one of its two most famous uses. Chlorine is used for sterilising water to drink, and in many swimming pools. Chlorine is also the poisonous choking gas which was used to such devastating effect during the First World War. Like many substances and most inventions, chlorine has powers that can be used for good or ill!

Fig. 1 Small amounts of chlorine are continuously added to our water supply. This is where the process is controlled.

What is chlorine like?

- ☐ Chlorine is a pale green gas.
- ☐ It is denser than many other gases, and it is very poisonous.
- ☐ It will dissolve in water, although not very well. The solution in water is acidic, but it bleaches indicators.
- ☐ The chemical **test for chlorine** is this bleaching effect. Moistened litmus and universal indicator papers turn whitish in chlorine.

How is chlorine used?

The best known use of chlorine gas is in water treatment to kill micro-organisms. Most chlorine is used, however, for making other chemicals:

Some uses of chlorine (in order of the quantities of chlorine used)

Use of chlorine to make . . .	From	Notes
chloroethene (vinyl chloride)	ethene	Used for making PVC (see 7.14).
'chlorinated solvents'	hydrocarbons	For example, 'Perklone' for dry cleaning, dichloromethane for paint stripping, trichloroethene for degreasing.
fluorocarbons	hydrocarbons and fluorine	Most fluorocarbons contain both F and Cl, for example CCl_2F_2, used in aerosols and refrigerators.
bleaches and disinfectants	sodium hydroxide (see opposite)	Usually done where chlorine is made, since both Cl_2 and NaOH are available 'on site' (see 7.10).
bromine	sea water	Sea water contains bromide ions.

Fig. 2 The use of chlorine as a war gas was one of the great atrocities of the 20th century. This is how it was launched.

> **Q1** Use information from this Section, and from the *Datapages* and *Index* to make a summary chart with the title: 'Products made from Chlorine'. Illustrate it with suitable pictures from magazines.

Fig. 3 Household bleaches containing chlorine. Many coloured materials lose their colour when they are oxidised. The bleach is an oxidising agent, and this is how it works.

What is the chemical nature of chlorine?

- ☐ Like the other halogens, chlorine is an oxidising agent. Its oxidising reactions are described more detail in 3.15. It will oxidise the ions of other halogens. For instance, when chlorine is passed into potassium iodide solution, iodine is formed:

$$Cl_2(g) + 2KI(aq) \rightarrow 2KCl(aq) + I_2(aq)$$

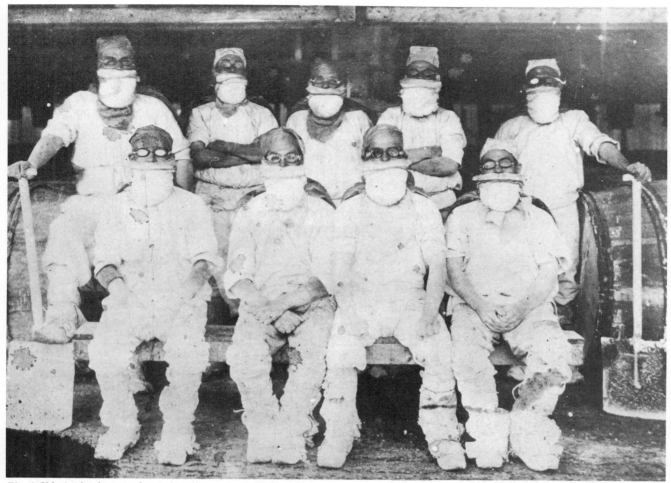

Fig. 4 Chlorine has been used to make a chemical called 'bleaching powder'. These workers, photographed in 1880, wear the only protection against chlorine which was available at the time.

☐ When chlorine dissolves in water, there is a reversible reaction, in which hypochlorous acid, HOCl, is formed:

$$Cl_2(g) + H_2O(l) \rightleftharpoons H^+(aq) + Cl^-(aq) + HOCl(aq)$$

☐ Many household bleaches contain the compound sodium hypochlorite, NaOCl, which is the sodium salt of hypochlorous acid. It is made by dissolving chlorine gas in sodium hydroxide solution:

$$Cl_2(g) + 2NaOH(aq) \rightarrow NaCl(aq) + NaOCl(aq) + H_2O(l)$$

☐ The reaction between chlorine and hydrogen gives hydrogen chloride:

$$H_2(g) + Cl_2(g) \rightarrow 2HCl(g)$$

Hydrogen chloride is a gas. Its molecules are covalently bonded. In solvents other than water it dissolves to give a solution which does *not* conduct electricity. In water it reacts to form ions:

$$HCl(g) + aq \rightarrow H^+(aq) + Cl^-(aq)$$

This is the widely used solution known as hydrochloric acid.

Q2 Explain why (a) a solution of chlorine in water is acidic; (b) it is dangerous to add acid to a household bleach; (c) hydrogen chloride gas will only affect *damp* indicator paper.

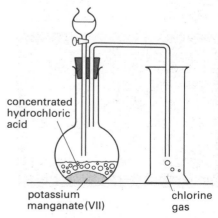

concentrated hydrochloric acid

potassium manganate(VII)

chlorine gas

Fig. 5 Making chlorine in the laboratory by oxidising hydrochloric acid.

Salt and other chlorides

Common salt, sodium chloride, is by far the best known chloride. It is an important part of our diet, though too much of it may cause high blood pressure and heart disease. Our average intake is about 10g per day. Huge quantities are found on the earth, both in the sea and below ground where prehistoric seas have evaporated and become covered over. The main British deposits are in Cheshire, where there are very large reserves. Salt may be obtained by underground mining (Fig. 4) or by pumping down water to make a solution, brine, which can be piped back to the surface.

Salt is often described as a 'typically ionic' substance. It has a high melting point (801 °C), dissolves in water, and forms cubic crystals (Fig. 1). These crystals are built up from a giant lattice of ions (Fig. 3).

Fig. 1 Crystals of sodium chloride, showing how they form into cubes.

Fig. 2 These pyramids have also been built up from regularly shaped blocks. What is the link with the pictures above and below?

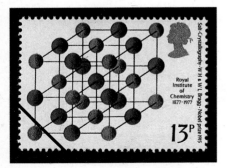

Fig. 3 This stamp shows how the ions are arranged in a crystal of sodium chloride.

Other chlorides

Salt is just one of the many chlorides which exist. Here are some others:

Some chlorides formed by metals and non-metals

Name of chloride	Formula	Notes
hydrogen chloride	HCl	gas, dissolves in water to form hydrochloric acid
sodium chloride	NaCl	crystalline solid, high M.P.
aluminium chloride	Al_2Cl_6	waxy solid, sublimes when heated
tetrachloromethane (carbon tetrachloride)	CCl_4	colourless liquid, does not conduct electricity
sulphur chloride	S_2Cl_2	orange liquid, does not conduct electricity
iron(II) chloride	$FeCl_2$	grey-green solid, made from iron and HCl gas
iron (III) chloride	$FeCl_3$	brown solid, made from iron and chlorine

Q1 List, with your reasons, the chlorides from the above table which appear to be (a) ionically bonded, and (b) covalently bonded. Where there is not enough evidence for you to decide, say so.

Q2 What predictions can you make about phosphorus chloride? (Phosphorus is a non-metal in Group 5 of the Periodic Table.)

Insoluble chlorides

Many chlorides are soluble in water, but those of silver and lead are not. Silver chloride is a white substance, obtained by a precipitation reaction, such as:

$$Ag^+(aq) + Cl^-(aq) \rightarrow AgCl(s)$$

It is not very stable, and breaks down if heated or even if exposed to daylight. A purplish colour is seen:

$$2AgCl(s) \rightarrow 2Ag(s) + Cl_2(g)$$

Fig. 4 *The Meadowbank mine at Winsford in Cheshire can produce nearly 2 million tonnes of salt per year. Very large mining machinery can be used because the rocksalt deposits are so thick.*

Silver and lead halides

The other halides of silver and lead have distinctive properties. All are insoluble in cold water, and here is some further information:

Silver and lead halides

Name of halide	Formula	Notes
silver chloride	$AgCl$	white solid, darkens quickly in daylight, soluble in ammonia solution
silver bromide	$AgBr$	creamy solid, darkens slowly in daylight, somewhat soluble in ammonia solution
silver iodide	AgI	pale yellow solid, little affected by light, not soluble in ammonia solution
lead chloride	$PbCl_2$	white solid, soluble in hot water
lead bromide	$PbBr_2$	creamy solid, somewhat soluble in hot water
lead iodide	PbI_2	bright yellow solid, slightly soluble in hot water

A test for the chloride ion

A solution suspected of containing chloride ions is usually checked by adding silver nitrate solution. Any chloride ions present would produce a white precipitate which quickly darkens in daylight, and does not dissolve in dilute nitric acid.

> **Q3** (a) Use information from the above table to explain this test.
> (b) How could you use a lead salt to test for chloride ions?

Fig. 5 *About 10% of the rocksalt mined in Britain is put on roads during the winter. Sand and grit are added to give vehicles a better grip.*

The chlor-alkali industry

Chlorine and sodium hydroxide are made from salt in a single process.

Chlorine

Chlorine is manufactured from rock salt, sodium chloride. There are two stages:

☐ The salt is dissolved in water, and purified.

☐ Electrolysis is used to oxidise the chloride ions to chlorine. (Go back to 4.9 if you want to remind yourself about electrolysis.)

The salt solution ('brine') contains hydrogen and hydroxyl ions from the water, together with sodium and chloride ions:

$$H_2O(l) \quad \rightleftharpoons \quad H^+(aq) + OH^-(aq)$$

$$NaCl(s) + H_2O(l) \quad \rightarrow \quad Na^+(aq) + Cl^-(aq)$$

The cells used for electrolysing brine are complicated. Several different types are in use, but they all produce three main products: chlorine, hydrogen and sodium hydroxide.

☐ Chlorine forms at the anodes, by oxidation of the chloride ions:

$$2Cl^-(aq) \quad \rightarrow \quad Cl_2 + 2e$$

☐ Hydrogen forms by the reduction of the hydrogen ions:

$$2H^+(aq) + 2e \quad \rightarrow \quad H_2(g)$$

☐ Sodium hydroxide remains when sodium ions (from the salt) and hydroxyl ions (from the water) are left after the electrolysis. So manufacturers of chlorine are also manufacturers of the alkali sodium hydroxide. This part of the chemical industry is often known as the **chlor-alkali industry**.

Q1 Make a summary chart of this process, starting with solid salt.

Sodium hydroxide

Sodium hydroxide is the most important cheap alkali. It is commonly known as 'caustic soda'. Floor and oven cleaners for home use may contain caustic soda, to remove grease and fats. These cleaners are dangerous materials, however. The word 'caustic' means 'burning', and this is the effect they have on your skin. Always wear rubber gloves to use cleaning materials like these, and be sure to store them well out of reach of children. About half of all the sodium hydroxide produced is used to make other chemicals. The rest is used:

☐ to make rayon – because it helps to dissolve wood pulp

☐ to make soaps and detergents – which are often sodium salts

☐ for purifying bauxite to make aluminium – because it dissolves aluminium oxide.

Q2 Sea water contains a lot of salt, but it is not used for making chlorine and sodium hydroxide. Suggest possible reasons for this.

Fig. 1 *Mercury cells for making chlorine and pure sodium hydroxide.*

Fig. 2 *Diaphragm cells for making chlorine and sodium hydroxide.*

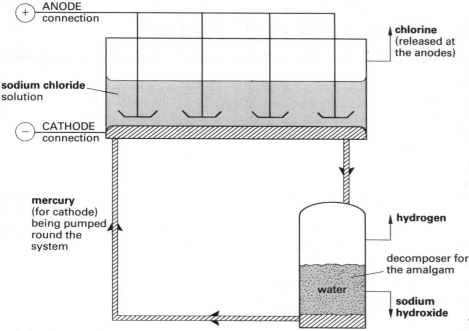

Fig. 3 *The Castner–Kellner mercury cell produces pure sodium hydroxide, but uses mercury as the cathode, which is expensive and toxic.*

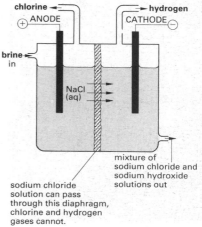

Fig. 4 *The Hooker diaphragm cell uses the diaphragm as a barrier to chlorine and hydrogen molecules.*

What types of cell can be used for making chlorine?

Two problems occur if brine is electrolysed in a simple container:

☐ Hydrogen and chlorine gases mix together.
  Problem: this mixture is explosive!
☐ Chlorine dissolves in the electrolyte.
  Problem: chlorine and sodium hydroxide react with one another.

This means that any cell for electrolysing brine must be designed to keep the chlorine, the hydrogen and the sodium hydroxide apart from one another throughout the process.

☐ In the **mercury cell** the cathode is a shallow layer of mercury. Sodium dissolves in this, forming an alloy known as an **amalgam**. The amalgam is allowed to flow into water (Fig. 3) where the sodium reacts to form hydrogen and sodium hydroxide solution. By keeping the water in a separate vessel, this reaction is kept safely away from the point where chlorine is produced.
☐ In the **diaphragm cell** the diaphragm acts as a barrier to the mixing of the ions, as they move towards the electrodes (Fig. 4).
☐ **Membrane cells** use a plastic membrane to separate anode and cathode compartments (Fig. 5). This membrane, which works on the 'ion-exchange' principle, allows only positive ions through.

All three types of cell produce pure chlorine, but there are differences in both the costs and the quality of the sodium hydroxide produced. Mercury cells produce pure sodium hydroxide, and for some industries this purity is vital. The other two types of cell do not use mercury, which is expensive and toxic. The newer membrane cells seem likely to replace diaphragm cells, once old installations become due for replacement.

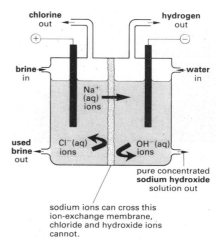

Fig. 5 *A membrane cell works on the 'ion-exchange' principle, and is the most modern type of cell.*

Fig. 1 *In some parts of the world we are lucky. We take our food for granted. What part does chemistry play?*

Fig. 2 *The pH of vinegar is low enough to prevent bacteria in these pickled onions from multiplying.*

Fig. 3 *Frozen food in transit for a large retailer.*

7.11

Chemistry and the food industry

Pictures in the press often give the impression that chemistry has a mysterious and harmful part to play in the production of our food. Of course, the skills of the chemist can be misused in the food industry, as elsewhere, and there are two sides to this story.

Food supply

The development of the fertiliser industry (see 7.2) has led to greatly increased yields of basic crops. Farming methods and seed quality have improved, too, so fertilisers alone are not responsible for the increase. Here are some figures for three important crops grown in England and Wales during the present century.

Yields of wheat, barley and potatoes (in tonnes per hectare)

Crop/Year	1905	1940	1964	1972	1981
wheat	2.0	2.3	3.4	4.2	5.8
barley	2.3	2.0	3.6	3.9	4.4
potatoes	15.1	16.3	15.6	29.9	34.0

Q1 Plot graphs to illustrate this information, and comment on any trends you notice. What factors, other than those mentioned above, might affect the crop yield in a given year?

Keeping food fresh

When food 'goes off' it is usually because of chemical reactions caused by exposure to air or micro-organisms. To keep food fresh you must kill the micro-organisms, or keep the food in conditions where the micro-organisms cannot multiply. **Salting** and **pickling** have been used for thousands of years to stop food from spoiling. Salt has a drying effect, and pickling solutions are acid. Most micro-organisms cannot live in dry or acid foods.

One of the most important modern methods for preserving food is **freezing** (see Fig. 3). Some foods, like packet soups, are prepared by **freeze-drying**. In this process the ingredients are rapidly cooled down to about −80°C, and the pressure is then reduced. At low pressure the ice crystals in the frozen food sublime, and water vapour is drawn off. When the food is allowed to warm up to room temperature it is thoroughly dried out. Its texture is undamaged because of the rapid freezing, which causes only very tiny ice crystals to form. When water is added later, the food regains its original form.

Food additives

Almost all the foodstuffs now offered for sale contain added substances of one kind or another. These 'additives' may be there for good reasons – helping to keep the food fresh, making it easier to use, improving our diet with vitamins, and so on. Other additives may be there simply to help the product to sell more easily. Colourings and flavourings are often added for this reason. There is a lot of debate about the use of food additives, and manufacturers often alter their products because of changes in public opinion.

Fig. 4 *These vegetables may contain minute traces of chemicals such as insecticides. Although these are not generally harmful in such small quantities, some people prefer to eat 'organically grown' vegetables, where no chemicals are used.*

What are E-numbers?

European rules now require all the food additives 'which are generally regarded as safe' to be given an E-number. Untested additives are not allowed. There is more information about this system on *Datapage M*.

Tartrazine (E102) – a colouring

The yellow colouring **tartrazine** is found in many drinks, sauces, sweets and snacks. To most people it is probably harmless, at least in small quantities. However, some children appear to be very badly affected by this substance. Different reports have suggested that hyperactivity, eczema, and asthma may be 'triggered' in some individuals. People respond differently to what they eat, so it is hard to make sensible rules which apply to all. Parents should certainly know that E102 has something of a bad reputation, and may decide not to give their children foods which contain it.

> **Q2** Keep all the labels from the foods you eat in a week. Make a systematic list of the additives they contain. (Use *Datapage M*.)

Did you know?

How many eggs are (a) laid by the average hen in its lifetime, and (b) eaten by the average person each year in the UK?

260 eggs per chicken, 180 eggs per person per year.

Fig 5 *Food packets showing E numbers.*

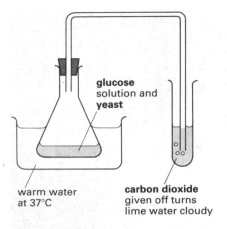

Fig. 1 *Fermenting glucose with yeast to obtain ethanol.*

Fig. 2 *Home-made beer in Zambia, a fermentation process.*

Fig. 3 *New foodstuffs are being developed in large fermenters. This one produces Pruteen, an animal food.*

Biotechnology: breaking down and building up!

Micro-organisms have been used in some methods of food-making for many centuries. Today these methods are often referred to as examples of 'biotechnology'. One of the oldest known biotechnologies is **fermentation**. This is a chemical change brought about by enzymes or by micro-organisms. It is used, for example, to make alcohol from carbohydrate materials like starch or sugar (see Fig. 2).

A simple apparatus for obtaining ethanol from glucose is shown in Fig. 1. The flask contains yeast, some added salts known as 'yeast nutrients', and a solution of glucose. If this mixture is kept warm, say around 35°C, the following reaction occurs:

$$\text{glucose} \quad \xrightarrow{\text{yeast}} \quad \text{ethanol} + \text{carbon dioxide}$$

$$C_6H_{12}O_6(aq) \quad \xrightarrow{\text{yeast}} \quad 2C_2H_5OH(aq) + 2CO_2(g)$$

In this process the enzymes in yeast are catalysts for the breaking down of glucose into simpler substances.

Fermentation is of course the basis for the drinks industry (beers, wines and spirits) and is also a vital step in bread-making. Drinks containing alcohol are popular in many places throughout the world. Yet some religions forbid alcohol completely, and many societies recognise its risks to health. Drink is a factor in many road accidents, and in many crimes of violence.

Q1 The alcohol content of three popular drinks is as follows: beer, 3.5% ethanol; table wine, 10% ethanol; whisky, 32% ethanol. How many grams of ethanol are there in (i) a pint of beer (568 cm³); (ii) a bottle of wine (700 cm³); (iii) a single whisky (43 cm³)?

Q2 The maximum 'blood alcohol concentration' permitted for drivers in many countries is 0.8 g ethanol per 100 cm³ of blood. This concentration can be reached by someone with an alcohol intake of 0.6 g ethanol per kilogram of body weight. How much beer, wine or whisky could produce this level for a 60 kg person?

New animal foods

Biotechnology can also be used for building up new foodstuffs from smaller molecules. One example is the animal food known as 'Pruteen', made in the fermenter shown in Fig. 3. In this case the basic chemical process is:

$$\text{air} + \text{ammonia} + \text{methane} \quad \xrightarrow{\text{micro-organisms}} \quad \text{Pruteen}$$

Foodstuffs like this contribute indirectly to the human food supply by making it easier and cheaper to feed farm animals.

Vinegar

Vinegar is a 5% solution of ethanoic acid, which has been traditionally made by fermenting ethanol with air and suitable micro-organisms. Malt

Fig. 4 Many traditional recipes involve yeast.

vinegar has caramel added to it, to give the brown colour. The essential chemistry is an oxidation reaction:

$$\text{ethanol} + \text{air} \xrightarrow{\text{micro-organisms}} \text{ethanoic acid}$$
$$\text{(alcohol)} \qquad\qquad\qquad \text{(vinegar)}$$

Margarine – a manufactured food

Not all food processing and manufacture can be called biotechnology. Fats for making margarine are made by reacting vegetable oils with hydrogen. No enzymes are used. The catalyst is nickel – a metal!

$$\text{vegetable oil} + \text{hydrogen} \xrightarrow{\text{catalyst}} \text{fat}$$

$$-CH=CH-\,(l) \xrightarrow{\text{catalyst}} -CH_2-CH_2-\,(s)$$

The molecules of the vegetable oil contain double bonds: they are 'unsaturated'. The hydrogen adds on to the molecule, forming the fat. The fat is then blended with salt, vitamins, water, colouring and flavouring to give a product which resembles butter. Margarine was originally produced as a cheap substitute for butter, but has now become very popular in its own right.

> **Q3** Find out more from a reference book about the manufacture of one of the foodstuffs mentioned in this section, and draw a flowchart to illustrate the production process.

Fig. 5 Making margarine.

Big molecules!

The molecules of many covalent substances, like water, sugar and petrol, are quite small: they contain 20 or 30 atoms at most. Other substances, like starch, silk, polystyrene and nylon, contain hundreds or even thousands of atoms in every molecule. Some of these molecules are extremely complicated, and their full structures are not yet understood. Others, although very large, have quite simple structures made up from 'repeating units'.

Monomers and polymers

Ethene, $CH_2=CH_2$, is a simple hydrocarbon (see 6.9). Under high-pressure conditions it is possible to make ethene molecules link together to form a substance called poly(ethene) – usually known as 'polythene'. The new molecules are made up from a large number of units:

$$-CH_2-CH_2-CH_2-CH_2-CH_2-CH_2-CH_2-CH_2-CH_2-CH_2-$$

This formula represents a small section from the middle of a poly(ethene) molecule. Molecules like this are called **polymers**, and the small molecules from which they are built are called **monomers**.

How are polymers different from other substances – and why?

Manufactured polymers are special because they can be tailor-made to suit the purposes for which they are needed. Only polymers can be drawn out into fine, strong threads. Only polymers can be made into solid materials which are strong, but also soft and flexible.

The reasons for these differences are all to do with the size and shape of the molecules. Polymer molecules are often said to be like long 'chains'. You can begin to build up a model of a polymer molecule by linking a few paper clips together. (The individual clips are 'monomer' molecules.) If you carry on doing this until you have used about 100 boxes of clips, you will have a reasonable scale model. Polymer molecules are incredibly long!

A lump of solid polymer contains vast numbers of these very long molecules, and they all get tangled up together. You could think of them like the strands in a plate of spaghetti which has been left to go cold. This gives a clue to the properties of the plastic or fibre. If the 'strands of spaghetti' are rigidly linked together you get a solid mass (like formica). If they are not so strongly held in place you get a bendy solid (like polythene). If they are drawn out by pulling them through a small hole, the molecules 'line up' alongside one another, and you get a fibre (like terylene).

How are plastics used?

New plastics have led to completely new techniques, both in the home and at work. Polymers made from oil chemicals have also changed the traditional ways of making everyday articles, for example:

☐ Terylene shirts, blouses, skirts and trousers are more hard-wearing, and easier to wash and iron, than cotton clothes.
☐ Poly(ethene) bags are stronger and more damp-proof than paper ones.
☐ Poly(propene) fishing nets are stronger than ones made from rope or twine, and they do not rot.
☐ Melamine cooking spoons are stronger and easier to keep clean than wooden ones.

Fig. 1 The natural fibres produced by silkworms have been highly prized for thousands of years.

Fig. 2 All fibrous materials are polymers. Some occur naturally, like wool, cotton, and silk. Most of the manufactured fibres are polymers made from chemicals obtained from crude oil.

Fig. 3 The molecules in a lump of plastic are often tangled up like this.

Fig. 4 A Victorian kitchen. Which items here would now be made from plastics?

Fig. 5 Today's plastic money is a magnetic sandwich! You can make telephone calls with this one.

Q1 Describe five more articles, now made from plastics. Explain what they used to be made from, and why plastics are now used instead.

Disposing of plastics

Huge quantities of plastics rubbish are thrown away each year. There are two main worries about this:

☐ Valuable chemicals have been used to make these materials. Once the plastic is thrown away they are lost for ever.

☐ Most plastics do not rot away or corrode, as natural materials do. This means that they remain in the earth indefinitely as possible pollutants. Micro-organisms which will rot paper and wood often have no effect on plastics.

The search is now on for plastics which can be broken down by natural biological processes into harmless waste, and for micro-organisms which will break down existing polymers. Substances which can be broken down by micro-organisms in this way are called **biodegradable**.

Fig. 6 This plant processes household waste. It turns plastics into RDF, 'Refuse Derived Fuel'.

Fig. 1 Expanded polystyrene is widely used for packaging. Even this cress arrives in a polystyrene box.

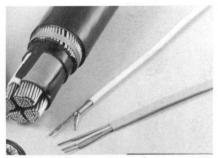

Fig. 2 These cables are insulated with PVC.

Fig. 3 This non-stick pan is coated with 'Teflon', PTFE.

7.14

Different types of polymer

Polymers which are made from a single type of monomer by linking together small molecules of the same kind are known as **addition polymers**. At its simplest, an addition polymer (made from monomers represented by 'A') looks like this:

$$-A-A-A-A-A-A-A-A-A-A-A-A-A-A-A-A-A-A-A-A-$$

Sometimes addition polymers are known as **step-growth polymers**, because they are built up step by step from the monomer:

$$A{=}A + A{=}A \quad \xrightarrow{\text{catalyst}} \quad -A-A-\ldots-A-A- \quad \rightarrow \quad -A-A-A-A-$$
monomers

$$-A-A-A-A- + A{=}A \quad \xrightarrow{\text{catalyst}} \quad -A-A-\ldots-A-A-A-A- \quad \rightarrow \quad -A-A-A-A-A-A-$$
(polymer)

A catalyst is nearly always needed to speed up this process.

Q1 The formula of ethene is $CH_2{=}CH_2$. Write a sequence for the formation of poly(ethene) from ethene. It follows the pattern shown above for the molecule $A{=}A$.

Q2 Addition polymers can only be formed from molecules which have double bonds. Explain why it is necessary for a molecule to contain a double bond if it is to be a suitable monomer for making an addition polymer.

Some addition polymers

Trade name of polymer	Chemical name of polymer	Name of monomer	Used for
Polythene	poly(ethene)	ethene	packaging
Polypropylene	poly(propene)	propene	kitchenware
Polystyrene	poly(phenylethene)	phenylethene	plastic cups
Polyvinyl chloride (PVC)	poly(chloroethene)	chloroethene	insulation, rainwear
Polytetrafluoro-ethylene (PTFE)	poly(tetrafluoro-ethene)	tetrafluoroethene	non-stick pans

Another type of polymer is made from two kinds of monomer which react together forming a chain-like molecule with the structure:

$$-X-Y-X-Y-X-Y-X-Y-X-Y-X-Y-X-Y-X-Y-X-Y-$$

This kind of molecule is known as a **condensation polymer**.

Some condensation polymers

Name	(Alternative names)	Used for
Nylon	(polyamide)	fishing line, clothing
Terylene	(polyester)	clothing
Bakelite	(phenolic resin)	electrical parts
Melamine		plastic houseware, electrical parts
Polyurethane		upholstery packing
Araldite		glue

Fig. 4 Making a model from a thermoplastic material. When the plastic is heated, it softens. Reducing the air pressure on one side of the soft plastic causes it to cave in to the shape of the mould. This process is used in vacuum-forming.

What happens when plastics are heated?

Heating causes the molecules in a solid to move about more. Eventually, when the substance melts, they part company with one another. When plastics are heated it is much more difficult to set the molecules free, because they are so long and tangled. Some kinds of plastics will soften and melt gradually, if the molecules are not too strongly linked. Others have molecules which are so firmly entangled that the heating just breaks down the molecules themselves.

Plastics which melt or soften when heated (like polythene and polystyrene) are called **thermoplastic** or **thermosoftening** materials. Plastics which char and decompose when heated (like bakelite and melamine), and will not melt, are known as **thermosetting** materials.

Thermoplastic materials are easy to shape. Once molten, they can be blown or injected into moulds, or even extruded like toothpaste. Thermosetting materials must be moulded into their final shape at the time the polymer is formed (see Fig. 4).

Fig. 5 Thermosetting plastics in use.

Questions

A. What can you remember?

** **1.** The activities of the chemical industry fall into a number of groups. List three of these, and name one major company involved in each. What are the main products in each case?

** **2.** Write an equation which represents the Haber process for making ammonia. How is this process carried out?

* **3.** Ammonia is an alkaline gas which dissolves in water. Describe one way of demonstrating this.

** **4.** A white solid, when heated with calcium hydroxide, gives off ammonia. The same substance, when dissolved in water, reacts with barium chloride solution, giving a white precipitate. State and explain the conclusions you can draw.

** **5.** Nitric acid is made from ammonia. Outline the process which is used.

** **6.** How, and under what conditions, does sulphuric acid react with (a) sodium hydroxide solution; (b) zinc; (c) copper; (d) sugar?

** **7.** Describe and explain all that happens when blue copper sulphate crystals are heated.

** **8.** Why is chlorine used (a) to purify water; (b) to make PVC; (c) in the extraction of bromine?

** **9.** Give the name of a chloride, different in each case, which (a) breaks down slowly when exposed to light; (b) is found in the earth in large quantities; (c) does not conduct electricity when molten or dissolved; (d) is a gas which forms an acid when dissolved in water. Explain your answer in each case.

** **10.** Chlorine and sodium hydroxide are manufactured by electrolysing brine. Draw a simple diagram (not illustrating a commercial process) which explains why this is possible.

* **11.** Explain why freezing and pickling are effective ways of preventing food from spoiling.

** **12.** Give one example of a fermentation process and explain how it works.

* **13.** What is a polymer? Give two examples of polymers, one natural and one which has been manufactured.

** **14.** Explain the difference between an *addition polymer* and a *condensation polymer*, and give one example of each.

* **15.** Explain what is meant by a *thermoplastic*. Give an example, and say how it is used.

B. What have you understood?

** **16.** Why is ammonia such an important compound for the fertiliser industry?

*** **17.** Explain why nitrates are *both* beneficial to crops, *and* a potential problem in the environment.

*** **18.** What is a 'hydrogensulphate'? How would you expect a solution of sodium hydrogensulphate to react with magnesium ribbon?

** **19.** A company with plans to build a new plant for manufacturing chlorine decides upon a site near the coast. Mercury cells are to be used for the process. A local enquiry has been arranged to consider the plans. As a member of the public with some chemical knowledge, what questions would you ask?

** **20.** Only about 10% of the gas mixture emerging from the Haber process is ammonia. Explain what happens to the rest.

** **21.** A solution of ammonia in water used to be known as 'ammonium hydroxide'. What do you know about this solution which would justify this name?

*** **22.** A textbook says that 'one of the ways in which nitric acid behaves as an oxidising agent is in its reaction with copper.' Explain this statement.

** **23.** Nitrates and nitric acid have always been important in making explosives. Why is this?

** **24.** Describe what is meant by *eutrophication*, and explain how it may arise.

* **25.** Explain why concentrated sulphuric acid will turn (a) copper sulphate crystals from blue to white, and (b) sugar from white to black.

** **26.** If you cut a strip from a poythene bag and grip it firmly in both hands, you can stretch it considerably. When you let go it remains stretched. Bearing in mind the 'spaghetti idea' (See 7.13), explain this behaviour.

** **27.** If you melt some nylon chippings and dip a wire into the molten material you can draw out a fine thread. What does this tell you about nylon?

C. Can you use this information?

* **28.** Here are some important grassland NPK fertilizers:
Morgrass (29:5:5)   Silage Special (24:0:15)
Nitromax (33.5:0:0)   All purpose (15:15:15)

State and explain which one would you choose
(a) for maximum nitrogen content
(b) if phosphorus alone was not required in the fertilizer
(c) for a balanced input of three nutrients

** **29.** A new fertiliser plant is to be set up in the south of England. It will produce several thousand tonnes of fertlisers each day. Its raw materials will need to be brought in both from other parts of Britain and abroad. About 300 people will be employed. What factors are likely to affect the company's decision on where to build the plant?

** **30.** Table 3 on *Datapage I* is about elements in the oceans. Study this information and suggest three elements which might be worth extracting from sea water. Outline a method for getting each one out.

* **31.** Using information from *Datapage M*, write down the purpose of the additives in the following products:
(a) Glace cherries containing E127, E202 and E220;
(b) Custard powder containing E102, E110 and E127;
(c) A grape juice drink containing E220 and E211;
(d) Chocolate biscuits containing E150 and E320.

** **32.** Draw a large pie chart to show the information about the different sections of the chemical industry given in *Datapage S1*. Why do you think the pharmaceutical industry is at the top of this list?

* **33.** Using information from Table 4 on *Datapage L* find out
(a) the name of a popular food which is 50% fat,
(b) the protein content of cooked ham,
(c) the energy content of a box of half a dozen Grade 2 eggs weighing an average of 66 g each.

D. Taking it further

*** **34.** Iron oxide, Fe_2O_3 is a base. It is one of the substances which make sand red. Ammonium chloride, NH_4Cl is a salt which sublimes. It dissociates when heated, forming hydrogen chloride (an acid gas) and ammonia (a base). If you heat red sand with ammonium chloride, the sand loses its colour. Explain what is going on.

** **35.** 'One litre of lemonade contains about 3 litres of dissolved carbon dioxide (measured at room temperature and pressure).' Describe an experiment you could carry out to check the truth of this statement.

*** **36.** Nitrogen compounds are formed when a high voltage spark passes through the air. How could you use this information to make nitric acid?

** **37.** Plastics have now replaced metal for the bumper bars on many motor vehicles. What reasons can you suggest for this?

*** **38.** One way of obtaining sulphur dioxide is to heat the mineral anhydrite, $CaSO_4$ with carbon. The overall reaction may be summarised by the equation:

$$2CaSO_4(s) \quad + \quad \rightarrow \quad 2CaO(s) \quad + \quad CO_2(g) \quad + \quad 2SO_2(g)$$

Anhydrite occurs naturally in the NE of England, and the process has been operated commercially. Explain why this might be a worthwhile enterprise.

** **39.** You have been asked to select a plastic for making beach sandals. What properties would you want the plastic to have? Where possible, explain how the plastic would be treated or chosen to fit your requirements.

*** **40.** There is information in 7.10 and on *Datapage R3* about the three different types of cell which can be used for manufacturing chlorine. Make a summary table showing their different features, and the advantages which each one has.

Quick questions

1. What gas is always given off when a nitrate is heated?

2. What are *agrochemicals*?

3. Give the formula for (a) ammonia, (b) the ammonium ion.

4. Name the important chemicals produced by these processes: Haber, Ostwald, Contact.

5. What is the meaning of the letters NPK, when applied to a fertiliser?

Appendix: Calculations in chemistry

1. Equations and formulae

Writing chemical equations

Chemical equations are written to sum up what happens in a chemical reaction. Think of what takes place when magnesium ribbon burns. There is a bright flame, and some white ash is left. The white ash is magnesium oxide. In chemical language, this is what happens: magnesium (a solid metal) burns with oxygen (a gas from the air) to form a new substance called magnesium oxide (which is a solid).

You could sum this up by writing:

magnesium(s) + oxygen(g) → magnesium oxide(s)

Chemical equations like this are called **word equations**. The small letters in the brackets are known as **state symbols**. They are used to show the physical state of the substances in the reaction. You should always write them down in chemical equations.

State symbols

Physical state of substance in reaction	State symbol
solid	(s)
liquid	(l)
gas	(g)
dissolved in water (aqueous)	(aq)

Moving from word equations to symbol equations

Look again at the word equation for the burning of magnesium:

magnesium(s) + oxygen(g) → magnesium oxide(s)

Write down the chemical formula for each substance:

$$Mg + O_2 \quad \rightarrow \quad MgO$$

Count the number of *atoms* on each side of the equation:

1 + 2   1 + 1

LHS total = 3   RHS total = 2

Something is wrong here! The equation cannot sum up what happens in the reaction unless every atom is accounted for. One of the oxygen atoms is missing!

All the oxygen used in this reaction is converted to magnesium oxide, so it must all be included on *both* sides of the equation. Fundamentally, all that happens in a chemical reaction is that atoms are re-arranged.

They emerge at the end linked together differently from when the reaction began, but no atoms are lost in the process. A chemical equation cannot sum up this process correctly unless it is **balanced**. This means that there must be the same number of atoms of every kind on both sides of the equation.

How do you balance an equation?

First you check that you have included *all* the substances taking part in the reaction and *all* the new substances that are formed. Then you check that all the formulae are correctly written. Then, and only then, can you balance up the number of atoms on each side. This is done by altering the number of particles until the numbers match.

If we go back to the case of magnesium burning in air, we can see that this equation is not balanced:

$$Mg + O_2 \quad \rightarrow \quad MgO$$

It becomes correct if *two* atoms of magnesium are used to react with *one* molecule of oxygen:

$$2Mg + O_2 \quad \rightarrow \quad 2MgO$$

Important note:
You might think that other ways of balancing the equation would be to use the 'extra' oxygen to write the formula of magnesium oxide as MgO_2, or to write oxygen itself simply as O. Neither of these are correct formulae for the substances, so they cannot be used. **Never alter the formula of any substance while balancing a chemical equation**.

The **balanced equation** can now be written in its final form:

$$2Mg(s) + O_2(g) \quad \rightarrow \quad 2MgO(s)$$

How heavy are atoms and molecules?

The atoms of the different elements are all different. The simplest atom, hydrogen, consists of just one proton and one electron. The hydrogen atom is the lightest of all, but heavier atoms may contain several hundred particles. Even the heaviest atom has much too small a mass to measure directly, however. We have to use indirect evidence (see 1.4) to work out the masses of atoms, *relative to one another*.

What is a 'relative' scale of masses?

When you buy shoes you do not tell the assistant that your feet are − let's say − 20cm long. You ask for a particular size. Everyone understands because there is an agreed scale of shoe sizes. These sizes are on a *relative* scale, where size 5 is bigger than size 2, and size

7 is bigger still. In a similar way, there is an agreed relative scale for the masses of atoms. This is how it works.

The carbon-12 atom is chosen as the standard atom for the scale. This is the atom which has 6 protons, 6 neutrons and 6 electrons. By international agreement, it has been given a mass of 12.0000 'atomic mass units'. The masses of all other atoms are given on a scale of masses which takes carbon-12 as the standard. These values are expressed *relative* to the mass of the standard atom, and this is why they are known as relative atomic mass values.

The **relative atomic mass** (symbol A_r) of an element is the average mass of its atoms, relative to one atom of carbon-12.

The symbol A_r is often used in writing down values of relative atomic masses. For instance, the statement 'The relative atomic mass of sodium is 23' is represented as A_r (Na) = 23.

Table 1: The relative atomic masses of some common elements

Atom	Symbol	Relative Atomic Mass (A_r) [all figures to the nearest 0.5]
hydrogen	H	1
carbon	C	12
nitrogen	N	14
oxygen	O	16
magnesium	Mg	24
aluminium	Al	27
sulphur	S	32
chlorine	Cl	35.5
iron	Fe	56
copper	Cu	63.5
silver	Ag	108
mercury	Hg	201
lead	Pb	207

[A fuller table of these figures is on *Datapage A*].

What do the relative atomic mass values mean?

1. The relative atomic mass (A_r) values tell you how much heavier one atom is than another. A carbon atom is 12 times as heavy as a hydrogen atom, for instance.

Q1 Which is the heavier atom, nitrogen or oxygen?
Q2 How much heavier is a magnesium atom than a carbon atom?

2. Some A_r values are not whole numbers. This is because of the existence of **isotopes** (see 1.6). You should re-read 1.6 if you are not sure what an isotope is.

Almost all naturally occurring samples of an element are mixtures of isotopes. Chlorine is a good example. It

contains two isotopes: chlorine-37 and chlorine-35. In ordinary chlorine gas these two isotopes are present in a ratio of about 3 to 1. This means that the *average* mass of the atoms in chlorine is somewhere between 35 and 37. This is how the relative atomic mass is worked out exactly.

Table 2: The isotopes in chlorine gas

Symbol	Percentage (= no. of atoms in 100 atoms)	Simplest ratio	Mass number (Z)
^{37}Cl	25	1	37
^{35}Cl	75	3	35

Worked example 1
Calculating the relative atomic mass of an element

Question
Work out the relative atomic mass chlorine from the information given in Table 2.

Answer
☐ In 100 atoms of chlorine there are 75 atoms of ^{35}Cl and 25 atoms of ^{37}Cl.
☐ So, the **total** mass of 100 atoms is $[(75 \times 35) + (25 \times 37)]$
☐ The **average** mass of these atoms is

$$\frac{(75 \times 35) + (25 \times 37)}{100}$$

$$= \frac{2625 + 925}{100}$$

$$= \frac{3550}{100}$$

$$= 35.5$$

☐ The **relative atomic mass of chlorine** is 35.5.

Q3 Magnesium contains the three isotopes: ^{24}Mg, ^{25}Mg, and ^{26}Mg, in the proportions 80:10:10. Work out the exact A_r value for magnesium, and compare this figure with the one given in Table 1.

How do you work out the relative masses of molecules?

It simple to work out the relative mass of a molecule if you know its formula. The **relative molecular mass** (symbol M_r) of a substance is the average mass of its molecules, relative to 1/12 of the mass of one *atom* of carbon-12. It is calculated by adding together the A_r values for all its atoms.

Note: This definition also applies to substances which are not made up of molecules. For example, M_r values for ionic substances are worked out *as if* the formula represented 'one molecule'.

Worked example 2
Calculating the relative molecular mass of a compound.

Question
Calculate the relative molecular masses of the following substances:
(a) chlorine gas (Cl_2), (b) sodium chloride (NaCl), (c) sodium nitrate ($NaNO_3$), (d) lead nitrate ($Pb(NO_3)_2$), (e) copper sulphate crystals ($CuSO_4.5H_2O$).

Answers
(a) Chlorine, Cl_2
  □ Look up the relative atomic mass of chlorine (Table 1): A_r (Cl) = 35.5
  □ Look at the formula for the chlorine molecule, and decide what must be done to the A_r value to work out the M_r value:
  M_r (Cl_2) = 2 x A_r (Cl)
  □ Calculate the M_r value:
  Cl_2 = 2 x 35.5 = 71
  M_r (Cl_2) = 71
(b) Sodium chloride, NaCl
  NaCl = 23 + 35.5 = 58.5
      Na   Cl
(c) Sodium nitrate, $NaNO_3$
  $NaNO_3$ = 23 + 14 + (3 x 16) = 85
       Na   N O_3
(d) Lead nitrate, $Pb(NO_3)_2$
  $Pb(NO_3)_2$ = 207 + 2(14 + [3 x 16]) = 331
          Pb   (2 x (NO_3))
(e) Copper sulphate crystals, $CuSO_4.5H_2O$
  $CuSO_4.5H_2O$ =
  63.5 + 32 + (4 x 16) + 5([2x1] + 16)
  Cu   S O_4 $5H_2O$
  = 249.5

Q4 Now use the A_r values given in Table 1 to calculate M_r values for the following: methane, CH_4; ethane, C_2H_6; aluminium oxide, Al_2O_3; magnesium chloride, $MgCl_2$; mercury(II) nitrate, $Hg(NO_3)_2$; iron(II) sulphate crystals, $FeSO_4.7H_2O$.

How do you find a chemical formula?

Before starting this section, look back at 1.8. The formula of a compound contains two pieces of information:

□ which **kinds of atom** the compound contains, and
□ the **numbers** of each kind of atom present in one molecule.

To write a chemical formula you need to know both of these things. For instance,

(1) Water molecules contain **two** kinds of atom, hydrogen and oxygen
(2) One water molecule contains **two** hydrogen atoms and **one** oxygen atom.

This is enough information to write the **formula** as H_2O.

How do you find out which kinds of atom are present?

This may be a job for the chemical analyst, or it may be simple enough for almost anyone to do. Here are two examples:

Water is known to contain hydrogen and oxygen because hydrogen gas and oxygen gas react together, giving just one product: water! What's more, if water is split up by electrolysis (see 4.10) the only substances produced are the two elements hydrogen and oxygen.

Methane is known to contain carbon and hydrogen only, because when it is completely burned in oxygen there are just two products: carbon dioxide and water. The carbon in the carbon dioxide, and the hydrogen in the water, can only have come from the methane.

How do you find out the numbers of each kind of atom?

Again, this may be a job for someone with special training, but simple substances can be worked out quite easily. You must first do an experiment like this one with silver oxide:

Silver oxide is a substance which breaks down to its elements when heated. The oxygen is released as a gas, and silver is left behind.

$$\text{silver oxide(s)} \xrightarrow{\text{heat}} \text{silver(s)} + \text{oxygen(g)}$$

The amount of oxygen given off can be worked out from the change in mass. Here are the results obtained by four people who heated some samples of silver oxide.

Table 3: Heating weighed amounts of silver oxide

Mass of silver oxide used in the expt (g)	Mass of silver left after heating (g)	Mass of oxygen given off during the expt (g)
Expt 1 20.0	18.6	1.4
Expt 2 19.0	17.7	1.3
Expt 3 16.0	15.9	1.1
Expt 4 13.0	12.1	0.9

Worked example 3
Using the results of a weighing experiment.

Question
Use the above information and the figures in Table 3 to work out (a) what mass of oxygen you would obtain by heating 14.25 g of silver oxide, and (b) what mass of silver is present in 14.25 g of silver oxide.

Answer
□ Plot a graph of the figures from Table 3, as shown in Fig. 1.
□ You can read off from this graph exactly how much oxygen would be released from a chosen weight of

silver oxide. The dotted lines show the answers you need:
(a) 14.5g of silver oxide gives off **1.0g of oxygen**, and
(b) **13.5g of silver** is left.

Q5 Write down the weights of oxygen you would obtain by heating (a) 22.0g, and (b) 16.75g of silver oxide.

Q6 Calculate the weights of silver present in the quantities of silver oxide given in Q5.

Worked example 4
Using the results of a weighing experiment to calculate a formula.

Question
Using the graph in Fig. 1 and the possible answers shown in Table 4, work out the formula of silver oxide.

Appendix Fig. 1
Heating silver oxide: the results of four experiments (see Table 3).

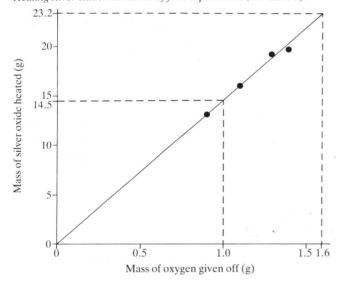

Table 4: Some possible formulae for silver oxide

Possible formula of silver oxide	Mass of silver (g)	Mass of oxygen (g)
AgO	108	16
AgO_2	108	32
AgO_3	108	48
Ag_2O	216	16
Ag_3O	324	16

Answer
☐ Look again at the graph. Notice which set of figures matches the ones from the experiment.
☐ You can see that 23.2g of silver oxide would give off 1.6g of oxygen when heated. This means that 232g of silver oxide (= 10 x 23.2g) would give 10 times as much oxygen.

☐ 232g of silver oxide therefore give off 10 x 1.6 (=16g) oxygen, leaving 216g of silver.
☐ The figures in Table 3 show that if a sample of silver oxide contains 216g of silver and 16g of oxygen, its **formula must be Ag_2O**.

The correct **formula of silver oxide** is Ag_2O.

Q7 Two pupils repeated the experiment with silver oxide. Jane heated 33.14g of silver oxide, and 2.28g of oxygen was given off. James heated 29.0g of silver oxide, and 28.0g of silver was left. Which pupil appears to have made an error?

2 How much material will react?

Combining masses from formulae
When two or more elements react to form one particular compound, the elements combine together in the *same proportion* by weight every time.

Worked example 5
Using the chemical formula of a compound to work out the mass of substance required for a chemical reaction.

Question
Iron and sulphur react together when heated, forming iron sulphide, FeS.
What mass of sulphur will combine with 7.0g of iron?

Answer
☐ Look up the A_r values for iron and sulphur:
$A_r(Fe) = 56$, $A_r(s) = 32$
☐ Decide how many atoms of iron combine with one atom of sulphur: The formula of iron sulphide is FeS, so 1 atom of iron combines with 1 atom of sulphur
☐ Write down the masses of iron and sulphur which combine together when one 'molecule' of FeS is formed: 1 iron atom of A_r 56 combines with 1 sulphur atom of A_r 32, so 56g iron combines with 32g sulphur
☐ Work out how many grams of sulphur will combine with just 1 gram of iron: 1g iron combines with 32/56g sulphur (There is no need to work this fraction out.)
☐ Work out how many grams of sulphur will combine with 7.0g of iron: 7.0g iron combines with
$\frac{7.0 \times 32}{56}$ g sulphur

 = 4.0 grams of sulphur
☐ **4.0g of sulphur** will combine with **7.0g of iron**.

Q8 Work out:
(a) the mass of oxygen which is taken from the air when 6.0g of magnesium ribbon is burned to form magnesium oxide, MgO, and
(b) the mass of chlorine which would be needed to convert 5.6g of iron wool to iron(III) chloride, $FeCl_3$.

Reacting masses from equations

If you know the chemical equation for a reaction it is possible to decide how much material is needed to carry out that reaction without wasting any material.

Worked example 6
Using the chemical equation for a reaction to work out the masses of the reactants and products.

Question
The equation for the 'thermite' reaction between aluminium and iron(III) oxide is

$$2Al(s) + Fe_2O_3(s) \rightarrow 2Fe(l) + Al_2O_3(s)$$

What mass of aluminium powder would be needed to react completely with 16g of dried iron(III) oxide?

Answer
☐ Work out the relative masses of the reacting substances:
A_r (Al) = 27; 2Al = (2 x 27) = 54
M (Fe$_2$O$_3$) = (2 x 56) + (3 x 16) = 160

☐ Write these figures down in a simple statement:
160g iron(III) oxide reacts with 54g aluminium

☐ Work out (if necessary) the mass of aluminium which would react with 1.0g of iron(III) oxide:
1.0g iron oxide reacts with 54/160g aluminium

☐ Work out the mass of aluminium which would be needed to react completely with 16g iron(III) oxide:
16g iron(III) oxide would react with
$\dfrac{54 \times 16}{160}$ g aluminium

= 5.4g aluminium

☐ **5.4g aluminium** reacts with **16g iron(III) oxide** in this reaction.

Q9 A similar reaction is used to extract uranium. Uranium oxide is reduced by heating it with calcium:

$$2Ca(s) + UO_2(s) \rightarrow 2CaO(s) + U(l)$$

How much calcium would be needed to reduce 27kg of uranium oxide, and what mass of uranium would be produced?

Q10 A sulphuric acid plant makes 500 tonnes of acid per week. How much sulphur would be needed for this?

Q11 A stock pile of iron ore, Fe$_2$O$_3$, is enough to run a blast furnace for a month. It weighs 5000 tonnes. How much iron could be made from it?

Q12 A sugar lump weighs 5.0g. Its formula is $C_{12}H_{22}O_{11}$. What mass of carbon does it contain?

Equations from reacting masses

Chemical equations are worked out from the results of experiments in which the amounts of material taking part in the reaction are measured.

Worked example 7
Working out the chemical equation for a reaction from the masses of the reactants and products.

Question
When 25.0g copper sulphate crystals were kept for two hours in an oven at 120°C, only water was removed. The final weight of the copper sulphate was 17.8g. Work out the equation for the reaction which occurred.

Answer
☐ Write down the formulae for the reactants and products, as far as you can. In this case, assume that the formula of the copper sulphate left at the end is CuSO$_4$.xH$_2$O. This meas that 'x' molecules of water remain with the copper sulphate, and so (5−x) molecules of water have been removed by heating:

$$CuSO_4.5H_2O(s) \rightarrow CuSO_4.xH_2O(s) + (5-x(g)$$

☐ Write down the M_r values for all the substances in the equation:

$$CuSO_4.5H_2O(s) \rightarrow CUSO_4.xH_2O(s) + (5-x)H_2O(g)$$
M_r values:
    250   160 + 18x 18(5−x)

☐ Now write underneath the known masses of substances taking part in the reaction:

$$CuSO_4.5H_2O(s) \rightarrow CuSO_4.xH_2O(s) + (5-x)H_2O(g)$$
M_r values:
    250   160 + 18x 18(5−x)
Masses:
    25.0g   17.8g   (25.0 − 17.8)g

☐ The ratio of the reacting masses to the M_r values is constant, so

$$\frac{250}{25.0} = \frac{160 + 18x}{17.8}$$

☐ This gives an equation which you can solve for 'x'.
Re-arrange as one line:
(160 + 18x) x 25.0 = 250 x 17.8
Divide both sides by 25:
(160 + 18x) x 1   10 x 17.8
Gather numbers to RHS of the equation:
18x = 178 − 160
18x = 18
x = 1

☐ The **formula of the copper sulphate** remaining is **CuSO$_4$.H$_2$O**, so so the **equation for the reaction** is

$$CuSO_4.5H_2O(s) \rightarrow CuSO_4.H_2O(s) + 4H_2O(g)$$

Q13 Use the information given here to work out equations for these two reactions:
(a) When 43 tonnes of gypsum, CaSO$_4x$H$_2$O, were heated to 500°C, all the water of crystallisation was removed. The remaining material, called anhydrite, weighed 34 tonnes.
(b) Magnesium sulphate crystals, MgSO$_4.x$H$_2$O, lose their water of crystallisation when heated to 500°C. A pupil who heated 2.5g of the crystals found that she had 1.0g of anhydrous magnesium sulphate at the end.

3 Calculating the percentage composition of a compound from its formula

The amount of each element present in a compound is easy to calculate from its chemical formula.

Worked example 8
Finding the percentage by mass of the elements in a compound.

Question
The mineral calcite is a pure form of calcium carbonate, $CaCO_3$.
What is the percentage by mass of each element present?

Answer
☐ Write down the formula of the substance, well spaced, with the A_r values for each element underneath:

	Ca	C	O_3
A_r value:	40	12	(3×16)

☐ Add up these figures to work out the relative molecular mass:
$$M_r = 40 + 12 + (3 \times 16) = 100$$

☐ Write down the A_r values for each element as a fraction of the relative molecular mass:

	Ca	C	O_3
Fraction:	$\dfrac{40}{100}$	$\dfrac{12}{100}$	$\dfrac{(3 \times 16)}{100}$

☐ Multiply each fraction by 100, to bring it to a percentage:

	Ca	C	O_3
Fraction: x 100:	$\dfrac{40 \times 100}{100}$	$\dfrac{12 \times 100}{100}$	$\dfrac{(3 \times 16) \times 100}{100}$

☐ Work out these fractions to determine the percentage composition of the compound:
$$Ca = 40\%, \quad C = 12\%, \quad O = 48\%$$

Calcium carbonate is a particularly easy example, because its relative molecular mass is 100. But the method is the same whatever the M_r value.

Worked example 9
Finding the percentage by mass of one particular element in a compound.

Question
What is the percentage of nitrogen in the fertiliser ammonium nitrate, NH_4NO_3?

Answer
☐ Work out the relative molecular mass of ammonium nitrate:
$$M_r (NH_4NO_3) = (2 \times N) + (4 \times H) + (3 \times O)$$
$$= (2 \times 14) + (4 \times 1) + (3 \times 16)$$
$$= 28 + 4 + 48$$
$$M_r (NH_4NO_3) = 80$$

☐ Write down the amount of nitrogen as a fraction of the total:
$$N = \frac{28}{80}$$
☐ Convert this to a percentage:
$$\% \text{ nitrogen} = \frac{28 \times 100}{80}$$
$$= 35\%$$

Q14 Work out the percentage by mass of each element in the following compounds:
(a) magnesium nitride, $M_r (Mg_3N_2) = 100$,
(b) calcium bromide, $M_r (CaBr_2) = 200$,
(c) chloromethane, $M_r (CH_3Cl) = 50$,
(d) glucose, $C_6H_{12}O_6$. (First work out the M_r for yourself).

Water of crystallisation as a percentage

Sometimes it is necessary to work out the percentage by mass of water in a hydrated salt. The method is the same as above, except that 'H_2O' is treated as an 'element' in the calculation.

Worked example 10
Finding the percentage by mass of water in a hydrated salt.

Question
What is the percentage by mass of water in the crystalline salt $Cr(NO_3)_3.9H_2O$? The M_r value for this substance is 400.

Answer
☐ Work out the fraction of the total mass which is water:
$$M_r (H_2O) = 18, \text{ so } 9H_2O = (9 \times 18) = 162$$
This mass as a fraction of the total mass is 162/400

☐ Convert this fraction to a percentage by multiplying by 100:
$$\text{percentage water} = \frac{100 \times 162}{400}$$
$$= 40.5$$

Chromium(III) nitrate crystals contain 40.5% water.

Q15 The following commercially important salts contain water of crystallisation. Work out the percentage of water in each.

Some important hydrated salts

Everyday name of salt	Formula	Relative molecular mass
Alum	$KAl(SO_4)_2.12H_2O$	474
Borax	$Na_2B_4O_7.10H_2O$	381
Photographers' hypo	$Na_2S_2O_3.5H_2O$	248
Washing soda	$Na_2CO_3.10H_2O$	286

4 The mole – a chemical unit

The mole is a unit on the internationally accepted SI system, like the metre, the kilogram and the second. Just as distances can be measured in metres, amounts of substances can be measured in moles.

One mole is the amount of substance which contains as many particles as there are carbon atoms in 12.0000g of carbon-12.

When using the mole unit it is essential to say what particle is being referred to. 'One mole of sulphur' means nothing until we know whether the statement refers to sulphur atoms, sulphur molecules (of stated formula), or even sulphide ions. The correct way to refer to amounts of substance is by their formulae, for example:

1 mole of S atoms
0.5 moles of S_8 molecules
4 moles of S^{2-}(aq) ions

It is even correct to write

1 mole of KCl(s) bonds
2 moles of >C=C< bonds
etc.

even though the 'particle' referred to may not really exist, as such.

An equation, such as

$$2K(s) + Cl_2(g) \rightarrow 2KCl(s)$$

is a short way of representing the statement:
'Two moles of potassium atoms (K) react with one mole of chlorine molecules (Cl_2), to form two moles of potassium chloride (KCl).'

Why is the mole unit useful?

One mole of *any* substance contains the same number of particles: the number of carbon atoms in 12 grams of carbon-12. This means that **equal numbers of moles** contain **equal numbers of particles**.

Chemical reactions occur, not according to the *masses* of the different substances taking part, but in proportion to the *numbers of particles* which react. This means that for working out what happens during a chemical reaction, knowing the numbers of particles present is more useful than knowing their mass.

If we turn the earlier statement round, we get **equal numbers of particles** make up **equal numbers of moles**. This means that if a reaction is represented by a balanced equation, such as

$$2Mg(s) + O_2(g) \rightarrow 2MgO(s)$$

you can work out the numbers of particles, the numbers of moles, and then the masses of the substances taking part in the reaction. For example:

$$\text{No. of particles:} \quad \underset{2}{2Mg(s)} + \underset{1}{O_2(g)} \rightarrow \underset{2}{2MgO(s)}$$

The equation shows that 2 particles of magnesium react with 1 particle of oxygen, forming 2 particles of magnesium oxide. This means that 2 *million* particles of magnesium will react with 1 *million* particles of oxygen, forming 2 *million* particles of magnesium oxide, and so on. So, 2 *moles* of particles of magnesium will react with 1 *mole* of particles of oxygen, forming 2 *moles* of particles of magnesium oxide.

Converting between 'mole quantities' and 'mass quantities'

You can find the mass of a substance in grams by using some kind of balance, but you cannot weigh directly in moles. If you know the A_r or M_r value of the substance being weighed, it is easy to convert to mole units. Oxygen is a simple example. Since $A_r(O) = 16$,

1 mole of O atoms weighs 16g
2 moles of O atoms weighs 32g
0.5 moles of O atoms weighs 8g

and

1 mole of O_2 molecules weighs 32g
3 moles of O_2 molecules weighs 96g

etc.

Worked example 11
Expressing amounts of substance as mole quantities.

Question
How many moles of substance are present in each of the following:
(a) 60g silicon dioxide, SiO_2?
(b) 50g heptane, C_7H_{16}?

Answer
☐ Work out the A_r and M_r values for each substance:
(a) $SiO_2 = 28 + (2 \times 16) = 60$
(b) $C_7H_{16} = (7 \times 12) + (16 \times 1) = 100$
☐ Write down the mass of 1 mole of each substance
(a) 1 mole of SiO_2 weighs 60g
(b) 1 mole of C_7H_{16} weighs 100g
☐ Calculate the required answers:
(a) 60g SiO_2 = 60/60 moles
    = 1.0 mole of SiO_2
(b) 50g C_7H_{16} = 50/100 moles
    = 0.5 moles of C_7H_{16}

Q16 Express the following amounts of substance as mole quantities:
(a) 150g arsenic, $A_r(As) = 75$
(b) 4g calcium, $A_r(Ca) = 40$
(c) 15g sulphur trioxide, $M_r(SO_3) = 80$
(d) 64g of oxygen gas
(e) 64g of copper
(f) 64g of magnesium oxide

Worked example 12
Converting mole quantities to masses in grams.

Question:
What is the mass of
(a) 1 mole of mercury atoms, Hg
(b) 2.5 moles of methane, CH_4
(c) 0.2 moles of 'Freon', CCl_2F_2?

Answer
☐ Work out the A_r and M_r values of each substance:
(a) A_r (Hg) = 200
(b) M_r (CH_4) = (12 + 4) = 16
(c) M_r (CCl_2F_2) = (12 + [2 x 35.5] + [2 x 19])
     = 120
☐ Calculate the required answers:
(a) 1 mole of Hg atoms weighs 200g
(b) 2.5 moles of CH_4 molecules weigh
     (2.5 x 16)g = 40g
(c) 0.2 moles of CCl_2F_2 molecules weigh
     (0.2 x 120)g = 24g

5 Calculating chemical formulae

The methods you have already learned can now be used to work out the exact formula of a compound. This is very important for anyone working on new chemical substances. The laboratory report from an analyst will contain figures for the percentage by mass of each element found in the substance.

Worked example 13
Finding the formula of a compound from its percentage composition by mass.

Question
A hydrocarbon with the formula C_xH_y contains 80% C and 20% H by mass. Its relative molecular mass is 30. What is its formula?

Answer
☐ Work out the mass of each element present in 1 mole of the hydrocarbon molecules:
     1 mole of the hydrocarbon weighs 30g,
so
     1 mole of hydrocarbon molecules contains (80% of 30)g of carbon atoms
          = 24g of carbon atoms, and
     1 mole of the hydrocarbon molecules contains (20% of 30)g of hydrogen atoms
          = 6g of hydrogen atoms

☐ Work out how many moles of carbon atoms and hydrogen atoms are present in 1 mole of the hydrocarbon molecules:

          24g C atoms = 24/12 moles
                      = 2 moles of C atoms
          6g H atoms = 6/1 moles
                      = 6 moles of H atoms

So, 1 mole of C_xH_y molecules contains 2 moles of C atoms and 6 moles of H atoms and 6 moles of H atoms, and

          x = 2 and y = 6

☐ **The formula of the hydrocarbon C_xH_y is C_2H_6**

Worked example 14
Finding the simplest (or 'empirical') formula of a compound from its percentage composition by mass.

Question
Another hydrocarbon, C_aH_b contains 90% C and 10% H by mass. Calculate its simplest (or 'empirical') formula.

Answer
☐ Work out the mass of each element present in 100g of the hydrocarbon molecules:
          100g C_aH_b molecules contains
          90g C atoms and 10g H atoms
☐ Work out how many moles of carbon and hydrogen atoms are present in 100g of the hydrocarbon molecules:
          90g C atoms = 90/12 moles of C atoms
                      = 7.5 moles of C atoms
          10g H atoms = 10/1 moles of H atoms
                      = 10.0 moles of H atoms
☐ Work out the simplest whole number ratio of 'moles of C atoms' to 'moles of H atoms'.
     'moles of of C atoms': 'moles of H atoms'
     =   7.5   :   10
     =   7.5/7.5 : 10/7.5
          (divide both by lower number)
     =   1   :   1.33
          (work out the ratio)
     =   3   :   4
          (work out the smallest
           whole number ratio)

☐ This means that a = 3 and b = 4.
☐ Since no information is given about the relative molecular mass of this hydrocarbon, all that can be said is that the **empirical formula is C_3H_4**. This means that for every 3 carbon atoms in the molecule there are 4 hydrogen atoms.

Worked example 15
Finding the molecular formula of a compound from its percentage composition by mass.

Question
The relative molecular mass of C_aH_b (the hydrocarbon from worked example 14) is 80. What is its molecular formula?

Answer
☐ Work out an M_r value for the empirical formula, C_3H_4:

$$M_r(C_3H_4) = (3 \times 12) + (4 \times 1) = 40$$

☐ Divide the M_r value supplied in the question by the M_r value worked out for the empirical formula:

$$\frac{M_r(C_3H_4)}{M_r(C_aH_b)} = \frac{80}{40}$$
$$= 2$$

☐ This means that the molecular formula of the hydrocarbon is *twice* the empirical formula. So 'a' becomes (2×3) and 'b' becomes (2×4), and **the hydrocarbon is C_6H_8**.

Q19 Work out the simplest formula for the following hydrocarbons. Then use the M_r values provided to find the molecular formula. Finally, look up the name of the hydrocarbon in *Datapage G*.
(a) 85.7% C, 14.3% H ($M_r = 28$); (b) 81.8% C, 18.2% H ($M_r = 84$); (c) 83.3% C, 16.7% H ($M_r = 170$).

Worked example 16
Finding the number of molecules of water of crystallisation in a salt from its percentage composition by mass.

Question
'Epsom salt' crystals have the formula $MgSO_4.xH_2O$. When heated they lose all of their water of crystallisation, forming anhydrous magnesium sulphate, $MgSO_4$. 12.3g of Epsom salt crystals weighed exactly 6.0g after being heated until there was no further change in mass. What is the value of x?

Answer
☐ Write an equation for the reaction which has taken place, together with the masses of each substance used and formed in the reaction:

$$MgSO_4.xH_2O(s) \rightarrow MgSO_4(s) + xH_2O(g)$$

Masses:
12.3g	6.0g	(12.3 − 6.0)g

☐ Now add the M_r values for each substance produced:

Masses:
$$MgSO_4.xH_2O(s) \rightarrow MgSO_4(s) + xH_2O(g)$$

		6.0g	6.3g
M_r values:		120	18

☐ Work out the number of moles of each substance formed:

No. of moles = 6.0/120 moles
$MgSO_4$ = 0.05 moles $MgSO_4$ formed.
No. of moles = 6.3/18 moles
H_2O = 0.35 moles H_2O given off.

☐ Use this information to calculate the number of moles of water molecules in 1 mole of Epsom salt:

When 0.05 moles of anhydrous magnesium sulphate are formed, 0.35 moles of water are given off. So, when 1 mole (= 20 x 0.05 moles) of anhydrous magnesium sulphate is formed, the number of moles of water molecules given off is 20 x 0.35 (= 7).

☐ **The formula of Epsom salt is $MgSO_4.7H_2O$.**

Q20 Use the information provided to work out the number of molecules of water of crystallisation in each of the following:
(a) 26.7g of strontium chloride crystals, $SrCl_2.aH_2O$, weighed 15.85g after being heated until they were completely anhydrous.
(b) 7.0g of nickel sulphate crystals, $NiSO_4.bH_2O$, lost 3.13g when heated until they were completely anhydrous.

---

6 Gases

In 1811 the Italian scientist Avogadro realised that all gases had something important in common. He suspected that under the same conditions of temperature and pressure, a fixed volume of any gas contained a fixed number of molecules. In other words, the number of H_2 molecules in 1 litre of hydrogen is the same as the number of CH_4 molecules in 1 litre of methane, and so on — so long as both gases are at the same temperature and pressure.

Avogadro suggested that 'equal volumes of all gases contain the same number of molecules'. The reverse of this statement is equally true: 'equal numbers of molecules of all gases occupy the same volume'. For these statements to be true, all measurements must be taken at *the same temperature and pressure*.

Since 1 mole of molecules of any gas contains a fixed number of molecules, it follows that the *volume* of 1 mole of gas molecules is the same — no matter what the gas may be. One mole of any gas at 0°C and '1 atmosphere' pressure (10^5Pa) occupies a volume of 22.4 litres. A convenient working version of this statement is this:

One mole of molecules of any gas at room temperature and pressure occupies a volume of approximately 24 litres.

Worked example 17
Finding the volume of a known mass of gas at room temperature and pressure.

Question
What is the volume of 1g of hydrogen gas at room temperature and pressure?

Answer
☐ Work out the number of moles of gas molecules present:

Hydrogen gas consists of *molecules*, H_2, and M_r

$(H_2) = 2$. Therefore 2g of hydrogen gas contains 1 mole of molecules, and 1g of hydrogen gas contains 0.5 moles of molecules.

☐ Use the statement '1 mole of molecules of hydrogen occupies 24 litres at room temperature and pressure' to work out the answer:

    1 mole $H_2(g)$ occupies 24 litres
    0.5 moles $H_2(g)$ occupies 0.5 x 24 (= 12) litres.

☐ **1g of hydrogen occupies 12 litres at room temperature and pressure.**

Worked example 18
Finding the number of moles of gas present in a known volume at room temperature and pressure.

Question
How many moles of oxygen molecules are present in the air inside a single-decker bus which measures 2m high x 2m wide x 10m long? Assume that 20% of the air is oxygen. [$1m^3 = 10^6$ litres]

Answer
☐ Work out the volume of oxygen inside the bus:
    Volume of air in bus $= 2 \times 2 \times 10 m^3$
  Volume of oxygen in bus $= 20\% \times$ (volume of air)
                    $= 0.2 \times (2 \times 2 \times 10) m^3$
                    $= 8m^3$
                    $= 8 \times 10^6$ litres

☐ Work out the answer, using the statement '24 litres of oxygen at room temperature and pressure contains 1 mole of oxygen molecules':

24 litres $O_2(g)$ contains 1 mole of O_2 molecules
Therefore, 1 litre $O_2(g)$ contains 1/24 moles of O_2 molecules, and 8×10^6 litres $O_2(g)$ contains
$\dfrac{8 \times 10^6}{24}$ moles of O_2 molecules
3.3×10^5 moles of oxygen molecules.

☐ **The bus contains 3.3×10^5 moles of oxygen molecules.**

Working out chemical equations for reactions involving gases

The same arguments can be used to work out chemical equations for reactions between gases. For instance, it is found that if 48 litres of hydrogen are exploded with 24 litres of oxygen, some water is formed, and there is no gas of either kind left over.

48 litres $H_2(g)$ + 24 litres $O_2(g) \rightarrow$ water
                        (and *no gas left over*)

In other words:

2 moles $H_2(g)$ + 1 mole $O_2(g) \rightarrow$ water
                        (and *no gas left over*)

If 2 moles $H_2(g)$ molecules react complete with 1 mole $O_2(g)$ molecules, then 2 molecules of hydrogen gas react completely with 1 molecule of oxygen gas to form water.

This is a long way of saying:

    $2H_2(g) + O_2(g) \rightarrow$ water (and *nothing else*)

so the equation for this reaction must be

$$2H_2(g) + O_2(g) \rightarrow 2H_2O(g)$$

Alternatively, you can work out the volumes of gas which would be needed for a chemical reaction if you know its equation.

Worked example 19
Finding the volume of gas produced in a chemical reaction.

Question (a)
How many cubic centimetres of carbon dioxide gas, measured at room temperature and pressure, are released when 1g of pure calcium carbonate is completely decomposed by heat.

Answer
☐ Write a balanced equation for the reaction, and put in the numbers of moles reacting:

$CaCO_3(s) \rightarrow CaO(s) + CO_2(g)$
1 mole $\rightarrow$ 1 mole   1 mole

☐ Write the M_r values of the substance for which you have a *mass* figure, and the *volume of 1 mole* of the substance whose volume you are asked to work out:

$CaCO_3(s) \rightarrow CaO(s) + CO_2(g)$
1 mole $\rightarrow$ 1 mole   1 mole
$M_r = 100$ 1mole = 24 litres

☐ 1g of calcium carbonate is 0.01 moles, and since

1 mole $CaCO_3$ $\rightarrow$ 1 mole CO_2
0.01 moles $CaCO_3$ $\rightarrow$ 0.01 moles CO_2

☐ The volume of 0.1 moles CO_2 is 0.01×24 litres
              = 0.24 litres carbon dioxide
              $= 240cm^3$ carbon dioxide.

☐ **1g of calcium carbonate produces $240cm^3$ of carbon dioxide when completely decomposed by heat.**

Question (b)
What volume of gas (if measured at room temperature and pressure) would be expelled from the exhaust system of a car during a 1-hour journey in which 4.4kg of LPG fuel is used? Assume that the LPG is the hydrocarbon propane, C_3H_8, which burns according to the equation:

    $C_3H_8(g) + 5O_2(g) \rightarrow 3CO_2(g) + 4H_2O(g)$

Answer
☐ Write out the equation for the reaction, and add all the information you can:

C_3H_8	+	$5O_2(g)$	$\rightarrow$	$3CO_2(g)$	+	$4H_2O(g)$
1 molecule	+	5 molecules	$\rightarrow$	3 molecules	+	4 molecules
1 mole of propane molecules	+	5 moles of oxygen molecules	$\rightarrow$	3 moles of carbon dioxide molecules	+	4 moles of water molecules

☐ $M_r (C_3H_8) =$
44, so 1 mole of LPG weighs 44g
44g of LPG gives (3×24) litres $+ (4 \times 24)$ litres of exhaust gases (if measured at room temperature and pressure)

226

□ Work out the answer from quantities given in the question:
4400g (= 4.4kg) gives 100 x [(3 x 24)litres + (4 x 24) litres]
So, the total volume of gases produced is
100 x [(3 x 24)litres + (4 x 24)litres]
    = 16800 litres

□ A total of **16800 litres of gas, measured at room temperature and pressure, is produced**. In practice, the volume of gas would be larger than this, because it is hot when it emerges from the engine — and all this comes from about 7 litres of liquid fuel!

> **Q21** Here are the results of three experiments with gases. All measurements are made at room temperature and pressure, so you may assume that 1 mole of gas molecules occupies 24 litres.
> (a) 4.8 litres of nitrogen monoxide reacted completely with 2.4 litres of oxygen
> (b) 2g of hydrogen reacted completely with 71g of chlorine
> (c) 1 litre of methane burned completely to carbon dioxide and steam in 2 litres of oxygen.
> Use this information to write chemical equations for each reaction.

7 Solutions

In 2.2 the concentration of a solution is defined as the mass of solute per 100g of solvent. For many purposes this is the most convenient system to use. Where reactions between solutions are being studied quantitatively, however, it is sometimes helpful to express the concentrations in terms of the *number of solute particles* present in a given volume of *solution*. The 'mole' unit provides a way of doing this.

Worked example 20
Finding the concentration of a solution in moles per litre.

Question
What are the concentrations, in moles of NaOH per litre, of solutions containing (a) 40g, (b) 80g, (c) 4g of sodium hydroxide in 1 litre of solution?

Answer
□ Work out the M_r value for the solute:
M_r (NaOH) = 23 + 16 + 1 = 40
□ So a solution containing 40g sodium hydroxide per litre has a concentration of 1 mole of NaOH per litre.
This is usually written as

$[NaOH] = 1\,molL^{-1}$, or
$[NaOH] = 1\,moldm^{-3}$.

□ One cubic decimetre, $1\,dm^3$, is the volume of a cube measuring 10cm x 10cm x 10cm. This is $1000\,cm^3$, which is the same as 1 litre.

$$1\,dm^3 = 1L$$

The square brackets [] are not just there for tidiness! They have a precise meaning: [X] means 'the concentration of substance X in moles of X particles per litre'.
□ The answers to the question are:
(a) 40g NaOH per litre of solution = 1 mole NaOH per litre $[NaOH] = 1\,molL^{-1}$
(b) 80g NaOH per litre of solution = 2 moles NaOH per litre $[NaOH] = 2\,molL^{-1}$
(c) 4g NaOH per litre of solution = 0.1 moles NaOH per litre $[NaOH] = 0.1\,molL^{-1}$

Reactions using solutions

You can calculate the volumes of solutions required for a chemical reaction if you know their concentrations in moles per litre.

Worked example 21
Finding the volume of a solution needed for a chemical reaction.

Question
A manufacturer has 1 tonne (1000kg) of ion-exchange resin which needs to be regenerated. To do this he must swap all the calcium ions on the resin for sodium ions by adding sodium chloride solution:

calcium resin +   →   sodium resin +
sodium chloride solution   calcium chloride solution

Two sodium ions must be added for every calcium ion replaced. The used resin contains 5 moles of calcium ions per kilogram. The sodium chloride solution has a concentration of 1 mole of sodium ions per litre. What volume of sodium chloride solution will be needed to regenerate the resin completely?

Answer
□ Write a balanced equation for the regeneration process:

$$Ca\text{-resin} + 2NaCl \rightarrow Na_2\text{-resin} + CaCl_2$$

□ Work out how many moles of calcium ions are in the Ca-resin: There are 5 moles of calcium ions in 1kg, therefore in 1000kg there are 1000 x 5 moles of calcium ions.
□ Decide how many moles of sodium ions are needed to replace these calcium ions:
2 sodium ions replace 1 calcium ion, so
2 x 5000 sodium ions will replace 5000 calcium ions, so
10000 *moles* of sodium ions will replace 5000 *moles* of calcium ions.
□ Calculate what volume of sodium chloride solution contains this number of sodium ions:
1 litre of sodium chloride solution contains 1 mole of sodium ions, so 10000 litres of sodium chloride solution contain 10000 moles of sodium ions.
□ **10000 litres of sodium chloride solution** (concentration 1 mole Na^+ ions per litre) will be needed to regenerate the resin.

Datapages

Basic information

A. The relative atomic masses (A_r) of some common elements

Element	Symbol	A_r	Element	Symbol	A_r
Aluminium	Al	27	Magnesium	Mg	24
Antimony	Sb	122	Manganese	Mn	55
Argon	Ar	40	Mercury	Hg	201
Arsenic	As	75	Neon	Ne	20
Barium	Ba	137	Nickel	Ni	59
Boron	B	11	Nitrogen	N	14
Bromine	Br	80	Oxygen	O	16
Calcium	Ca	40	Phosphorus	P	31
Carbon	C	12	Platinum	Pt	195
Chlorine	Cl	35.5	Potassium	K	39
Chromium	Cr	52	Silicon	Si	28
Cobalt	Co	59	Silver	Ag	108
Copper	Cu	63.5	Sodium	Na	23
Fluorine	F	19	Strontium	Sr	88
Gold	Au	197	Sulphur	S	32
Helium	He	4	Tin	Sn	119
Hydrogen	H	1	Titanium	Ti	48
Iodine	I	127	Tungsten	W	184
Iron	Fe	56	Uranium	U	238
Lead	Pb	207	Vanadium	V	51
Lithium	Li	7	Zinc	Zn	55

Note: These values are given to the nearest whole number, except in the cases of chlorine and copper.

B. Elements in order of atomic number

1	Hydrogen	H	35	Bromine	Br	69	Thulium	Tm
2	Helium	He	36	Krypton	Kr	70	Ytterbium	Yb
3	Lithium	Li	37	Rubidium	Rb	71	Lutetium	Lu
4	Beryllium	Be	38	Strontium	Sr	72	Hafnium	Hf
5	Boron	B	39	Yttrium	Y	73	Tantalum	Ta
6	Carbon	C	40	Zirconium	Zr	74	Tungsten	W
7	Nitrogen	N	41	Niobium	Nb	75	Rhenium	Re
8	Oxygen	O	42	Molybdenum	Mo	76	Osmium	Os
9	Fluorine	F	43	Technetium	Tc	77	Iridium	Ir
10	Neon	Ne	44	Ruthenium	Ru	78	Platinum	Pt
11	Sodium	Na	45	Rhodium	Rh	79	Gold	Au
12	Magnesium	Mg	46	Palladium	Pd	80	Mercury	Hg
13	Aluminium	Al	47	Silver	Ag	81	Thallium	Tl
14	Silicon	Si	48	Cadmium	Cd	82	Lead	Pb
15	Phosphorus	P	49	Indium	In	83	Bismuth	Bi
16	Sulphur	S	50	Tin	Sn	84	Polonium	Po
17	Chlorine	Cl	51	Antimony	Sb	85	Astatine	At
18	Argon	Ar	52	Tellurium	Te	86	Radon	Rn
19	Potassium	K	53	Iodine	I	87	Francium	Fr
20	Calcium	Ca	54	Xenon	Xe	88	Radium	Ra
21	Scandium	Sc	55	Caesium	Cs	89	Actinium	Ac
22	Titanium	Ti	56	Barium	Ba	90	Thorium	Th
23	Vanadium	V	57	Lanthanum	La	91	Protactinium	Pa
24	Chromium	Cr	58	Cerium	Ce	92	Uranium	U
25	Manganese	Mn	59	Praesodymium	Pr	93	Neptunium	Np
26	Iron	Fe	60	Neodymium	Nd	94	Plutonium	Pu
27	Cobalt	Co	61	Palmium	Pm	95	Americium	Am
28	Nickel	Ni	62	Samarium	Sm	96	Curium	Cu
29	Copper	Cu	63	Europium	Eu	97	Berkelium	Bk
30	Zinc	Zn	64	Gadolinium	Gd	98	Californium	Cf
31	Gallium	Ga	65	Terbium	Tb	99	Einsteinium	Es
32	Germanium	Ge	66	Dysprosium	Dy	100	Fermium	Fm
33	Arsenic	As	67	Holmium	Ho	101	Mendelevium	Md
34	Selenium	Se	68	Erbium	Er	102	Nobelium	No

C. What are the elements like?

Element	Symbol	Density (g cm^{-3})	MP (°C)	BP (°C)	
Aluminium	Al	2.7	660	2470	light silvery metal
Antimony	Sb	6.6	630	1380	grey semi-metal
Argon	Ar	(gas)	−189	−186	colourless Noble Gas
Arsenic	As	5.7	−	613*	grey semi-metal
Barium	Ba	3.5	714	1140	soft grey metal
Boron	B	2.3	2300	2530	brown solid non-metal
Bromine	Br	3.1	−7	59	dark brown liquid
Calcium	Ca	1.5	850	1487	grey metal
Carbon	C	2.25 (graphite)			soft, black solid
		3.51 (diamond)	3730*	4800	very hard, colourless
Chlorine	Cl	(gas)	−101	−35	green choking gas
Chromium	Cr	7.2	1890	2482	hard silvery metal
Cobalt	Co	8.9	1492	2900	hard grey metal
Copper	Cu	8.9	1083	2595	reddish metal
Fluorine	F	(gas)	−220	−188	colourless choking gas
Gold	Au	19.3	1063	2970	dense yellow metal
Helium	He	(gas)	−270	−269	light colourless gas
Hydrogen	H	(gas)	−259	−252	light colourless gas
Iodine	I	4.9	114*	184	blackish shiny solid
Iron	Fe	7.9	1535	2750	greyish metal
Lead	Pb	11.3	327	1744	dense grey metal
Lithium	Li	0.5	180	1330	lightest metal, grey
Magnesium	Mg	1.7	650	1110	light silvery metal
Manganese	Mn	7.2	1240	2100	grey metal
Mercury	Hg	13.6	−39	357	silvery liquid metal
Neon	Ne	(gas)	−249	−246	colourless gas
Nickel	Ni	8.9	1453	2730	silver-grey metal
Nitrogen	N	(gas)	−210	−196	colourless gas
Oxygen	O	(gas)	−218	−183	colourless gas
Phosphorus	P	1.82 (white) 2.34 (red)	44	280	waxy non-metal, with white and red alltropes
Platinum	Pt	21.4	1769	3830	v. dense silvery metal
Potassium	K	0.9	64	774	v. light, v. soft metal
Silicon	Si	2.3	1410	2360	blackish shiny non-metal
Silver	Ag	10.5	961	2210	dense silver metal
Sodium	Na	1.0	98	890	light soft metal
Strontium	Sr	2.6	768	1380	soft silvery metal
Sulphur	S	2.1	115	444	yellow crumbly non-metal
Tin	Sn	7.3	232	2270	silver metal
Titanium	Ti	4.5	1675	3260	hard silver metal
Tungsten	W	19.4	3410	5930	hardest metal
Uranium	U	19.1	1130	3820	grey metal
Vanadium	V	6.0	1900	3000	silvery tough metal
Zinc	Zn	7.1	420	907	silvery metal

* These elements sublime when heated at atmospheric pressure.

D. Some common ions

	Name of cation	Symbol or formula		Name of anion	Symbol or formula
3+	Aluminium	Al^{3+}	3–	Phosphate	PO_4^{3-}
	Iron(III)	Fe^{3+}			
2+	Barium	Ba^{2+}	2–	Carbonate	CO_3^{2-}
	Calcium	Ca^{2+}		Oxide	O^{2-}
	Copper	Cu^{2+}		Sulphide	S^{2-}
	Iron(II)	Fe^{2+}		Sulphate(IV)	SO_3^{2-}
	Lead	Pb^{2+}		Sulphate(VI)	SO_4^{2-}
	Magnesium	Mg^{2+}			
	Zinc	Zn^{2+}			
1+	Ammonium	NH_4^+	1–	Bromide	Br^-
	Hydrogen	H^+		Chloride	Cl^-
	Lithium	Li^+		Fluoride	F^-
	Potassium	K^+		Hydrogencarbonate	HCO_3^-
	Silver	Ag^+		Hydrogensulphate	HSO_4^-
	Sodium	Na^+		Hydroxide	OH^-
				Iodide	I^-
				Nitrate	NO_3^-

E. How well do substances dissolve?

1. How well do some common substances dissolve in cold water?

Anion:	carbonate	chloride	hydroxide	nitrate	sulphate
Cation:					
calcium	I	★★★	★	★★★	★
copper	I	★★	I	★★★	★★
iron (Fe^{2+})	I	★★★	I	–	★★
iron (Fe^{3+})	I	★★★	–	★★★	★★
lead	I	I	I	★★	I
magnesium	I	★★	I	★★	★★
potassium	★★★	★★	★★★	★★	★★
silver	–	I	–	★★	★
sodium	★★	★★	★★★	★★★	★★
zinc	I	★★★	I	★★★	★★

Key:
  I   = insoluble or very slightly soluble, will form a precipitate
  ★   = somewhat soluble, only a little will dissolve
  ★★ = soluble, a fair amount will dissolve
★★★ = very soluble
  –   = compound unstable under ordinary room conditions

2. How does the solubility of different salts vary with temperature?

Salt:	Solubility (g/100g water) at				
	10°C	30°C	50°C	70°C	90°C
Ammonium chloride	33.3	41.4	50.4	60.2	71.3
Calcium hydroxide	0.125	0.109	0.092	0.070	0.059
Copper sulphate	17.4	24.2	33.8	47.0	67.5
Lead nitrate	44.0	60.7	78.6	97.7	117.4
Potassium chlorate(V)	5.1	10.1	18.5	30.2	46.0
Potassium chloride	31.3	37.6	43.2	48.6	53.8
Potassium nitrate	21.2	45.3	83.5	135	203
Sodium chloride	35.8	36.2	36.8	37.6	38.6
Sodium nitrate	80.5	96.2	114	135	161

F. The reactivity series

High reactivity	potassium	Metal **difficult** to obtain from ore
	sodium	
	lithium	
	barium	
	calcium	
	magnesium	
	aluminium	
	(carbon)	
	zinc	
	iron	
	tin	
	lead	
	(hydrogen)	
	copper	
	mercury	
	silver	
	gold	
Low reactivity	platinum	Metal **easy** to obtain from ore

G. The properties of some hydrocarbons

Name	Formula	MP (°C)	BP (°C)	Density of liquid (g cm^{-3} at 25°C)
Alkanes				
methane	CH_4	−182	−162	
ethane	C_2H_4	−183	−89	
propane	C_3H_8	−188	−42	
★ butane	C_4H_{10}	−138	−0.5	0.60 (at BP)
★ 2-methylpropane	C_4H_{10}	−160	−12	0.50 (at BP)
★★ pentane	C_5H_{12}	−130	+36	0.63
★★ 2-methylbutane	C_5H_{12}	−158	+28	0.62
★★ 2,2-dimethylpropane	C_5H_{12}	−16	+9	0.59 (at BP)
hexane	C_6H_{14}	−95	+69	0.66
nonane	C_9H_{20}	−51	+150	0.72
dodecane	$C_{12}H_{26}$	−10	+216	0.75
hexadecane	$C_{16}H_{34}$	+18	+287	0.78
Alkenes				
ethene	C_2H_4	−169	−104	
propene	C_3H_6	−185	−48	
but-1-ene	C_4H_8	−185	−6	0.60 (at BP)
pent-1-ene	C_5H_{10}	−138	+30	0.64
hex-1-ene	C_6H_{12}	−98	+64	0.67

Note:
★ These compounds are isomers of butane
★★ These compounds are isomers of pentane

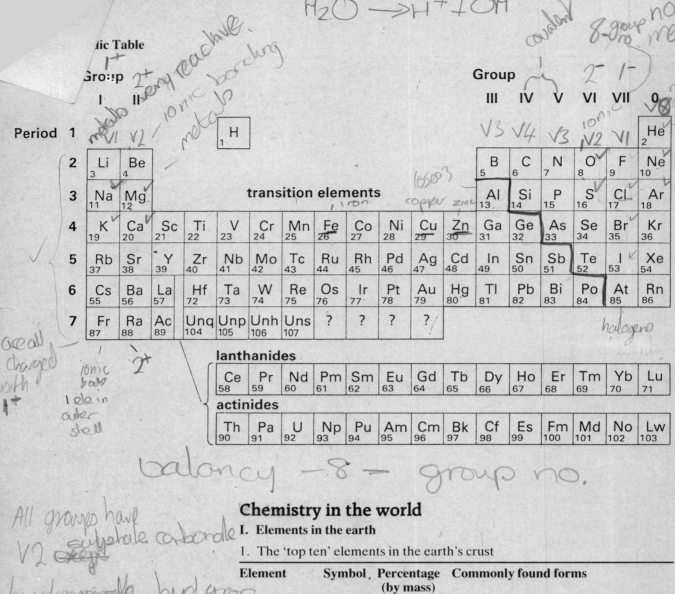

$H_2O \rightarrow H^+ + OH^-$

balancy — 8 — group no.

Chemistry in the world

I. Elements in the earth

1. The 'top ten' elements in the earth's crust

Element	Symbol	Percentage (by mass)	Commonly found forms
Oxygen	O	46.6	as oxides, 'oxy-anions' and water
Silicon	Si	27.7	in sand, clays, and many igneous rocks
Aluminium	Al	8.1	in clays and many minerals
Iron	Fe	5.0	widely dispersed, often as iron oxides
Calcium	Ca	3.6	limestone, chalk and marble
Sodium	Na	2.8	in many clays and minerals
Potassium	K	2.6	in many clays and minerals
Magnesium	Mg	2.1	
Titanium	Ti	0.4	
Phosphorus	P	0.1	widely dispersed
All other elements		1.0	

$MgO - Mg^{2+} + O^{2-}$

Sulphate $- SO_4$

Carbonate $- CO_3$

234

2. The gases in pure air

Gas	Formula	M_r	% in atmosphere (by volume)	BP (K)	BP (°C)
Nitrogen	N_2	28	78.9	77	−196
Oxygen	O_2	32	20.95	90	−183
Argon	Ar	40	0.93	87	−186
Carbon dioxide	CO_2	44	0.03	195★	−78★
Helium	He	4	0.0005	4	−269
Neon	Ne	20	0.018	27	−246
Krypton	Kr	84	0.001	121	−152
Xenon	Xe	131	0.0001	166	−107
Radon	Rn	222	variable	211	−62

★ Carbon dioxide sublimes at this temperature at atmospheric pressure

3. The 'top ten' elements in the oceans

Element	Symbol	Percentage (by mass)	Commonly found forms
Oxygen	O	85.7	as $H_2O(l)$, and as dissolved $O_2(g)$
Hydrogen	H	10.8	as water, $H_2O(l)$
Chlorine	Cl	1.9	as the chloride ion, $Cl^-(aq)$
Sodium	Na	1.1	as the sodium ion, $Na^+(aq)$
Magnesium	Mg	0.14	as the magnesium ion, $Mg^{2+}(aq)$
Sulphur	S	0.09	as the sulphate ion, $SO_4^{2-}(aq)$
Calcium	Ca	0.04	as the calcium ion, $Ca^{2+}(aq)$
Potassium	K	0.04	as the potassium ion, $K^+(aq)$
Bromine	Br	0.007	as the bromide ion, $Br^-(aq)$
Carbon	C	0.003	as the carbonate, $CO_3^{2-}(aq)$, and hydrogencarbonate, $HCO_3^-(aq)$, ions

J. The public water supply

1. Using water at home

In the UK we use at home, on average, about 120 litres (26 gallons) of tap water per person each day.

L/day	Use	Percentage of total home usage
42	Washing up, drinking, cooking, washing clothes by hand	35
40	Flushing the toilet	33
20	Personal washing, showers and baths	17
14	Washing clothes by machine	12
4	Watering the garden, washing the car, etc.	3
120	**Total**	**100%**

Another 200 L/day per person is used on our behalf by industry, at work and so on. Total use per person 320 L/day 72 gallons/day.
[Source: *Water Services Yearbook, 1986* and *Sunday Times Magazine* 10.8.86 p.36]

2. How hard is the water supply?

(a) Some examples from the Severn/Trent Water Authority

Water	Temporary hardness mg/l	Permanent hardness mg/l	Total mg/l
Derbyshire (parts)			
Derwent valley	14	37	51
Chesterfield	50–250	0–220	50–300
High Peak	50–300	30–50	45–200
Amber Valley	60–250	40–50	140–160
Worcestershire (parts)			
River Severn	22–237	20–247	66–484
Gloucestershire (parts)			
River Wye	24–276	20–145	44–414
Birmingham area			
Elan Valley	7	14	21
Bourne & Blythe	140	150	290
Staffordshire			
Stafford Boro (E)	155	85	240
Stafford Boro (W)	250	150	400
Stone	155	85	240
Stoke on Trent (N)	45	55	100
Stoke on Trent (cent.)	155	60	215
Stoke on Trent (S)	140	60	200
Newcastle-u-Lyme	145	25	170

[Source: *Water Services Yearbook, 1986*]

(b) Water hardness in some major cities

City	Temporary hardness mg/l	Permanent hardness mg/l	Total mg/l
Bath	100-250	70-155	204-400
Birmingham	7	14	21
Cardiff	20	10	30
Glasgow	8	4	12
Leeds	–	–	60-200
Liverpool	–	–	30-100
London	–	–	230-360
Manchester	5-62	0-50	12-93
Norwich	200	120	320
Nottingham	95	50	145
Rugby	130	150	280
Salisbury	215	40	255
Southampton	190-270	30-60	220-310

[**Important note**: Water hardness varies a good deal even within the same city, because different areas get their water from different sources. Notice the figures for Birmingham in Table (a) above.]

Chemistry at work

K. Some alloys

Name of alloy	Main metals	Approximate percentages* (NB most are variable)
Aluminium alloy (see 5.3)		
Duralumin	alumininium, copper, manganese, magnesium	95:3:1:1
Copper alloys (see 5.8)		
Brass	copper, zinc	70:30
Bronze	copper, tin	90:10
German silver	copper, zinc, nickel	60:25:15
Cupronickel	copper, nickel	75:25
Gold		

Pure 100% gold would be '24 carat' gold. Hallmarked items are made from one of the following alloys. The proportion of gold is fixed, but the proportions of copper and silver may vary.

22 carat	gold, silver, copper	91.7:5.5:2.8
18 carat	gold, silver, copper	75.0:12.5:12.5
14 carat	gold, copper, silver	58.5:21.0:20.5
9 carat	gold, copper, silver	37.5:31.25:31.25
White gold	(Same gold content, also contains nickel or palladium)	
Nickel alloys		
Invar	iron, nickel	64:36
Monel	nickel, copper	70:30
Lead alloys		
Solder	tin, lead	50:50
Type metal	lead, antimony, tin	70:20:10
'Silver' coins in Britain (see 5.10)		
Until 1920	silver, copper	92.5:7.5
1921–1946	silver, copper, nickel, zinc	50:40:5:5
since 1947	copper, nickel	75:25
Steels (see 5.6)		
Mild steel	iron, carbon and other non-metals	99:0.2:08
Stainless steel	iron, chromium, nickel	74:18:8

* Listed in the same order as the metals in column 2.

L. Food

1. Why do we need vitamins?

Vitamin	Main benefits	What happens if your diet is short of it?	Recommended daily amount (micrograms)
A	healthy eyesight and skin	can't see in the dark, liable to infection	750 [1]
B1	helps to convert glucose into energy	tiredness, nausea DD: beri-beri [2]	1500
B2	maintains condition of body tissues	eye and skin problems	1700
B6	maintains condition of nerves and blood	skin problems, anaemia	2000
B12	maintains condition of nerves and blood	DD: pernicious anaemia	3
C	helps resistance to infection	weakness, ulcers DD: scurvy	60,000
D	helps you to absorb calcium from food	bone pain, tiredness DD: rickets	10

Notes:

1. The recommended daily intake of vitamins varies according to your age, sex, and state of health. These are only approximate figures.

2. DD = 'deficiency disease', a serious condition affecting people who are very short of the vitamin. These only occur in cases of starvation, or where the person is restricted to one particular kind of food.

2. What are the best sources of different vitamins?

Vitamin	Best food sources, in order of the quantity of vitamin they contain
A	Halibut liver oil, liver, margarine, butter, cheese, eggs
B1	Yeast and yeast extracts, brown rice, wheatgerm, nuts
B2	Yeast and yeast extracts, liver, wheatgerm, cheese, eggs
B6	Yeast and yeast extracts, bran, wheatgerm, oatflakes
B12	Liver and kidneys (pig's), fish, pork, beef, lamb
C	Many fruit juices and green vegetables
D	Cod liver oil, kippers, many kinds of fish, eggs

3. What about fibre?

High fibre food	Grams of fibre in 100g of the uncooked food
Wheat bran	44
Haricot beans	25
Butter beans	22
Puffed wheat	15
Coconut	14
Cornflakes	11
Wholemeal flour	10
Peanuts	8
Muesli	7
Brown rice	6
Lentils	4

4. Information from some food labels

Food	Protein (g per 100g)	Carbohydrate (g per 100g)	Fat (g per 100g)	Energy (kJ per 100g)
Fresh cream	2.7	3.9	18.6	795
Cooked ham	20.0	1.0	9.3	700
Coleslaw	1.3	7.5	10.0	513
Eggs	12.3	0.4	10.9	619
Soft cheese	8.0	3.0	31.0	1350
Roasted peanuts	24.0	20.0	50.0	2600
Orange juice	0.6	11.4	–	192

5. What's in a fizzy drink

Drink	Added flavour	Added colour	% Sugar (g/100 g water)	Added acid	Acid conc'n (g/litre of syrup)
Orangeade	oil of orange orange juice	caramel	12	citric	7.5
Ginger beer	ginger root	caramel	7-11	citric	7.5
Cola	kola nut extract	caramel	11-12	phosphoric	4.5
Lemon & lime	oil of lemon oil of lime	none	10-11	citric	7.5

The volume of carbon dioxide gas dissolved, at room temperature and pressure, is from 1 to 4 times the volume of the drink, depending on its fizziness.

[Source: Kirk Othmer Encyc. Vol 4 page 717, modified]

M. Food additives

When you read the label on a food packet you will often find that some of the ingredients are listed by their E-numbers. These numbers refer to 'permitted additives'. Here are some widely used examples:

Commonly used additives

Number Name	Effect	Uses
E100-E180 Colours		
E102 Tartrazine	yellow colouring	drinks, sweets, packet foods
E110 Sunset Yellow	yellow colouring	sweets, squashes, jams
E120 Cochineal	red colouring	many traditional uses, becoming expensive (made from insects)
E122 Carmoisine	red colouring	packet foods, sweets, sauces
E124 Ponceau 4R	red colouring	packet foods, tinned fruit, pie fillings
E127 Erythrosine	red colouring	glace cherries, disclosing tablets
E150 Caramel	brown colouring	products made to resemble chocolate, sauces, gravy browning
E200-E290 Preservatives		
E200 Sorbic acid -203 & its salts	stops growth of moulds	many milk products, cakes and sweets
E210 Benzoic acid -219 & related compounds	stops growth of bacteria and fungi	jams, beer, sauces
E220 Sulphur dioxide	preservative	wide range of fruit & veg products
E250 sodium nitrite	stops bacterial growth	cured and processed meats
E260 Ethanoic acid	kills bacteria	vinegar: widely used in pickles and sauces
E300-E321 Anti-oxidants		
E300 Ascorbic acid (Vitamin C)	anti-oxidant	stops browning of fruit and discolouration of meat
E320 BHA [1]	anti-oxidant for fats	biscuits, butter, margarine
E322-E494 Emulsifiers and stabilizers (not all numbers allocated)		
E330 Citric acid	stabilizer	drinks, jams, bakery products
E338 Phosphoric acid	various, incl. flavouring	fizzy drinks, cooked meat
E450 Phosphates	emulsifers	cheese and milk products
E466 CMC [2]	thickening agent	fruit fillings, soups, ice cream, mousses, processed cheeses
E621 MSG [3]	flavour enhancer	many "convenience foods"

[1] BHA Butylated hydroxyanisole
[2] CMC Sodium salt of carboxymethylcellulose
[3] MSG Monosodium glutamate

Definitions

Anti-oxidant   substance which slows down deterioration of food caused by oxygen from the air

Bacteria   single-celled organisms which may cause disease

Emulsifier   substance which stabilises mixtures of liquids like oil and water which do not normally mix

Flavour enhancer substance which affects our sense of taste, making food seem tastier.

Mould   powdery growth produced by fungi

Preservative   substance which slows down or prevents growth of micro-organisms

Stabiliser   substance which helps to support the structure of the food product

Thickening agent substance which prevents food products from becoming too "watery"

Note: In addition to the additives listed here there are a number of miscellaneous additives, with E numbers between E170 and E927.

N. Flame Tests

Metal ion	Flame colour	Flame colour when seen through blue glass
Sodium	golden yellow	none
Potassium	lilac	crimson
Copper	sharp green	–
Barium	dull green	blue-green
Lithium	bright red	–
Calcium	brick red	light green
Strontium	crimson	purple
Lead	bluish	white

The following common metal ions give no visible colour to the flame:

aluminium, iron, magnesium, nickel, silver, tin, zinc

O. Where does our energy come from?

1. UK energy sources

Date	Coal %	Oil %	Natural Gas %	Nuclear %	Hydro-electric %
1950	89.6	10.0			0.4
1955	85.4	14.2			0.4
1960	74.0	25.4			0.6
1965	61.8	35.0	0.4	2.0	0.7
1970	46.6	44.6	5.3	0.8	2.7
1975	36.9	42.0	17.1	3.3	0.6
1980	36.7	37.0	21.6	4.1	0.6
1985	32.2	35.2	25.2	6.8	0.6

[Source: 'United Kingdom Energy Statistics, 1986' (Dept. of Energy)]

2. World energy sources

Date	Solid fuel %	Oil %	Natural gas %	Nuclear and hydro-electric %
1950	62.3	25.2	10.8	1.6
1960	52.1	31.3	14.6	2.0
1970	35.0	41.9	20.8	2.3
1980	29.3	43.6	18.6	8.4

3. Where are the world's nuclear reactors?

Country	Total nuclear power generating capacity ('000s of Megawatts of electricity)	Number of reactors installed
USA	77.8	93
France	37.5	43
USSR	26.8	50
Japan	23.7	33
W. Germany	16.4	20
UK	10.1	38
Canada	9.5	16
Sweden	9.5	12
Spain	5.6	8
Belgium	5.5	8
(16 other countries)	26.1	53
World total	248.5 thousand Megawatts	374 reactors

[Source: 'Atom' no. 354 p19]

P. Facts and figures about the oil industry

1. What can you get from a tonne of crude oil?

2.2 tonnes of North Sea crude oil was produced in 1985 for every man, woman and child in the UK. The conversion of this into products depends upon the changing demands of customers. In 1985, for every tonne of crude oil entering a refinery in the UK, we produced:

Oil product group	Product	Uses	Amount produced from 1 tonne of crude oil
Liquefied petroleum gas (LPG)	propane	metal cutting, welding heating and cooking in homes without main gas supply	
	butane	mainly for making other chemicals also in gas lighters, paint stripping torches, etc.	21 kg
Light distillate	naphtha	for making other chemicals as an industrial solvent	40 kg
Gasoline	Aviation spirit	High octane fuel for piston engined aircraft	
	Motor spirit	Petrol	310 kg
	Industrial spirits	White spirit for paints, solvents and dry cleaning	
Kerosene	Jet fuel	For aircraft	106 kg
	Paraffin	For small heaters, etc.	
	Burning oil	For domestic oil-fired central heating	
	Vapourising oil	For farm tractors (non-diesel)	
Gas oil	Derv	For Diesel Engine Road Vehicles	
	Heating oil	for domestic 'oil fired central heating	302 kg
Heavy distillate	Fuel oil	For industrial heating, for ships, and electric power generation	180 kg
Lubricating oil	'Lube' oil	For oiling machinery	17 kg
Bitumen	Tar	For road making	24 kg

[Source: Oil Data Sheet No. 8, Institute of Petroleum]

2. How much motor fuel is used in the UK?

Fuel	Millions of tonnes delivered to customers in 1985	%
★★★★ petrol	17.91	65.1
★★★ petrol	0.16	0.6
★★ petrol	2.33	8.5
DERV	7.11	25.8
Total	27.51	100.0%

[Source: Inst of Petroleum UK Petroleum Industry Statistics 1984 & 1985, modified]

3. How many 'miles per gallon'?

Method of transport	No. of persons carried	Passenger miles per gallon equivalent
Bicycle	1	1600
Train	250	625
Double deck bus	70	490
Walking	1	400
Electric car	2	122
Aircraft	320	96
Petrol car	2	60

Source: 'Living with energy' (Lothian Energy Group) p. 10

4. World oil production

Country	Oil production in a typical 1980's year (Mt)	%
USSR	620	22
USA	490	18
Saudi Arabia	240	9
Mexico	150	5
UK	120	4
China	110	)
Iran	100	)
Venezuela	95	)
Canada	80	)
Indonesia	70	)
Nigeria	65	)
Iraq	60	)
Kuwait	60	)
Libya	50	) 42%
Egypt	40	)
Abu Dhabi	40	)
Norway	35	)
Algeria	30	)
Argentina	25	)
India	25	)
55 Other countries	280	)
Total (approx.)	2785 million tonnes per year	100%

[Source: Mining Annual Review and 'Know more about oil: World Statistics' (Institute of Petroleum)]

Q. Facts and figures about coal

1. Who uses coal?

Customer for coal	Percentage of total sales
Power stations	83
Coke manufacture	9
Household use	8
Industry	9
Export	5
Other markets	4

[Source: NCB Facts & Figs about Britain's Coal Industry, 1981/2]

2. Which are the main coal-producing countries?

Country	Coal production in a typical year (1980's)		
	Hard coal (Mt)	Brown coal 'lignite' (Mt)	TOTAL (Mt)
USA	690	50	740
China	690	30	720
USSR	550	150	700
E. Germany	–	290	290
Poland	190	50	240
W. Germany	90	130	220
S. Africa	160	–	160
India	150	10	160
Australia	120	30	150
UK	120	–	120

[Source: Mining Annual Review, 1985 p99]

R. Extracting the elements

1. How much metal is in the ore?

Metal	Common ore	Formula	% Metal in ore as found (typical value)
Aluminium	bauxite	$Al_2O_3.3H_2O$	28
Copper	chalcopyrite	$CuFeS_2$	0.5
Gold	native	Au	0.001
Iron	haematite	Fe_2O_3	30–60
Lead	galena	PbS	5–10
Mercury	cinnabar	HgS	0.3
Nickel	pentlandite	$NiS.(FeS)_2$	2.0
Platinum	cooperite	PtS (also native)	0.01
Silver	argentite	Ag_2S	0.6
Tin	cassiterite	SnO_2	1.5
Titanium	rutile	TiO_2	2.5–25
Uranium	uranium oxide	U_3O_8	0.1–0.9
Zinc	zinc blende	ZnS	10–30

[Source: Kirk Othmer Encyc. Vol 8 page 742, modified]

2. What goes into a blast furnace?

What goes IN	% by mass	What comes OUT	% by mass
Iron ore, sinter, scrap, etc.	43	Molten iron	26
Limestone	1	Slag	8
Coke	12	Gases	66
Air	44		
Total	100%		100%

[Source: Kirk Othmer Encyc. Vol 13 page 743, modified]

3. Making elements by electrolysis

Element	Anode	Cathode	Electrolyte	Temp. (°C, approx.)	Cell voltage
Molten electrolytes					
Aluminium	graphite	steel	cryolite 80-85% alumina 2-8%	950	4.1
Sodium	graphite	steel	sodium chloride 42% calcium chloride 58%	700	6.0
Electrolytes in solution					
Chlorine					
(mercury)	titanium	mercury	sodium chloride (aq)	90-95	4.3
(diaphragm)	titanium	steel	sodium chloride (aq)	90-95	3.4
(membrane)	titanium	steel	sodium chloride (aq)	90-95	3.7
Copper	lead	copper	copper sulphate (aq)	30-35	2.2
Zinc	lead	aluminium	zinc sulphate (aq)	35	3.5

[Source: Kirk Othmer Encyc. Vol 8 page 688-9, modified]

4. How has the production of metals grown during this century?

Date	Aluminium '000 tonne	Copper '000 tonne	Lead '000 tonne	Silver '000 tonne
1900	15	500	850	5
1905	30	700	1000	5
1910	60	850	1150	7
1915	65	1050	1050	6
1920	150	950	950	5
1925	250	1400	1600	8
1930	300	1550	1600	8
1935	300	1450	1350	7
1940	750	2350	1750	8
1945	650	2150	1200	5
1950	1450	2500	1700	5
1955	3000	3150	2150	6
1960	4700	4400	2450	7
1965	6350	5100	2750	8
1970	10300	6450	3400	10
1975	13100	7300	3550	10
1980	16050	7850	3550	11
1984	13400	8250	3350	13

[Source: Adapted from Mining Annual Review, 1985, page 23 in which C.J. Schmitz, *World Non-ferrous Metal Production and Prices 1700-1976*, Frank Cass & Co., Ltd. is acknowledged as the original source.]

S. The chemical industry

1. What does the UK chemical industry produce?

Products	Percentage of the industry (mid-1980's) expressed in terms of 'gross value added'
Pharmaceuticals	24%
Industrial and Agricultural chemicals	18%
Organic chemicals	13%
Soaps, toilet preparations	9%
Paints, varnishes, printing inks	8%
Synthetic resins, plastics and rubbers	7%
Inorganic chemicals	7%
Fertilizers	6%
Dyestuffs and pigments	4%
Household and office products	4%

[Source: Chemical Industries Association]

2. How much do ordinary chemicals cost?

Well, it all depends ………! It depends upon how much you buy, who you buy it from, whether you have to pay for transport charges, how pure the stuff is, and so on. Here are a few examples.

Chemical	Approx. industrial price (per tonne)	Approx. price of 1 kg (laboratory grade)
Barium sulphate	£130	£6.00
Bromine	£475	£7.50
Calcium carbonate	£35	£3.00
Graphite, lump	£700	£9.00
Iodine	£10 000	£25.00
Manganese(IV) oxide	£125	£5.00
Rocksalt	£15	£1.00
Potassium chloride	£80	£4.00
Sodium nitrate	£120	£9.00
Sulphur	£100	£4.00

3. How much do precious metals cost?

Metal	Typical price (£/kg) in the mid-1980's
Rhodium	£11000 per kilogram
Platinum	£8500
Gold	£8000
Iridium	£7500
Palladium	£3300
Silver	£200

[Source: Adapted from Mining Annual Review, 1985, page 45]

4. How much do ordinary metals cost?

Metal	Typical price (£/tonne) in the mid-1980's
Tin	£8000, but dropped below £4000 per tonne in 1985/6
Nickel	£3600
Copper	£1000
Aluminium	£900
Zinc	£600
Lead	£350

[Source: Adapted from Mining Annual Review, 1985, page 23 in which C.J. Schmitz, 'World Non-ferrous Metal Production and Prices 1700-1976', Frank Cass & Co., Ltd. is acknowledged as the original source.]

5. How have metal prices changed during this century?

Many factors influence the price of metals. The balance between supply and demand is only one, and different metals have shown quite different patterns of price movement during the present century.

Date	Aluminium £/tonne	Copper £/tonne	Lead £/tonne	Silver £/kg
	Note: all prices index-linked to mid-1980's			
1900	–	2204	487	109
1905	4823	2023	388	103
1910	1877	1563	339	86
1915	1800	1640	460	64
1920	1596	1080	367	81
1925	1668	926	505	60
1930	1424	954	282	38
1935	1691	604	242	67
1940	1450	820	336	40
1945	1072	743	329	50
1950	1195	1877	1109	93
1955	1343	2826	849	82
1960	1312	1735	509	79
1965	1163	2779	681	95
1970	1233	2836	612	116
1975	1021	1454	486	167
1980	1080	1256	522	387
1984	929	1052	333	200

[Source: Mining Annual Review, 1985, page 23 in which C.J. Schmitz, 'World Non-ferrous Metal Production and Prices 1700-1976', Frank Cass & Co., Ltd. is acknowledged as the original source.]

Historical information

T. Who discovered the elements and gave them their names?

Element and symbol Isolated by	Date	Country	Origin of name
Aluminium, Al Wohler	1827	Germany	Latin: *alumen* = alum. Alum is an aluminium salt which has been used since ancient times in the dyeing of cloth. It prevents the dye from washing out too easily.
Antimony, Sb ancient			Latin: *stibium* a mark. The word 'stibium' referred to marks made on the face, because black antimony sulphide was used in ancient times for eye make-up.
Argon, Ar Ramsay	1894	UK	Greek: *argos* = idle. Argon was given its name because it is so inactive!
Arsenic, As Albertus	1250	Germany	Greek: *arsenikon* = orpiment. Orpiment is the naturally occurring yellow sulphide of arsenic, once used as a pigment.
Barium, Ba Davy	1808	UK	Greek: *barys* = heavy. Barium minerals are surprisingly dense. One is still known as 'heavy spar'.
Boron, B Davy	1808	UK	Arabic: *baraqa* = to glisten. Borax, a naturally occurring compound of boron known since ancient times, is a glistening crystalline substance.
Bromine, Br Balard	1826	France	Greek: *bromos* = strong smell. Bromine has an extremely pungent smell. It is very harmful to the eyes and lungs.
Calcium, Ca Davy	1808	UK	Latin: *calx* = lime. Lime was one of the earliest known compounds of calcium.
Carbon, C ancient			Latin: *carbo* = charcoal. Charcoal was the earliest form of carbon to be recognised.
Chlorine, Cl Scheele	1774	Sweden	Greek: *chloros* = light green. Chlorine is a pale green gas.
Chromium, Cr Vauquelin	1797	France	Greek: *chroma* = colour. Many chromium compounds are strongly coloured.
Cobalt, Co Brandt	1735	Sweden	German: *Kobold* = wicked goblin, or 'demon of the mines'. Cobalt ore was at first thought to be a worthless and troublesome material.
Copper, Cu ancient			Latin: *cuprum* = from Cyprus. The first copper in the Western world was found in Cyprus.

Fluorine, F
Moissan   1886   France

Latin: *fluere* = to flow. Naturally occurring minerals containing fluorine, such as fluorspar, were so named because they melted (and therefore flowed) easily.

Gold, Au
ancient

Latin: *aurum* = gold or yellow coloured. Gold was the only yellow metal known.

Helium, He
Ramsay   1895   UK

Greek: *helios* = sun. The existence of an element in the sun, then unknown on earth, was realised by Lockyer in 1868 while studying its spectrum.

Hydrogen, H
Cavendish   1766   UK

Greek = water-producing. The French chemist, Lavoisier, realised that water is formed when hydrogen burns, and gave the element its name.

Iodine, I
Courtois   1811   France

Greek: *iodes* = violet. Iodine has a violet-coloured vapour.

Iron, Fe
ancient

Latin: *ferrum* = iron.

Lead, Pb
ancient

Latin: *plumbum* = lead

Lithium, Li
Bunsen   1855   Germany

Greek: *lithos* = stone. Lithium was (wrongly) believed to exist only in rocks and minerals.

Magnesium, Mg
Davy   1808   UK

The name may possibly have come from the Greek place name, *Magnesia*. Davy called it Magnium because of the confusion with manganese (see below).

Manganese, Mn
Gahn   1774   Sweden

German: *mangan* = manganese, after some confusion with the use of the same name for magnesium!

Mercury, Hg
ancient

Greek words '*hydor argyros*' = liquid silver. Mercury, once known as quicksilver, takes its name from Mercury the nimble Greek messenger of the Gods.

Neon, Ne
Ramsay   1898   UK

Greek: *neos* = new. Until 1892 the existence of the Noble Gases was completely unanticipated.

Nickel, Ni
Cronstedt   1751   Sweden

German: *cupfernickel* = false copper. 'Old Nick' was the devil, Old Nick's copper was a deception!

Nitrogen, N
D.Rutherford   1772   UK

Latin: nitre-producing. Nitre, is potassium nitrate, known to contain nitrogen.

Oxygen, O
Priestley   1774   UK
Scheele   1774   Sweden

Greek: acid-producing. The French chemist, Lavoisier, who named this element, mistakenly thought that all acids contained oxygen.

Element	Discoverer	Year	Country	Origin of name
Phosphorus, P	Brand	1669	Germany	Greek: light bearer. Phosphorus gives out light as it oxidises (hence 'phosphorescence').
Platinum, Pt	de Ulloa	1735	Spain	Spanish: *platina* = silver colour. Platinum is a bright shiny silver-coloured metal.
Potassium, K	Davy	1807	UK	Latin: *kalium* = potash, or wood ashes. Note the link with the word alKALI.
Silicon, Si	Berzelius	1817	Sweden	Latin: *silex* = flint. Flint is one form of silicon oxide.
Silver, Ag	ancient			Latin: *argentum* = white and shining, silver-coloured. The S. American country of Argentina takes its name from the belief of the Spanish, who reached the country in the 16th century, that they would find silver there. They were wrong!
Sodium, Na	Davy	1807	UK	Latin: *natrium* = 'natron', a Hebrew name for deposits of naturally occurring sodium salts. The word 'soda' is Arabic for a splitting headache! Sodium salts were said to bring relief.
Strontium, Sr	Davy	1808	UK	The ore was first found at Strontian in Scotland during the 1790's. No other element takes its name from a British place-name.
Sulphur, S	ancient			Latin: *sulphurium* = sulphur, an element well known in Italy because of its association with volcanoes. A volcanic area to the north of Naples is still called Solfatara.
Tin, Sn	ancient			Latin: *stannum* = tin.
Titanium, Ti	Berzelius	1825	Sweden	Greek: *Titans* = mythological figures of great strength.
Tungsten, W	d'Elhuyar	1783	Spain	Swedish = heavy stone. Tungsten ore is extremely dense.
Uranium, U	Peligot	1841	France	Uranium was named after the planet Uranus, which had been discovered in 1781, a few years before the existence of the element was recognised.
Vanadium, V	Sefstrom	1830	Sweden	From the Scandinavian goddess Vanadis, also known as Freya.
Zinc, Zn	ancient		India	German: *zink* = a word applied to various ores.

[⋆ Ancient = known for thousands of years, often to the peoples of Africa, India, China, Egypt, Greece and Rome.]

U. Popular or old-fashioned names used for chemical substances

Chemical Name	Popular or old-fashioned name(s)
Aluminium potassium sulphate	alum
Aluminium oxide	alumina
Ammonia	spirit of hartshorn
Ammonia solution	ammonium hydroxide
Ammonium chloride	sal ammoniac
Ammonium sulphate	sulphate of ammonia
Barium sulphate	barytes
Calcium carbonate	chalk, limestone, marble, calcite
Calcium hydroxide	slaked lime
Calcium hydroxide solution	lime water
Calcium oxide	quicklime
Calcium sulphate	plaster of Paris, Gypsum
Carbon (graphite)	plumbago, black lead
Copper sulphate crystals	blue vitriol
Ethanol	spirits of wine
Ethanoic acid	acetic acid, pyroligneous acid
Hydrochoric acid	muriatic acid
Hydrogen chloride	spirit of salt
Iron(II) salts	ferrous salts
Iron(III) salts	ferric salts
Iron(II) sulphate crystals	green vitriol, copper
Iron(III) oxide	jewellers' rouge
Lead(II) acetate	sugar of lead
Lead(II) carbonate hydroxide	basic lead carbonate, white lead
Lead(II) oxide	litharge, massicot
Dilead(II) lead(IV) oxide	red lead
Mangesium sulphate crystals	Epsom salt
Mercury	quicksilver
Mercury (I) chloride	calomel
Mercury sulphide	cinnabar
Methanol	wood alcohol, wood spirit
Methane	marsh gas, firedamp
Nitric acid (conc.)	aqua fortis
Nitrogen monoxide	nitric oxide
Dinitrogen monoxide	nitrous oxide
Potassium chloride	potash, muriate of potash
Potassium hydroxide	caustic potash
Potassium nitrate	saltpetre, nitre
Potassium manganate(VII)	potassium permanganate
Potassium sulphate	sulphate of potash
Silicon oxide	silica, sand
Silver nitrate	lunar caustic
Sodium carbonate (anhydrous)	soda ash
Sodium carbonate crystals	washing soda
Sodium hydrogencarbonate	bicarbonate of soda, baking soda
Sodium hydrogensulphate	sodium bisulphate
Sodium hydroxide	caustic soda
Sodium nitrate	Chile saltpetre
Sodium silicate solution	water glass
Sodium sulphate crystals	Glauber's salt
Sodium thiosulphate	hypo
Sulphuric acid (conc.)	oil of vitriol
Sulphuric acid ('fuming')	oleum
Tetrachloromethane	carbon tetrachloride
Zinc carbonate	calamine
Zinc oxide	Chinese white
Zinc sulphate crystals	white vitriol

Index